Migration Trauma, Culture, and Finding the Psychological Home Within

Migration Trauma, Culture, and Finding the Psychological Home Within

Views from British Object Relations Theory

Grace P. Conroy

ROWMAN & LITTLEFIELD
Lanham • Boulder • New York • London

Published by Rowman & Littlefield
A wholly owned subsidiary of The Rowman & Littlefield Publishing Group, Inc.
4501 Forbes Boulevard, Suite 200, Lanham, Maryland 20706
www.rowman.com

Unit A, Whitacre Mews, 26-34 Stannary Street, London SE11 4AB

British Library Cataloguing in Publication Information Available

Library of Congress Cataloging-in-Publication Data Available

ISBN: 978-1-4422-3151-1 (cloth : alk. paper)
ISBN: 978-1-4422-3152-8 (electronic)

∞™ The paper used in this publication meets the minimum requirements of American National Standard for Information Sciences—Permanence of Paper for Printed Library Materials, ANSI/NISO Z39.48-1992.

Printed in the United States of America

Prologue

*"The Journey"**

One day you finally knew
what you had to do, and began,
though the voices around you
kept shouting
their bad advice—
though the whole house
began to tremble
and you felt the old tug
at your ankles.
"Mend my life!"
each voice cried.
But you didn't stop.
You knew what you had to do,
though the wind pried
with its stiff fingers
at the very foundations,
though their melancholy
was terrible.
It was already late
enough, and a wild night,
and the road full of fallen
branches and stones.
But little by little,
as you left their voices behind,
the stars began to burn
through the sheets of clouds,
and there was a new voice
which you slowly
recognized as your own,
that kept you company
as you strode deeper and deeper
into the world
determined to do
the only thing you could do—
determined to save
the only life you could save.

—Mary Oliver

To my mother, Alicja, and my uncle, Dr. Pawel Przybylski, who endured exile and many migrations in great spirit and with an inner flame that was passed on to my generation.

Contents

Acknowledgments

This book is the outcome of a long experiential and professional journey from Eastern Europe through the United Kingdom and, finally, to the United States of America. It was experientially conceived back in Eastern Europe and come to fruition many years later, here in the United States.

Many of my ideas on migration, culture and psychic home within have been influenced by multiple teachers, supervisors, migrant patients, colleagues, and other mental health professionals. Without these helpmates and guides along the way, and especially my patients, this work would not have come to fruition.

I am especially deeply appreciative to Nasir Ilahi, LLM and Dr. Alan Roland, internationally well-known psychoanalysts, who contributed their profound knowledge, wisdom and understanding about migration, identity and culture. Nasir Ilahi, LLM, a gifted psychoanalyst and migrant himself has been a source of ongoing inspiration for me. As my mentor for many years, he has fundamentally influenced my personal and professional development. I wish to express my most deep gratitude for his invaluable guidance. Dr. Alan Roland, a third-generation migrant and American psychoanalyst has made many original contributions to cross-cultural psychoanalytic studies. His deep wisdom and profound understanding of cross-cultural differences immensely enriched and clarified my thinking and focus about radically different cultures. I am deeply thankful for his generosity.

Dr. Jeffrey B. Rubin, whose work challenges psychoanalytic reductionism and proposes a much broader approach to psychoanalysis, has helped me to broaden my approach in addressing the issues of migration, identity and culture. I appreciate his support of my work.

Dr. Don Shapiro who is knowledgeable in the field of psychoanalysis and human development gave me a lot of encouragement and motivation. He understood my struggles as a writer, provided positive influence, and was available for questions, suggestions and clarifications. I am grateful for his guidance.

Dr. Linda B. Hopkins is a teacher and psychoanalytic writer who generously contributed her insight and knowledge of psychoanalysis to this project. Dr. Jose Cedillos, a migrant himself and a talented artist, to whom I am thankful for his efforts in reading my work and providing vital feedback. Drs. Karen Kaufman and Steven Lansky, my fellow colleagues along this journey were important sources of encouragement and I truly appreciate their support.

I am thankful to my niece, Jacqueline Rall, who is a second-generation migrant, for her drawings representing "psychic home," the road on which the journey takes place, as well as illustrations of Rumi's and Mary Oliver's poems. She spent many hours expressing artistically, through her art, her feelings and ideas related to the migration process.

My assistant and editing partner, Helene Towers, conducted literature searches, reviewed my manuscripts and provided solid support and good "writer feedback" which improved the quality of my writing. I would like to acknowledge her for her great consistency and vital support of this book.

I am grateful to Rowman & Littlefield associate editors Amy King and Alison Pavan for commenting and revising this manuscript. Without these helpmates and many others who contributed many hours and ongoing support to this project, it would have been quite impossible to complete this work.

Above all, I am thankful for my mother and uncle Pawel to whom this book is dedicated. Together they taught me about the trauma of migration and exile through their own examples. They experienced exile and multiple migrations, but their inner flames and psychic homes remained regardless of their surroundings.

Introduction

Almost every individual or a family in this increasingly globalized world has experienced the impact of "migration and relocation phenomenon." The topic of migration goes back to the dawn of our civilization and the myth of Adam and Eve captures the original story of migration and exile from Eden. This book about migration trauma and its relationship to identity and primary culture has the potential to be of interest to most migrants and mental health professionals working with migrants in many countries, most especially, in a country of immigrants such as the United States which has large influxes of people coming from different parts of the world and settling here.

The phenomenon of migration in its broader cultural context seems to be present everywhere and yet its complexity is often taken for granted. The psychological effects of the immigration process and its relationship to internal culture and identity have seldom been studied by psychoanalysts. It is rather perplexing that so little study has been done on the subject of migration, culture, and identity given that many of the pioneers of psychoanalysis were themselves immigrants who came from diverse cultural and ethnic backgrounds.

Generally, mainstream psychoanalysis favors a focus on the intra-psychic internal world, and much less attention is given to cultural, sociological, and historical factors (for many different reasons which are outside the scope of this study to explore). Little literature is available about the psychological adjustment to relocation and the different types of anxieties such as persecutory, annihilation, and depressive anxiety activated by the trauma of migration. How can one work through powerful anxieties and losses activated by the phenomenon of migration? What effects do the various types of migration have on the individual's basic identity, and how do we mourn real losses and expand and transform our basic identity into an integrated sense of self? This book explores such specific questions as how migration, internalized culture, and identity influence immigrants and why some immigrants adjust to a new culture while others have great difficulties doing so.

The larger question that I wanted to explore in-depth was what psychoanalysis can contribute to the migrant experience and the degree to which psychoanalysis can penetrate the process of authentic integration into a new culture and finding the psychological home within.

In this book, the factors that lead to successful psychological migration, as well as the factors that lead to failure, have been examined. The phenomenon of migration has been investigated both as a trauma of psychological losses, on the one hand, and as a significant opportunity for self-discovery and satisfying psychological integration into a new culture on the other.

This study is a microcosmic psychoanalytic exploration of the phenomena of migration. It is concerned with the details and nuances of inner psychological struggles and transformations of individual migrant patients in the process of working through the migration trauma.

My clinical work and psychoanalytic thinking has been primarily influenced by the work of S. Freud, M. Klein, W. Bion, D. Winnicott, and others. I found their psychoanalytic orientation helpful in this study because it addresses, in great detail, the early infant development that is dependent on and greatly influenced by the maternal matrix and therefore by different cultural child rearing practices in a given culture. Particular attention in this study was paid to premigration experiences and very early psychological factors, which perhaps are most important in the outcome of the psychological migration process.

The scope of this book addresses the following dimensions: (1) psychoanalytic perspectives on migration, culture, identity, and development of the psychological home within; (2) presentation of the three clinical composite case studies illustrating the migration process and working through the migration trauma; and (3) concluding analysis as to what leads to a degree of successful migration and what may end in failure of the migratory process.

The basic psychoanalytic framework that helped to organize my thinking and this book's conclusions highlights three fundamental elements: premigration experience, identity, and the environment (primary culture). While there are other factors and themes that I consider, I pay special attention to these three dimensions.

In my clinical work, I only know the premigration experiences and oral history from migrant patients' descriptions and their memories. I am aware of and pay attention to what extent migrant patients talk about the actual premigration experience and to what extent by talking about their premigration experience they are really talking about their early psychic life before migrating into the new world.

As a psychoanalyst I look at migration experience as an internal experience which has some relationship with the external world. In this study I am particularly concerned with the internal psychic world focus but in a dialectic with cultural environment. My knowledge about migrant's external world experience comes mostly from my clinical work itself with migrant patients.

In this book I do not independently assess what the premigration experience was. Therefore, in my work, I pay attention to specific external criteria related to premigration experience but seen through migrants' subjective internal world.

For instance, we may wonder if a migrant comes from a country which is a dictatorship to the United States' democratic system, and his or her life was persecuted there as compared to somebody who came from a society that is also democratic and offers economic opportunities. Would that make a significant difference in a premigration experience? These external factors will play some role in shaping the internalized experience, but the internalized experience may be shaped by the psychic factors in their country of origin.

The second factor area related to identity is addressed throughout the study in terms of finding a psychological home within and in terms of what leads to a degree of successful (or unsuccessful) migration. Therefore the type of migrant that has a relatively well-integrated sense of self-identity has a chance of going through a healthy process of migration. The other type of migrant with a more precarious identity will go through a psychological type of migration, which is more traumatic.

The other factor that I pay special attention to is the environment, and therefore the circumstances to which migrants arrive, which include family and other support systems. However, I do not talk about the environment independently, but more in terms of a person's psychological experience of the environment. I may pay particular attention to some broad notions about the environment such as what sort of culture the migrant comes from, as well as what social, economic, and personal factors influenced their development.

For instance, an external situation, where a minority person migrated in order to escape persecution in their own country, may be a very important factor in shaping up the internal world of the migrant patient. Different people with different internal worlds will experience these external factors in different ways, even though it would be traumatic to be in that type of oppressive persecutory environment for anyone. However, the kind of trauma someone would experience would be influenced by their own inner psychological framework. There will be a connection between the internal and external worlds but not in terms of simple one-on-one impact, where migrants with that type of internal psychic framework will react in the same way to the phenomena of migration. Generally speaking, migrants with a relatively well-integrated inner psychic world will have a very different experience with migration (possibly more positive) than migrants with a precarious sense of identity.

We cannot ignore the significant external factors and the reality of the external world of particular culture and society in which people live. There is a reality of a particular culture that will have an impact on a migrant's life and psyche. There is also a reality of the internal psychic world shaped by internal and external factors which will influence one's perception of the environment and external reality.

The essential foundation of this study is in-depth clinical work with migrant patients in the process of migration and integration into a new culture. The clinical cases of Eastern European migrants that I have selected illustrate the various stages of the transformational process of self-integration, and therefore the process of finding the psychological home within (with different degrees of it).

I chose to use composite cases in my study in order to maintain the confidentiality of specific patients' cases. These composite cases were rooted in clinical experience and other direct observations. In order to create the composite cases, I selected cases whose subjects had comparable attributes, responses and life experiences (i.e., migration). This approach has been employed by internationally acclaimed psychoanalysts Wilfred Bion and Juliet Mitchell, as well as other psychoanalysts and mental health professionals, in order to protect their patients' privacy.

For example, Juliet Mitchell, the internationally well-known psychoanalyst and author of such groundbreaking books as *Psychoanalysis and Feminism* (1974), has adopted this approach in the very well received book published by Basic Books, *Mad Man and Medusas: Reclaiming Hysteria* (2000).

Mitchell (2000) writes:

> In the interests of illustrating these phenomena (hysteria) and furthering my argument without making it unnecessarily discursive, I propose to amalgamate a number of patients who, despite their different histories, have comparable hysterical responses . . . this fictional being is like a character in a "true story"—all the elements come from direct observations, although the combination does not. The combination is entirely plausible. (p. 226)

In *Ethical Issues in the Publication of Clinical Material*, published in the *Journal of Analytical Psychology* (50, 1), Barbara Wharton writes:

> material from several patients (can be used by researchers) to build up a composite patient, in that way seeking to free themselves from the obligation to ask permission, and safeguarding the anonymity of the patient. (2005, p. 87)

Among many other mental health professionals, Peter D. Kramer, psychiatrist and author of the landmark bestseller, *Listening to Prozac*, in his most recent book, *Should You Leave*, used this approach and created a wide range of composite patients.

Similarly, I created the composite cases, rooted in direct observations and clinical experiences, and arrange them based on similar attributes and migration experiences. All the elements of this composite being are based on the true life stories of migrants, but the combination does not.

I do not believe this distorts any of the clinical discussion, implications, or the clinical concerns about the phenomena of migration, identity and culture that I have presented. In my selection of clinical data, I had to exercise my clinical judgment in order to ensure that the phenomena discussed here properly represent authentic experiences of migrant clients.

In order to preserve the authenticity of composite cases I have included two but not more than three patients per composite case being in this study. Each composite case illustrates particular clinical dynamics and clinical issues related to migration trauma, culture, and identity which are similar and compatible.

Instead of writing about any one individual in this study, I considered the treatment of different combined cases, and focused mostly on the relevant themes related to migration, identity, and culture. Hence, in this study, I was not concerned with describing the full chronological development of the treatment but only different relevant aspects of such treatment.

The usage of the composite cases is simultaneously a strength and limitation of this study. It is strength because it provides a wealth of clinical information from a few patients experiencing similar issues and the phenomena of migration. Therefore, the findings and conclusions about one particular case are supported and reinforced by a few other cases concerning patients who are experiencing similar issues, which add depth and richness of clinical information. On the other hand, the use of composite cases is a limitation because it does not describe or present any particular case study in full length.

Another key aspect of my work in this study and my understanding of the subject matter is my personal relocation and migration experience from Eastern Europe to the United Kingdom and to the United States. My interest in the topics of migration, identity, and culture comes from my experience of living in different cultures.

When approaching this study I thought through the implication of migration in terms of my own life and my work. Many of my thoughts and ideas on migration, identity, and culture have been based on direct observations and personal experiences of migration. The actual clinical psychoanalytic work with immigrant patients in another culture in ongoing psychoanalytic therapy can contribute to a much greater level of psychic depth and understanding of the process of cultural integration. Through such psychoanalytic psychotherapeutic work, one can investigate the process of changes in psychic structures that take place when the individual is in prolonged contact with another culture that is different from his or her native culture.

One can study the often slow development of inner psychic structures and the integration of the self in two cultures. One can also observe the universal similarities of the intrapsychic self and the differences according to cultural patterns and different internalized world views, that is, value systems that give different meaning to everyday experiences.

My patients from Eastern European countries were part of the American cosmopolitan culture, yet internally and psychologically they have only partially integrated the two different cultures. They were authentically and often painfully working through the processes of self-integration and integration into an American culture. They were highly motivated to move through their inner conflicts, feelings, and emotions, and to transform their difficulties and traumas. A greater in-depth psychoanalytic understanding could be ensured by such a long-term psychoanalytic treatment.

I set out to explore how in-depth psychoanalytic work with individual composite case patients from Eastern European countries coming to the United States can provide answers to much broader questions, such as determining what leads to successful adaptation to a new place of living, what leads to the development of an expanded "bicultural *self*" (Roland, 1988), and how we can find the psychic home within ourselves regardless of external hardships.

I studied the essential psychological elements of the process of integrating into a new culture. It seems that one of the essential factors in the process of integration is the capacity to deal with painful emotions and to mourn losses. A painful emotion with which most newcomers must struggle is the feeling of guilt for having abandoned the family and friends left in the old community.

Yet another very powerful feeling most migrants experience is shame and fear of exposing themselves to new things, new situations, and, often, a new language. We all have a powerful need to cling to the old and familiar patterns that enable us to face our futures with a degree of confidence.

It was my intention to explore the effects of different reasons for migration, whether motivated by a voluntary or involuntary move. In other words, one could readily expect that the effects of migration and the degree of pain experienced as a result of separation from the country of origin would vary as a function of the degree to which the immigrant had been an integrated member of that country or not, and whether migration was a matter of life or death (e.g., the migration of the refugee) or a matter of improving their quality of life (e.g., migration to make a better living). Is the immigrant fleeing mistreatment or rushing toward what she or he hopes will be better opportunities?

The clinical case material strongly indicated that those migrants who had very early psychological disturbances had much greater difficulties in dealing with the psychological trauma of migration. Migrants with basic psychological capacities to mourn, to form healthy relationships, and endure difficult feelings had a much greater chance of successfully going through a migration.

The surprising discovery was that there is a much more significantly traumatic element to the process of migration, which is not sufficiently recognized by psychological literature. There is a considerable psychological literature on sociological, historical, cultural, and anthropological aspects of migration. However, they do not focus on the traumatic factors of the migration process (see Chapter 1). There is only a small section of psychoanalytic literature that speaks about the traumatic aspects of the migratory process. My book is in agreement with these psychoanalytic studies which consider migration in its traumatic aspects. Finally, the psychic and physical migration often brings out more vividly not only the traumatic aspects of the migration process but, also, the possibilities for creative change and future psychic development.

This book opens up further this new and only scantly charted territory of human migration trauma and the potential of creative psychic change. It helps to fill the existing gap and build the recognition and attention it deserves and needs. As previously stated, what is notable about my study is that I provide very detailed clinical case studies of Eastern European migrants coming to the United States and psychologically working through the migration trauma. Perhaps the image and metaphor of the psychic home (used throughout this book) and the road on which a psychic and physical journey takes place to some distant destination captures the predicament of most migrants (or other travelers).

There is a traumatic aspect of the migration process which introduces more explicitly the element of multiple losses but also a factor of a psychic destruction and psychic creation within the human psyche. The migrant by leaving the native world to which he used to belong and entering the new world not only suffers the multiple losses but, also, necessarily psychologically destroys some aspects of the old world. It is possible that a migrant more vividly than others (nonmigrants) always carries in his or her psyche an element of psychic destruction of the parts of the old world. Perhaps some level of psychic destruction on the migrant's journey (psychic and physical) is inescapable, provided that there is also the capacity for creative potential. In reality, a migrant "traveling down the road" in search of a new psychological and physical home, to some degree, has to psychologically destroy the world left behind in order to come to a different new world. We may wonder how much one can keep the aspects of the old world alive and how much other aspects are inevitably destroyed.

It is possible that the task that migrants need to face (more explicitly than other human beings) is how to keep a degree of inner balance between the psychic destructive forces and creative forces (when possible), and therefore the balance between keeping alive the aspects of the old world and also the elements of the new world.

One may hope to be able to create a psychic movement back and forth between the old and new world and keep both of them alive in various degrees. However, we may wonder how much of the old culture has to be, to some degree, psychologically destroyed so the new world can be created within and without. The nonmigrant may not have to face the above dilemmas because they have not quite left and to some degree psychologically destroyed their native world.

All societies are developing and growing entities but they are doing it in the same cultural and historical context of a given county. If a particular person is living, growing, and changing within the same society than for him or her leaving and relocation have different meanings than for a migrant leaving the whole society behind. Migrants who have left one's society and moved to another country to take a refuge in another world face different implications. Since a migrant's original connections are left behind these have different meanings in comparison to those who stayed and changed within the same society. That kind of migrant who has left one's culture is often faced with the task of creating new psychological and physical links and connections (more urgently than others) and the idea of creation of the new expanded psychological and physical home (when possible).

Chapter 1

Psychoanalytic Perspectives on Migration, Identity, Culture, and its Differentiation from Psychosocial Approaches

In *Psychoanalytic Perspectives on Migration and Exile* (Grinberg & Grinberg, 1989) psychoanalysts Leon Grinberg, M.D., and Rebeca Grinberg, M.D., observe that human migration has been examined by sociologists, historians, and scholars from other disciplines, but they believe that the outcomes of migration have not been examined in-depth from a psychoanalytic perspectives. Grinberg and Grinberg address the phenomena of migration in detail and in terms of different types of fears, phantasies, and lost parts of the self. According to them, such fears may trigger unconscious/conscious phantasies that produce what they refer to as "the psychopathology of migration." The ability to work through these fears promotes the development of a more mature and expanded sense of cultural identity in migrants.

Migration from one place to another is a very complex psychosocial process, one that involves profound changes and losses, and yet also the possibility of enormous growth and creative expansion. In this process, all that is known and familiar, including the motherland (or fatherland) and often the mother tongue, are given up. Can the psychic shock of losing one's country and one's native language be psychologically survived? This often sudden change due to migration activates tremendous anxieties that threaten the very sense of self and therefore the individual's sense of coherent existence and psychological stability. The migrant is faced not merely with the fundamental existential process of yet another separation-individuation from the motherland but also the possibility of enormous identity transformation.

What is the psychosocial transformational process involved in identity change of the newcomer? How can psychoanalysis illuminate the deeper levels and dimensions of the process of relocation, existential separationindividual, and identity maturation? I have used psychoanalytic concepts to shed some light on the process of cultural integration and identity reorganization, for example, the drastic change that is a consequence of migration can affect the psychological balance of the self. The profound change of dislocation can lead to self-regression and the overuse of more primitive psychological defenses such as splitting, projection, fragmentation, idealization, devaluation, and so on, all of which weaken the integrity of the self and the psychic home.

In the *Psychoanalytic Quarterly* (1974), Falk suggests that on an unconscious level the old and the new countries often represent the early mother and father. The country of birth (the motherland) may represent the mother, and the new country the father, or vice versa. This can activate unconscious Oedipal phantasies and their reenactment in the new country. Comprehension of these unconscious Oedipal phantasies might be helpful in the process of integration.

On the other hand, some of these unconscious Oedipal phantasies might be worked through by an immigrant (with the well-integrated sense of self) without necessarily being fully comprehended and made fully conscious. In immigrants who have an integrated inner sense of self, there is an inner work (conscious and unconscious) that is taking place and they might be able to work through the challenge of migration to a greater or lesser degree without fully comprehending the maternal and paternal unconscious and conscious phantasies and aspects of the personality.

D. W. Winnicott formulated his theory of the true and false self in his 1960 paper "Ego Distortion in Terms of True and False Self" (Winnicott, 1960) where he states:

> The development of a false self is one of *the most successful defense organizations* designed for the protection of the true self's core, and its existence results in the sense of futility. (p. 292)

For Winnicott the fundamental factor that facilitates and leads to the sense of feeling real and good is a good-enough facilitating environment which holds and contains.

The conceptualization of true/false structures as presented in *The Maturational Processes and the Facilitating Environment* (Winnicott, 1960) captures the essence of true and false identifications with the new culture. A true and deeper integration begins if the holding environment (provided by a good-enough environment) in the new world and culture provide enough emotional support to allow the process of mourning and reintegration (Winnicott, 1960). The environment must contain aggression sufficiently to lead to further true internal/external integration. Failure of the holding environment and the process of mourning may lead to helplessness and a desperate search for the often idealized lost old world of objects and devaluation of the new world of objects that are available or vice versa.

In facing the loss and mental pain of separation, the immigrant may resort to the defense of idealization of the future and be unable to live in the "now moment" and the internal emotional home. The process of idealization/devaluation resulting from fear of loss always robs the "now moment" of its vitality, and leads to the creation of an artificial psychic home. Such a migrant needs to face the process of de-idealization of the lost old world of objects and with it, the painful processes of mourning and letting go, so that it may be possible to live in the emotional home and the now moment.

The fundamental element in the process of immigrant integration into a new culture is integration on the intrapsychic level of splitting and fragmentation of the self and the internal world of object relations. In order to move through the process of integration, the individual needs to have some basic emotional capability for intrapsychic separation and mourning, and the capacity to experience painful emotions such as guilt, anger, shame, and so forth. In situations where character structure is problematic, the powerful ongoing processes of mourning and integration may not be possible.

In the book *In Search of Self in India and: Toward a Cross-Cultural Psychology* (Roland, 1988), the author asserted that the result of authentic integration is a new, more mature, expanded *cultural self* (Roland, 1988) that emerges with new emotional capacities for ambivalence toward both the old and the new worlds. This expanded cultural self may possess greater flexibility, spaciousness, depth of emotions, and wisdom, as well as a broader spectrum of feelings and response. On the other hand, such a self may also be impoverished if deprived of various factors and ingredients available only in the old world and culture.

Heinz Kohut was an American analyst born in Vienna (an immigrant himself) who was founder of self-psychology that is a distinct psychoanalytic theory of development and psychotherapy. The pivotal concept of self-psychology is the "selfobject." *The Psychology of the Self: A Casebook* (1978) conceptualized a very important link between the self and the object which he called the selfobject. This link is fundamental in the development of the self.

In Allen Siegel's book *Heinz Kohut and the Psychology of the Self* (1996), he states:

> In 1978 Kohut removed the hyphen from the term "selfobject" to provide the idea that the function-providing object is not experienced as separate from the self. . . . The non-hyphenated "selfobject" first appeared in a joint publication later that same year (Kohut & Wolf, 1978). (p. 72)

In contrast to a selfobject, a true object is psychologically separate and distinct from the self. "It can be 'loved and hated by a psyche that has separated itself from the archaic objects, has acquired autonomous structures, has accepted the independent motivations and responses of others, and has grasped the notion of mutuality' (1971, p. 51)" (Siegel, 1996, p. 72).

Broadly speaking, the selfobject is experienced in terms of the specific psychological need-fulfilling functions it provides for the self which include attunement to affective states, validation of subjective experience, affect containment, tension regulation, soothing, sustaining, organizing or restoring a weakened sense of self disrupted by selfobject failure and recognition of uniqueness and creative potential.

Self-psychology has talked about the fact that the individual needs a good selfobject that can facilitate and enhance the person's development as well as contribute to strengthening the sense of self. If one did not have good selfobject experiences, then the sense of self will be undermined and one will not be able to reach a more mature level of development.

Kohut's view in which the object world (including environment) is experienced as providing various sustaining functions throughout life can shed some light on a migrant's dilemma, namely, suffering a rupture of the object world (culture), and therefore possibly needing such cultural selfobject functions in a new and unknown world.

The themes that D. Winnicott and W. Bion talked about are similar to *The Psychology of the Self: A Casebook* (Kohut, 1978) "selfobject" functions. Particularly in *Deprivation and Delinquency* (Winnicott, 1955) the concept of a "holding" and in *Learning from Experience* (Bion, 1962) the idea of "containing" object and the role of such a containing and holding object in helping with development and integration of the self might be compared to Kohut's notion of "selfobject."

American psychoanalyst Eric Erikson, who is well known for his many original ideas on how human beings develop a sense of self and identity, emphasized the continual development of a person's identity and awareness one has of oneself as a whole person throughout an eight-stage life cycle. He also maintained that cultural and social influences are very important parts of human development. Erikson is best known for his ideas on adolescence and adolescent identity crisis before moving into the next stage of adulthood.

> In their search for a new sense of continuity and sameness, adolescents have to refight many of the battles of earlier years, even though to do so they must artificially appoint perfectly well-meaning people to play the role of adversaries; and they are ever ready to install lasting idols and ideals as guardians of a final identity. (Erikson, 1950b, p. 261)

The author's ideas about cultural and social influences on human development throughout the life cycle are very helpful in understanding the development and ongoing maturation of our psyche. However, Erikson's ideas about self and identity development and how one takes on identity as an adolescent in relation to cultural values and ego ideal address a higher level of identity development than the British object relations approach used in this study. Therefore, Erikson's ideas about identity are less relevant to this study, which addresses very early levels of self-integration, as well as impediments to self-integration, cohesion and development.

The focus of this book is on the primary identity development (primary identifications) where the individual person has to distinguish his/her sense of self from that of his/her objects. According to *A Critical Dictionary of Psychoanalysis* (Rycroft, 1968), the primary identity is related to the early process of self and other differentiation, where the individual has to distinguish his/her identity from that of his objects. The secondary identification is part of further self-development, which is the process of identifying with an object (i.e., parent) whose separate identity has already been discovered.

Due to early unworked-through traumas, parts of the self (primary identity) are often split off and disowned and they need to be re-owned and brought together by an individual in order to find a psychic home within and become more integrated. The migrants presented in this work engaged in a massive splitting and disowning of large parts of themselves (due to early traumas), which leads to a fragile sense of identity formation.

In such circumstances, the migration becomes yet another trauma in which these early tendencies to disown parts of oneself become reactivated in a migrant's life. The focus in treatment is to help such a migrant to re-own and bring these parts together. Such a migrant, who is working through the migration trauma, is often trying to get ownership of the fundamental aspects of the self in order to become more fully alive.

If a migrant tries to disown large parts of the self and then tries to put on top of such a fragmented self another cultural identity or image, this will lead to a false sense of security, false image/identity solution and pseudo-adjustment to a new culture (different levels of falseness and authenticity).

With the loss of a holding culture, the migration frequently becomes a new trauma that becomes a threat to early fragile sense of identity. The inner sense of self needs to be *owned up to*—reclaimed—by a migrant first, before he or she can engage—*authentically engage*—in a new culture, and internalize the new culture in a productive way.

Therefore, if there is not such a primary well-integrated and grounded sense of self, a migrant may not be able to learn from new experiences and arrives at false identifications with the new culture.

In contrast, if the migrant has a well-integrated primary identity and capacity to deal with the internal psychic reality and the outside world, and is able to come up with some type of authentic relationship between the two, then there is a chance for more authentic integration into a new culture.

As already stated, in this study I primarily used the concepts and ideas that I derived from the object relations approach, which have been informed by the works of S. Freud, M. Klein, D. Winnicott, W. Bion, and others.

Broadly speaking Nasir Ilahi, LLM, describes this particular approach and the understanding of its transference and countertransference aspects in *The Psychoanalytic Study of the Child* in the following ways:

> It is also worth noting that in these British approaches a great deal of attention is paid to the earliest interaction between eros and the aggressive drive (death drive for Klein and certain others) including the role of the latter in either promoting or inhibiting development or promoting too rapid a progress leading to precocity and "premature ego development". . . . Note that this view of aggression broadens our understanding of it as it is not limited to negative themes such as anger, frustration, envy, etc. . . . far greater attention (is) paid to unconscious phantasies, anxieties and defenses and these may be communicated by the more disturbed patient . . . symbolically (or more accurately, often proto symbolically) to us via a variety of means, including enactments in the transference of split off relations between parts of the self and objects, gaps, somatizations, concretizations, projective identifications, corporeal and emotional behavior, nonverbal gestures, and so forth. (Ilahi, cited in King, 2003, pp. 130–31)

In general, my perspectives and way of thinking, as well as the way that I work with patients clinically (which is reflected in this study) have been greatly influenced by the above way of working, which is mostly informed by works by British object theorists.

Alan Roland, author of such books as *In Search of Self in India and Japan: Toward a Cross-Cultural Psychology* and *Cultural Pluralism and Psychoanalysis: The Asian and North American Experience* has made many original and important contributions to cross-cultural psychoanalytic studies. He speaks about universalities of human nature and also the profound psychological differences from culture to culture. He emphasizes a comparative pluralistic cross-cultural paradigm, and the cultural dimension of psychoanalysis.

Roland writes about such issues as the cultural self, the personal self, and the familiar self, multiculturalism, cross-cultural communication, and how the construction of self differs in other cultures, and the benefits that can ensue from interdisciplinary collaboration and away from psychoanalytic reductionism.

In *Cultural Pluralism and Psychoanalysis: The Asian and North American Experience,* Roland (1996) has asserted that essential to psychoanalytic theory is the developmental schema that were formulated first incorporating the Freudian notions of psychosexual development and, followed by other analysts such as Klein (1957), notions of early childhood development and have paranoid-schizoid and depressive psychic organizations. Because developmental schema have been developed according to the Western clinical data, nonetheless many psychoanalysts tend to assume that such developmental schema are universal and therefore tend to assume the primacy of psychic reality and that psychology determines culture.

Roland writes in *In Search of Self in India and Japan* (1988):

> The psychoanalytic formulation of the primacy of psychic reality and psychic determinism usually reads that the character formation brought about through the particular vicissitude of universal early childhood psychosexual stages is a strong determinant of the sociocultural patterns of a given society. (p. 230)

Roland points out that according to the traditional psychoanalytic formulations of the primacy of psychic reality there are some universal built-in psychosexual stages of development and they influence social and cultural patterns of a given society. The influence is from the built-in psychosexual stages to society, rather than also from society toward structuring the internal world.

Roland further points out that psychoanalysis has under-emphasized the value of culture; in other words, culture plays a more important role than psychoanalytic theory has traditionally granted it. There is a dynamic interaction between the psychic world and cultural reality.

I recognize that the subject of the relationship of psychoanalysis, migration, and culture is vast. There are many ways of investigating and examining the topic of culture, which has been studied through such perspectives as the sociological and the anthropological as well. It is not within the purview of my work to examine this subject from many perspectives. Rather, I have considered the topic of culture mostly from an internal perspectives, and accordingly have addressed internal culture and its relation to migration and identity issues. I wanted to analyze my clients' internal world along with their internal culture and their relationship to migration.

In his book *Cultural Pluralism and Psychoanalysis: The Asian and North American Experience* (1996), Alan Roland writes about the development of the *cultural self* on a higher, more integrated level, and an outcome of working through the process of separation-individuation (Mahler). He also speaks of such broad psychoanalytic categories as the *bicultural self,* the *familial self,* and the *individualized self.*[1] I intend to expand on some of the above

1. The concepts such as *Cultural Self, Bicultural Self, Expanded Self,* etc., were originally used by A. Roland. I make references to and use of these concepts throughout this study.

broad psychoanalytic terms (such as bicultural self) and apply them to Eastern European immigrants.

Roland also speaks of bicultural selves as coexisting together, more integrated, in dialogue with each other and available for use in different ways so the individual is able to function in two cultures. Such a broad, universal psychoanalytic category as the bicultural self could be filled in with the different types of self that are either more or less integrated and more split off. Thus there could be the higher level, more integrated bicultural self or the lower level, more split off, fragmented, and conflictual bicultural self.

Depending on prior trauma and the individual's psychological equipment, the individual could develop the *bicultural self* (Roland, 1996) with different degrees of falseness or authenticity. I suspect that when dismissing his or her past history and culture, the individual is also rejecting the culture represented by the parents and other early relationships. The individual could create here the idealized cultural self (false self) and in this way deny hate for the individual's culture and parents. Such an idealized bicultural self is not created out of love, but out of hate, and therefore it is false. The process of migration can trigger some of these early conflicts related to the individual's parents and culture.

On the other hand, within the bicultural self, for instance the *Eastern European Self* may be in conflict with the *American Self.* I believe that the two different selves represent two different ways of being, and thus may be in conflict, or even split off from each other. It is necessary to explore just how deep such conflicts and splits are within the bicultural self. The bicultural self split may be used by other types of splitting, where, for example, anger or sexuality gets split between the two selves.

I suspect that if the basic structure of the self is already split off due to early traumatic relationships, then the bicultural self may be used for further division. On the other hand, even if the immigrant is more integrated, he or she will still have to navigate through the issue of two different cultures, but will be able to navigate with a more integrated sense of self rather than a precarious sense of self.

I would conceptualize the *cultural self* (Roland, 1996) as more peculiar to a particular culture. What makes human beings different from one another are their individual experiences and talents, and also their internalized cultures. Therefore, broadly speaking, the cultural self is a self that has been acquired and carries the imprint of the particular culture, whereas what I characterize as the true elemental self is there irrespective of culture and is intrinsically related to our humanity. Thus, at a more fundamental level, generally speaking, if the individual functions more from the true elemental self than the cultural self of the individual will be more authentic. On the other hand, if the individual operates from the early (or later) "false self" (Winnicott, 1960) than the cultural self will be less authentic. There are different levels and shades of this particular dilemma.

I would further conceptualize the elemental self as the most basic self that exists in each human being; it is out of this elemental self that the "true self" (Winnicott, 1960) evolves. Such an elemental self is related to our deeper humanity, vulnerability, and is present irrespective of any culture from which the individual comes. All human beings can connect with one another through this basic and elemental self. Such an elemental self connects all humanity regardless of cultural differences and personal heritage.

I believe that when a migrant comes from a different culture to, for example, the United States, there is some rupture of the cultural self but the true elemental self (Winnicott, 1960) that is beneath our cultural conditioning stays intact. To simplify the picture, such a rupture of cultural self and multiple cultural attachments (family, language, etc.) can be paralyzing to some degree to the individual (due to multiple losses) and a false self structure may be created to cover up the losses but this leads to a more artificial life style. On the other hand, if the individual is able to work through the losses, there is the possibility of something elemental and creative breaking through, which is often enriching to the migrant's identity.

All of this depends upon the immigrant's psychological equipment, prior traumas, personal history, and emotional and psychological capacities.

In 1967, Winnicott examined the theme of cultural experience in his paper "The Location of Cultural Experience" where he states:

> I have used the term cultural experience as an extension of the idea of transitional phenomena and of play without being certain that I can define the word "culture." The accent indeed is on experience. In using the word culture I am thinking of the inherited tradition. I am thinking of something that is in the common pool of humanity, into which individuals and groups of people may contribute, and from which we may all draw *if we have somewhere to put what we fund.* (pp. 98–99)

For Winnicott, culture is at the very center of the merged experience of the mother/infant, at the beginning of life. Thus the primary culture is the early mother and infant relationship. Cultural customs, language, etc. emerge from this *primary culture*. Winnicott also conceptualizes a third area, the transitional space where we are when we are *doing* (Winnicott, 1951). He uses the term "cultural experience" as an extension of that idea and of play. Therefore, the cultural experience takes place in the transitional space, and if *doing* comes from the true self, then the individual's life and cultural experience will feel real and fulfilling.

I suspect that the culture becomes internalized by the infant through the mother from the start of the infant's life, and goes into the formation of the early sense of self. The infant's interaction with the mother is essential in building up the sense of self. Winnicott writes of the *environmental mother*, which is the entire environment that the mother sets up for the baby (Winnicott, 1963).

We may wonder what the infant internalizes at this early interaction with the mother. According to Winnicott, the early self is in bits that coexist and the mother, through her holding and containing function, helps the bits to coalesce—the beginning of the process of integration of the true self (Winnicott, 1945). Through the mother's holding and containing matrix, the infant mind is able to come together. In fact, both the mother and the infant are playing a role in gathering things together. The mother helps the process of integration to begin, and then the infant, having identified in a primitive way with the mother's holding function (which in turn becomes internal capacity), is able to carry on this process. Through the mother's holding function, the psyche and the instinctual experience can be related to each other. In the more integrated state, there is some ownership of the instinctual life and psyche and soma can come together.

On the other hand, if there has not been this type of holding by the mother, some level of false integration (false self) will take place that the infant needs to make in order to survive. Underneath this false self is going to be the true self in some precarious state, and dependent on the false self structures. The false self can come to existence early or later in life as well.

We may also ask what role the mother's internal world and her specific culture play in establishing the internal world of the infant. According to Winnicott (1945) and Bion (1962), the mother's unconscious (and conscious) mind and experiences, including culture, are relevant in the formation of the infant mind. A mother's unconscious mind is communicated to the infant through all her interactions, her holding and containing functions, and the whole environment that she sets up. From the start, the *being* aspect of the infant, which belongs to the true self and the "inherited potential" (Winnicott, 1960), is influenced by the mother's unconscious. Through this mother/infant object relationship, the mother instinctually is communicating her unconscious, which thus is a building block with which the infant's own potential is interacting and building up the internal world and the psyche.

Winnicott, in his book *Playing and Reality* (1971), spoke about the relevance of the primary culture but he did not investigate different cultural realms and their meanings. For Winnicott and Bion the unconscious content of the mother's internal world was very important to a child's development. However, they did not talk about the different cultural content of the mother's unconscious psyche.

Generally speaking, the content of the mother's internal world differs from one culture to another. For instance, in Western culture the mother's psyche tends to be much more internally structured to treat her child to a far greater degree as an individual than an Eastern culture mother who may feel more comfortable with merged experiences with her child. In this respect culture comes into play through the interaction between the mother and the infant from the beginning of the infant's life, and goes into the formation of the (infant's) early sense of self.

In his two books, *Psychotherapy and Buddhism: Toward an Integration* and *A Psychoanalysis for Our Time: Exploring the Blindness of the Seeing I*, Jeffrey B. Rubin reveals and challenges psychoanalytic reductionism, a hidden authoritarianism, residual sexism, and overly simplistic conceptualizations of "self" and therefore our basic identity. He also explores the psychoanalytic concepts of *self* (and therefore our basic identity); alienation from self and others, ontological homelessness, psychological dislocation, cross-cultural communication, and the Eurocentrism of psychoanalysis, and so forth. In *A Psychoanalysis for Our Time: Exploring the Blindness of the Seeing I* (1988), he states:

> As studies of non-Western cultures teach us, other meaningful ways of being exist. For example, certain non-pathological, non-achievement oriented, non-self-centered states of being may be more important for many people than pursuing ambitions and ideals. These alternative ways of being are either missed or pathologized when one assumes that the individualistic ethos of the Northern European and North American individualized self is a universally valid and superior mode of being. (p. 118)

Rubin emphasizes that culture and cultural differences matter and, in his work, supports many of Roland's original ideas about cultural differences. In his study, Rubin provides useful discussion about some of the object relations theorists, such as Winnicott, that I am also writing about in this study. However, my focus has been specifically related to migration, identity and primary culture as he does not write about the topic of migration.

In his book *Immigration and Identity* (1999), Salmon Akhtar has also written on the theme of migration from one country to another and the long-lasting effects of such a move on an individual's identity. According to Akhtar:

> Immigration from one country to another is a complex psychosocial process with significant and lasting effects on an individual's identity. Leaving one's country involves profound losses. Often one has to give up familiar food, native music, unquestioned social customs, and even one's language. The new country offers strange tasting food, new songs, different political concerns, unfamiliar

> language, pale festivals, unknown heroes, psychically unearned history, and a visually unfamiliar landscape. However, alongside these losses is a renewed opportunity for psychic growth and alternation. New channels of self-expression become available. There are new identification models, different superego dictates, and fresh ideals. (p. 5)

He explores in his study such questions as the following: What determines the psychological outcomes of immigration? Can one ever mourn the loss of one's country? Why do people migrate from one country to another? and many more.

However, he has looked at these questions largely from the Ego Psychology approach and M. Mahler's separation-individuation theory (Mahler, 1971) which does not take into account some of the more primitive issues in psychological development, whereas my orientation in this study has been more focused on object relations theory perspectives and early development, which leads to differences in how one understands the presented clinical material.

In general, he also considers migration as a radical change in one's cultural and psychological environment and a form of trauma. He considers the tasks that a migrant is confronted with in dealing with multiple losses that migration brings about. He explores specific guidelines for psychotherapy and psychoanalysis for immigrant patients and what contributes to a healthy type of migration.

DIFFERENTIATION OF PSYCHOSOCIAL APPROACHES FROM PSYCHOANALYTIC PERSPECTIVES

There is massive literature in psychology on the phenomena of acculturation, ethnic identity and acculturative stress. One of the best examples is the best-selling textbook *Cross-Cultural Psychology* (1992) which examines the fast-growing field of cross-cultural psychology. The authors discuss concepts such as acculturation stress, migration motivation factors affecting acculturative stress and adoption, in addition to various factors that affect an individual in the process of migration and acculturation. They also address the moderating factors prior to migration and acculturation such as age, gender, education and language, as well as social support, social attitudes and coping strategies.

The psychosocial research based on very broad social and psychological concepts is useful in understanding the phenomena of acculturation. However, it does not attend to the kinds of issues that I am addressing in my book. My study uses in-depth psychoanalytic theories and I focus much more on how the inner adaptations and inner world transformations take place and what may promote a successful (or unsuccessful) migration.

In the book *Cross-Cultural Psychology*, we find the following definition of the concept of cultural identity:

> A parallel approach to understanding intercultural strategies uses the concept of **cultural identity** (Aboud, 1981; Berry, 1999a; Liebkind, 1996; Phinney, 2000). This notion refers to a complex set of beliefs and attitudes that people have about themselves in relation to their culture group membership; usually these come to the fore when people are in contact with another culture, rather than when living entirely within a single culture. (Salazar & Salazar, 1998, pp. 357–58)

This definition is very helpful in conceptualizing cultural identity from sociological and sociopsychological perspectives. However, on the other hand, this definition addresses identity on a very broad level of cultural, national and civic identity.

The in-depth psychoanalytic definitions of identity and acculturation stress and their unconscious dimensions are very different than the definitions used in the psychosocial approaches. In my study I address the concept of identity from a very different psychoanalytic level (see identity section) which is more based on such internal processes as: psychic internalizations, identifications, unconscious and conscious feelings and phantasies about subjective sense of identity and inner psychological home.

My book focuses more on the feelings and phantasies related to inner identity and inner psychological home. This work is more concerned with psychoanalytic concepts of identity and less with social-psychological broad concepts of cultural identity which address different level of cross-cultural psychological research.

Sociopsychological studies on acculturation stress and intercultural relationships are often carried out by questioners' method and do not tend to utilize in-depth psychology concepts and methods of psychoanalytical therapy. While the information presented in the studies about culture and cultural stress is very helpful, it does not directly pertain to the focus of my work in this study, which intends to address the process of migration and finding psychological home from a very different psychoanalytic perspectives based on clinical work. In particular, I am very concerned with taking a very microscopic look at what is happening in the internal world of the individual in terms of premigration issues and in what way the migration itself becomes a psychologically traumatic event.

The social psychological level addressed in the study about ethnic identity and acculturation strategies is very useful in providing the background for deeper psychoanalytic explanations of migration and finding an inner identity and psychological home within.

The research on acculturation provides many useful general conclusions which overlap with some of my own observations. For instance, in *Cross-Cultural Psychology* (1997) we read:

> Despite this lack of information for many societies, there is a clear trend indicating that acculturating people (individuals and groups) prefer, and adapt better, when they are attached to both their heritage culture and to the larger national society. (i.e. integration) (pp. 381–82)

However, my book also explores much more specific questions and nuances related to the process of migration and acculturation. For instance, in my composite case studies I explore different types of attachments to both the native culture and the larger new national society. For example, in the composite case of Zbyszek, the title character has a very ambivalent attachment and attitude toward his own heritage, which should not be mistaken to mean that he wanted to give up his ambivalent attachment.

In this study I explore many forms of attachment as observed in individual migrants: positive, negative, idealized, devalued or ambivalent, sometimes to both the heritage culture and the larger national society, all from a psychoanalytical point of view. I have drawn many of my general conclusions from my clinical work with individual migrant clients and some of them overlap with general conclusions on the study of acculturation which addresses very broad social levels.

Whereas my book presents in detail how individual migrant clients adapt and what is successful adaptation. I am looking at the specific individual migrants and a particular migration situation from Eastern Europe to the United States. I am not necessarily extending these principles and conclusions to other types of migrations, that is, from Eastern Europe to Japan.

The existing study on the acculturation process generalizes what acculturation is from the level of broad social psychological studies. Through the social psychological lens the research on acculturation looks at such factors as acculturation stress, acculturation attitudes and contact.

There are other approaches in existence which address the issue of multicultural assessment and its clinical, psychological and educational applications. Psychologist Joseph G. Ponterotto has written extensively on the subject of multicultural counseling and he uses qualitative and quantitative methods to explore the subject of multicultural counseling. Similarly Lisa A. Suzuki's psychological research has been focused on the areas of multicultural assessment.

The *Handbook of Multicultural Assessment, Clinical, Psychological and Educational Applications* (2001), coedited by Lisa A. Suzuki, Joseph G. Ponterotto, and Paul J. Meller is a comprehensive text addressing major multicultural assessment issues and their applications to diverse populations. Such important concepts as acculturation, ethnic and racial identity are mentioned in different contextual frameworks for multicultural assessment. Their work is focused on psychosocial, cognitive multicultural assessment which is most directly related to the external factors and not necessarily focused on in-depth psychoanalytic approaches.

They do not look at inner psychic world stressors, conflicts and processes that would be a part of psychoanalytic study. In my work I use in-depth psychoanalytic approaches wherein my focus is on allowing the issues related to unconscious and conscious culture to come out in a dynamic way in the course of psychoanalytic treatment. I do not specifically do multicultural interviews and ask specific questions but I am simply attentive in psychotherapy treatment to the themes related to culture and migration as they unfold. I pay particular attention to unconscious dimensions of psyche and the issues of trauma and conflicts. For instance, the conflict between the unconscious cultural values of one culture and another culture in mutual interaction may produce certain traumatic situations which are not consciously recognizable by a migrant client.

The psychological approaches of Suzuki, Ponterotto, and Meller about multicultural assessment, acculturation and ethnic identity are focused on broad social psychological dimensions and understanding of these concepts from a macrocosmic level. The broad social psychological formulations are helpful and valid in general understanding of the phenomena of acculturation and migration. However, they do not address the particular migrant situations and specific individual migrant clients in the process of acculturation.

Writing from a psychological-sociological perspective, Berry, Suzuki, and Ponterotto have also written on ethnic identity and they provide useful definitions of cultural and national identity based on different cultural beliefs, value systems and world views. These writers, however, define identity differently than psychoanalytic approaches do. While their discussions are very useful, they do not quite address the issue of inner identity at the very basic and fundamental level.

My book is making a contribution by providing a deeper microcosmic psychoanalytic exploration of the phenomena of migration and finding a psychic home within. In my study I explore the inner struggles and processes of individual migrant patients in the process of working through the migration trauma.

I approach the process of migration and acculturation from a very microscopic level. I focus on the detail and minute understanding of the very early development of unconscious psychic phantasies and unconscious traumas. I am concerned with understanding inner psychological transformation and focus less on broad social psychological understanding of the phenomena of migration.

It is only through the psychoanalytic approach that we get data on the unconscious life related to immigration and the way that early life experience impacts the migrant existence. However, the broad socio-psychological level and the deeper more detail-oriented psychoanalytic level can in some ways complement each other. The broad psychological level can provide a useful background to the deeper psychoanalytic detail exploration.

The systems theory of Monica McGoldrick and Froma Walsh, family therapy practitioners and researchers, is based on the Internal Family Systems Therapy which integrates intrapsychic and family theory and technique.

In the book *Ethnicity and Family Therapy* (1982), Monica McGoldrick talks about the stresses of migration, and how the effects of the migration process can persist over generations.

According to Monica McGoldrick (1982):

> Therapists need to be attuned to the stresses of migration even several generations late. (Sluzki, 1979; Cassim, 1982). All families in this country have experienced the complex stresses of migration; they may be "buried" or forgotten, but they will continue, albeit at times subtly, to influence the family's outlook. Under the pressure of accommodating to the new situation, and because of the pain of what was left behind, many immigrant groups have been forced to abandon much of their ethnic heritage (Greeley, 1979; Winawer-Steiner & Wetzel, Chapter 12; Hines & Boyd-Franklin, Chap. 4) and thus have lost a part of their identity. The effects of this cutting off of the past may be all the more powerful for being hidden. Families will be more vulnerable in the present; the more they have repressed their past. (p. 12)

The author is strongly emphasizing the need to be sensitive and attuned to stressors of the migration process. She clearly recognizes the stressors of migration and the complex impact that migration has which often endures over many generations.

What I bring about in my psychoanalytic exploration is how the migration trauma affects real migrants who are in the process of integrating into the new culture. I study how the migration trauma affects real migrant patients and how they work through the stresses of migration. Through the psychoanalytic framework I study the deeper levels of unconscious and conscious aspects of the psyche and the impact of migration on psychological functions.

With its emphasis on understanding the language of the unconscious, the psychoanalytic framework provides one with access to understanding the deeper unconscious effects of migration. The sociopsychological approaches, which do not subscribe to the psychoanalytic framework with its emphasis on understanding the language of the unconscious, do not address such unconscious effects of migration.

Many of Monica McGoldrick's general comments about migration stresses, ethnicity and family therapy are in agreement with my observations and thinking. However, in my book I also focus on how these stresses, conflicts and issues were present clinically in the work with individual migrant clients. Her work addresses the issue of culture, ethnicity and migration from the family's point of view (not individual psychotherapy). Therefore, her recommendations for psychotherapy are essentially suggestions for family therapy where she emphasizes the awareness of cultural conflicts:

> Appreciation of cultural variability leads to a radically new conceptual modal of clinical intervention. Restoring a stronger sense of identify may require resolving cultural conflicts within the family, between the family and the community, or in the wider context in which the family is embedded. A part of differentiation involves selecting from our ethnic traditions those values we wish to retain and carry on. Families may need coaching to sort out deeply held convictions from values asserted for emotional reasons. (McGoldrick, 1982, p. 23)

In my study I look at the family context but, fundamentally, I study the individual migrants and their unconscious and conscious internal conflicts, which could only be addressed through an in-depth psychoanalytic orientation. Through such an in-depth psychoanalytic approach one can understand how these cultural conflicts work inside the individual migrant and the different ways that migrants cope with them or escape them.

In this study I attempt to understand these cultural conflicts at their unconscious roots. I am interested in how individual, family and cultural conflicts are represented in the unconscious/conscious psyche and interpersonal life.

The systems theory writers and family practitioners such as Froma Walsh and Monica McGoldrick have made many valuable contributions to the subject of culture, ethnicity and family therapy. Although the systems theory and in-depth psychoanalytic orientation follow two different forms of thinking and different theoretical approaches, I believe that some of my study conclusions can be linked to observations and contributions made by systems theory.

Migration Complex and Losses Related to Cultural Dimensions

The shifting sands of our multi-globalized world have an impact on our psyche, culture, and world views. This is an area of massive migrations and the age of displaced and dislocated individuals who often lost place in their own culture and, therefore, their place in the world.

The displaced migrant's voyage from one culture to another can be seen as a metaphor for a physical and psychological journey of multiple losses and great potential for self-exploration of often unconscious and unacceptable, or acceptable but yet not known parts of our psyche, and hidden aspects of our deeper cultural selves often unnoticed in our culture of origin.

In comparison to migrants, those who have never been displaced from their own cultures of origin may continue their process of self-exploration in their native culture, often unaware of the power of holding and containing aspects of a given culture and their cultural selves with its particular modes of being and thinking.

Migration is a symbol and metaphor for human beings transitory and impermanent condition in this world and one's inner psychic reality. Almost any migrant by necessity develops greater sensing capacity of self/other in order to be able to see and observe the subtle differences and nuances in cultural modes of being and thinking in order to be able to navigate their new culture with more flexibility.

What makes us different as a human being is our specific cultural conditioning and particular holding/containing of a given culture. The loss of such cultural holding environment is generally deeply felt by each migrant. Most human beings are mostly aware of one culture of their origin, migrants are aware of at least two or more.

In this book I am looking at the idea of culture mostly from the perspectives of migration complex and the consequent multiple losses it entails including the loss of cultural dimension. I am less concerned with the psychological and cultural conflicts this tends to create in migrants lives and psyche. The in-depth exploration of migration complex in migrants coming from Eastern Europe stimulated my thinking about the possible existence of a category called Eastern European self. Is there such a category that may be called Eastern European self, psychological structure that operates on some deeper level that may have some clinical relevance? Will the loss of Eastern European self create conflicts inside a migrant's personality?

Eastern European culture includes many different countries and regions. There will be many differences and variations between regions. However, broadly speaking there are some commonalities between Eastern European cultures, especially when compared to Western European/Northern American type of cultures. The migration process itself is deeply affected by cultural changes and shifts in cross-cultural paradigms.

The Eastern European culture and its different regions have been under studied, possibly due to the socialist past and consequent freedom limitations. What is different and deeply ingrained in Eastern European psyche that is passed from generation to generation compared to Northern American and Western European self? The understanding of Eastern European psyche and delineation of Eastern European self is an uncharted territory in psychoanalysis that entails further deeper clinical and theoretical work and discussion.

Many subtle unconscious dimensions of the Eastern European self have not been explored and conceptualized, yet they may have much clinical relevance, which presents an interesting psychoanalytic exploration for a future study.

Psychoanalysis took root in different counties and has been influenced by culture, national heritage, and beliefs of a given country. According to Edith Kurzweil (1998) different countries unconsciously create the psychoanalysis it needs. In her book, *The Freudians: A Comparative Perspective (Psychiatry and Social Psychology Series)* (1998), she further states that the Freudian doctrine has been transmuted by aesthetic values, behavioral mores, and political traditions of different cultures. She suggests that culture and broader national traditions have influenced psychoanalysis. However, she does not go into a deeper unconscious psyche and its inner psychological structures created by different cultural beliefs and child rearing practices based on different cultural paradigms and assumptions.

Is there such a category as Eastern European psychoanalysis that is different from Western European psychoanalysis? The pioneering Eastern European psychoanalyst, Sandor Ferenczi's contributions to psychoanalysis represent different ways of thinking from Western European Freud's way of thinking. In *Disappearing and Reviving: Sandor Ferenczi in the History of Psychoanalysis* (2002), psychoanalyst Andre E. Haynal states that Ferenczi is the founder of all relationship-based psychoanalysis and explorer of traumatisms. Ferenczi focused on the relationship aspects and countertransference implications in psychoanalysts. He was one of the first important seminal thinkers who emphasized the whole idea of the actual role of the environment and how an environmental trauma may confuse or even derail developments of the individuals, which has implications for transference and countertransference relationship with the psychoanalyst.

In his book, Haynal states the following:

> Whereas Freud followed in the footsteps of the *Aufklarung*, the German Enlightenment, emphasizing human *liberation* through *rational knowledge*, Ferenczi belongs more in the romantic tradition, stressing as he did the *personal*, individual and *subjective*, which takes place first and foremost in "I-Thou" encounters. . . . (p. 69)

Ferenczi brings the psychoanalytic perspectives that is different from the German Enlightenment perspectives that Freud was emphasizing. He introduced more of two- and three-body psychoanalysis compared to one-person psychoanalysis emphasized by Freud. Freud's psychoanalysis is called one-person psychoanalysis because he was heavily focusing on what happened inside of the individual and did not give sufficient importance to the influence of relationships that could have had a damaging effect on the individual.

Freud was much more interested in the vicissitudes of instincts and the struggle between different instinctual forces. He gave greater significance to projections of internal conflict.

Ferenczi introduced the Eastern European psychoanalysis and movement away from one-person psychology that Freud emphasized to object relations psychology. The world of the object in Freud's thinking was marginal, and Ferenczi introduced the role of the object in a much more central way.

Historically one could argue that there have been differences between Eastern and Western European psychoanalysts and therefore different ways of thinking and being. One could begin to see in the differences between Freud and Ferenczi's thinking, and also differences in Eastern European psyche and Western European psyche, and its inner structure, the birth of Eastern European psychoanalysis. The Eastern European psychoanalytic tradition, with a more central role of the object and environment, was different from Western European tradition being focused on the individual, and one-person psychology.

Clearly there are culturally based differences in Eastern European thinking compared to Western European/Northern American thinking. What are the differences and similarities between Eastern European and Western European/Northern American cultures and a sense of underlying different cultural selves? There is a lot of literature in sociology, anthropology, and psychology about culture of individualism and collectivism. In fact, the world could be broadly divided between these two different cultural paradigms with its different shades and modes of being, on an individual and collective level. There are certainly shades and gradations of individualism and collectivism within each cultural paradigm. For instance, a migrant in individualistic culture coming from the American village to a cosmopolitan city such as New York City may feel that he/she left a more collectivistic sense of American village existence compared to New York City's type of existence. He/she may feel that village life offers a greater sense of community, extended family relations, compared to a very isolating individualistic culture of New York City.

Alan Roland, one of the contemporary pioneers in cross-cultural psychoanalysis, has written extensively about cross-cultural issues related to radically different cultures in terms of collectivism and individualism. In *Journeys to Foreign Selves: Asians and Asian Americans in a Global Era* (Roland, 2011), he states the following:

> I later realized that much of the rest of the world has one variation or another of the familial self, and that it is primarily the Northern European/North American culture area in modern Western history that has developed the individualized self. (p. 33)

Roland worked deeply and extensively with more Eastern collectivist, family-centered and radically different cultures. His observations about the familial self are relevant for Eastern European cultures, even though I am not speaking about radically different cultures. I am talking about Eastern European cultures that may possibly be in the middle of the spectrum related to individualistic and collectivistic cultures and ways of being with greater emphasis on collectivism without further clinical elaboration.

In *Search of Self in India and Japan,* Roland (1988) states the following about the familial self that he found in his clinical work with patients from radically different cultures:

> The familial self encompasses several important suborganizations: *symbiosis-reciprocity* that involves intensely emotional intimacy relationships, with their emotional connectedness and interdependence, in relationship-centered cultures where there is a constant affective exchange through permeable outer ego boundaries, where a highly private self in maintained, where high levels of empathy and receptivity to others are cultivated, and where the experiential sense of self is of a "we-self" that is felt to be highly relational in different social contexts. (pp. 7–8)

Even though Roland's notion of familial self applies to more radically different cultures, I think that, to a certain degree, this category of "we-self" will apply to the Eastern European culture which is more family oriented with greater emphasis on interdependence. The Eastern European culture broadly speaking falls into the category of collectivism, which may create more subtle cultural conflicts for Eastern European migrants than for migrants coming from radically different cultures, who are likely to experience more difficulties in migration because of significant cultural/psychological conflicts and issues.

In *Search of Self in India and Japan* (Ronald, 1988), he states:

> The individualized self in characterized by inner representational organizations that emphasize: an *individualistic "I-ness"* with relatively self-contained outer ego boundaries, sharp differentiation between inner images of self and other, and considerable social individuation orienting the person toward relatively autonomous functioning, inner separateness, and initiatives. . . . (Roland, p. 8)

He further differentiates the Western self which he called individualized self, from familial self which he thinks can be seen in terms of the "we-self." I suspect that Eastern European self will take some form of the familial self, but we may wonder what type and what form?

The mother and child early relationship is a living illustration and microcosm of our culture and society. According to our approach toward individualism and collectivism most of the world cultures can be separated into two broad-based dimensions regarding child rearing practices. In the North American/Western European cultures deeply ingrained value system regarding child development places great emphasis on a child's independence, self-reliance, highly verbal skills, and capacities to control emotions. In individualistic societies these characteristics are highly valued and appreciated.

Broadly speaking in Eastern cultures, which are the majority of our globalized world, the greater emphasis is placed on interdependence, we-self, and deeper appreciation of the extended family notion. The dependent behaviors are reinforced, such as appropriate levels of relatedness, self-effacing, unassuming attitudes are highly reinforced in child rearing practices. An individual is often responsible for a family's respect. The most painful punishment is the rejection by the family or primary group where the person is left alone. This is in contrast to the Northern American cultural icon of the self sufficient, "lonely cowboy" who represents the epitome of individualism and self reliance.

The psyche gets structured differently from the beginning of life, in the early interaction between mother and child. The culture of collectivism and individualism will be embedded from the beginning of life, in a human being's psyche, due to different child rearing practices. The mother will be acting in accordance with practices of a culture of collectivism or individualism. She would have internalized within herself the values of each culture and that would be automatically represented in the way she would relate to her child/or others. The particular culture is part of her inner framework that would be unconsciously and consciously transmitted to the child. The cultural individualized inner framework will be transmitting different values and practices to the child than familial inner cultural framework. This would lead to differences in psychic structure formations.

Early family expectations are different for Eastern cultures, including Eastern European people. The idea of the individualized self carries less importance. There is less emphasis on the development of the individualized self, which is built into early child rearing experiences and less thinking in terms of "me" and "I." In Western cultures there is a greater individualistic emphasis and more thinking about oneself. To think about oneself primarily may not come naturally to a person from collectivist backgrounds such as Eastern Europeans. The more individualized the given culture, the more importance the materialistic dimension of life will acquire. These individualistic dimensions are present in the more Eastern cultures too, but there is more emphasis on sharing, family values, and interdependence. There is a greater importance on not emphasizing the self which is part of child rearing practices.

In Western cultures the greater significance is placed on the development of separate you/me, subject/object, and sharper ego boundaries. The Western rational thinking is very much an achievement of the individualized culture, where there is an emphasis on rationally processing situations, ideas, and feelings. In individualistic societies greater prominence is placed on language and what is verbally communicated and less importance is given to nonverbal communication in the form of sensing self/other. One may argue there is an over emphasis in Western cultures on putting thoughts and feelings into words. The communication in the nonlinguistic modes has greater significance in Eastern cultures. In Western tradition and practice, people may attend to nonverbal communication to a lesser degree.

We all have our cultures; however, migrants coming from collectivistic culture to individualistic culture have different inner psychological makeup and the loss of that cultural dimension is deeply felt and often disorienting to a migrant. Migrants from more collectivistic cultures including Eastern European migrants typically feel a more familial type of self which allows for a greater dependence, emotionally, with less-structured ego boundaries; coming to a more individualized cultural set up such as the United States, migrants may experience greater loss and trauma in the migration process compared to Western migrant. They possibly repress or split off to a greater degree the more emotional familial self that may not be valued or even recognized in the new culture. They become very American, often prematurely. However, at some deeper level they have this familial side split off and coexisting with an American self. This process of splitting would create future complications in the process of migration and authentic integration into a new world and deeper psychic integration (see the cases of Zbyszek and Bruno).

Migrants come from cultures that value different ideas and ways of thinking and that generally creates cultural conflicts. A migrant brings his/her internalized culture and cultural psychic boundaries into a new world and culture. We may wonder how the internal worlds of a migrant and a native person living in the given culture relate to each other? There will be the internal culture of a migrant and inner culture of a person who belongs to the new world which often creates difference and confusion. For instance, the obvious differences may be sharply visible at the level of food and eating habits. In the familial type of cultures the idea of having your own plate setting at the dinner table may not be as clear cut idea as it is in Western cultures. One may have their own plate setting but may want to share food with others too. There may be a different concept of how people eat together in the East compared to a more formal eating structure in the Western world. There are different concepts of how people eat together that migrants may not take into account, which may create greater distress in the migration process.

The other different concept is the idea of standing in queue in the systematic and structured way. In the Western world it is an important way of behaving and organizing in social situations. In many Eastern cultures if one remains very strict about following the queue and attending to only one person at a time, he or she may upset others waiting who are not being given special considerations. For instance, it may be quite common in Eastern cultures that an Eastern government official may be helping one person standing in a less-structured queue, and at the same time attending to a few other people standing close by who are also asking for help. One can think here about a father or mother representative helping a few children simultaneously. The family dynamics are deeply internalized into a human psyche and get enacted in different life situations (such as above). In contrast the Western person or government official may feel that not giving strict attention to one person at a time standing in a well-formed queue is inappropriate and outright rude. In the individualized Western world that is more formalized and structured, one-on-one focus is highly valued. In the Eastern culture if one remains very strict and follows the strict line/queue, others may feel that one is inconsiderate and rude. There are different cultural internal psychological frameworks that are at play here that may create a lot of mystification when a migrant enters a new culture.

Different embedded cultural assumptions based on culture of collectivism and individualism, if misunderstood, create a lot of confusion, additional stress and conflict in the process of migration. When a migrant crosses different cultural boundaries there is great scope for misunderstanding and incertitude.

The unconscious different cultural assumptions that migrants carry within their selves become much more visible when they (migrants) come across radically different cultures. When migrants travel across cultural boundaries the cultural conflicts inevitably get activated. If one does not make a cross-cultural journey than there is no cultural conflict issue as one is in one's culture.

Since the Eastern European culture is more of the collectivistic, family-centered culture, this will create conflicts for Eastern European migrants that carry within them more of the familial self. The loss of such a familial cultural dimension often adds stress to the migration process.

I suspect that there are no radical differences between Eastern European and Northern American culture compared to radically different cultures that Roland (1988) writes about. However, there are many subtle cultural conflicts manifested in migration that may have important ramifications for migration trauma. The subject of more subtle cultural/psychological conflicts in the lives of Eastern European migrants in North America, in clinical work, will require further clinical and theoretical exploration.

In this book I am addressing the Eastern European self from a higher level than the deeper understanding of unconscious psychic structure formation level. I gave more general descriptions of Eastern European self and Northern American self in the context of collectivistic and individualistic cultures. The deeper cultural study of Eastern European and Northern American selves underlying different types of psychic structure, and psychological profiles will require further studies.

From the migration point of view, we may wonder if Eastern European migrants will encounter greater problems in the process of migration because their psychological self carries within the familial self dimension that might be differently structured compared to the Northern American self. The Eastern European self has different grades and gradations of familial self within. I suspect that Eastern European self will have some version of the "familial self" that Roland (1988) speaks about; with greater sense of emotionality, more relationship oriented, with a lesser need for sharply differentiated self/object structures, more permeable ego boundaries, and greater interdependency needs.

As already stated, the important shades of differences between Eastern European and Western European cultural selves were greatly evident in different ways of thinking of Eastern European psychoanalyst, Ferenczi who has brought much more of the Eastern European family-centered emphasis in his psychoanalytic writing compared to Freud. We could argue that he was an originator of Eastern European version of psychoanalysis based on cultural differences and different ways of being and thinking when compared to Western psychoanalytic writings. Roland (1988) wrote about cultural and psychological conflicts and distinctly different cultural experiences and cultural selves that are kept apart. There is a sharper contrast of cultural differences when we talk about radically different cultures. The Eastern European familial type of self is much more within manageable area of difficulties in understanding such a familial self in Eastern European migrants. I also suspect that cultural boundaries at the psychological level in Eastern European migrants were not radically different compared to the Western sense of cultural boundaries. Broadly speaking the psychological differences relate to dissimilarities in deeper structural psychological makeup of familial self and individualized self. There is a more subtle unconscious cultural structural dimension related to familial and individualized selves in the migration process, that migrants may not be consciously aware of, and yet feel deeply its loss and the conflicts that it causes in migrants lives.

As previously stated, in this book I am not looking at intrinsic psychic structure differences between Eastern European and America selves. I am looking at split-off cultural experiences and not necessarily bicultural identity conflicts (on a psychic structure level). The split-off unintegrated cultural experiences may reinforce further inner splitting of the self and greatly affect the process of migration and integration into a new culture. For instance, in the clinical case of Bruno, I speak about the particular splits that he makes inside of his psychological self due to different cultural experiences that he connects with Eastern Europe and the United States. I am not necessarily looking at the intrinsic cultural differences between different cultural selves. I am more concerned with the splits in his psyche which are invested with some type of cultural experience which affects the process of inner and outer integration and migration trauma.

To reiterate, in this book I am not talking about radical differences related to moving from Eastern European culture to the North American culture. I am pointing out some cultural differences related to Eastern European migration that are within the more manageable range of human experience, which does not cause deep confusion but may cause some cultural conflicts inside the migrants internal world. I look at my clinical cases mostly from the migration point of view and the migration trauma that was there irrespective of culture. I also speak about culture mostly in the context of the migration situation. I study culture at a level of a migrant coming from a different culture to another culture and dealing with consequent multiple losses and cultural conflicts. I am not necessarily speaking about cultural/psychological conflicts, which migration may create on a psychic structural level, and how such a conflict may manifest itself in migrant patients carrying within deeply internalized cultural identities different from Northern American patients.

The loss of familiar cultural objects and cultural dimension adds additional stress to the migration process. The migrant is not only moving away from home and loved ones, he/she is also loosing elements and ingredients that may be part of only their native culture, and may not be available in a different culture. Migration can become a more traumatic event when the cultural dimension is lost. As a remedy migrants often try to recreate their cultures by living in their own cultural communities in order to have some cultural familiarity around them, as will be seen in the case of Ela.

"Interpretation of Dreams in Light of British Object Relations Theory and Other Thoughts on Methodology"

Freud regarded *The Interpretation of Dreams* as his paramount psychoanalytic work. He states in this book, third English edition published in 1932, the following:

> It contains, even according to my present-day judgment, the most valuable of all the discoveries it has been my good fortune to make. Insight such as this falls to one's lot but once in a lifetime. (SE4, XXXI)

He further states in the same book edition, his well-known phrase: "The interpretation of dreams is the royal road to a knowledge of the unconscious activities of the mind" (p. 608).

Freud felt that dreams are the royal road to the unconscious mind, because certain material about the human psyche can be attainable only in dreams. Freud's theory of dreams is called wish-fulfillment theory which contends that dreams have psychological meanings and express fulfilled wishes.

In *A Critical Dictionary of Psychoanalysis* (1995), Rycroft states:

> According to Freud's original formulations, dreams have (a) *a manifest content,* which is the dream as experienced, reported, or remembered (see also manifest), and (b) *a latent content,* which is discovered by interpretation (see also latent). He also held that the dreamer performs work (the *dream-work)* in translating the latent into the manifest content, and that; therefore, dream-interpretation is the reverse of dream-work. According to his wish-fulfillment theory of dreams, the latent content is a wish, which is fulfilled in the dream in hallucinatory form (see hallucination), the translation into the manifest content being necessitated by two factors: (a) the physiological conditions of sleep which determine that dreaming is, in the main, a visual not a verbal process, and (b) that the wish is unacceptable to the waking ego; it has therefore to be disguised in order to pass the censor. Nightmares and anxiety dreams constitute failures in the dream-work; traumatic dreams (see trauma), in which the dream merely repeats the traumatic experience, are exceptions to the theory. (pp. 40–41)

The basic psychological model of the mind on which the idea of the manifest and latent dream content is based is called topographic model of the mind and theory of neurosis. In the topographical model the major distinction is between unconscious, preconscious, and conscious mind. This is in contrast to Freud's second theory of the psychological apparatus called the structural model of the mind where he differentiates the three agencies of id, ego, and superego. The topographical model of the mind is the one Freud applied to his dream interpretations. Freud felt that the contents of the unconscious mind were not allowed to come to consciousness, because human beings engage in the process of disguising and censoring of the unconscious content, owing to the fact that it is too dangerous to bring out unconscious content into consciousness. Therefore, the unconscious content that is disguised in the waking life. However, in dreams the unconscious content attempts to come out and express itself more directly. Based on Freud's theory of dreams the unconscious is always trying to express itself via different avenues. In the dream life there is still some level of censorship present and that is one of the reasons why Freud spoke about latent and manifest dream content. The censoring process is present in the dream via manifest content which is a disguise and cover up for latent underlying content. To understand the dream one has to go beyond the manifest content in order to perceive the hidden meanings in the latent content. Freud felt that dreams are basically the repressed content of the unconscious mind trying to come out in a waking life which activates the censorship that attempts to conceal the process. The unconscious carries content that one may not want to get in touch with, because it is in conflict with becoming aware of these unconscious issues in one's consciousness. There are ideas and feelings that one cannot allow to fully come into consciousness (they are unacceptable or intolerable) and therefore they are pushed down and repressed into the unconscious mind. However, while they are suppressed in the unconscious mind, they always try to come out in one form or another, and that is what is causing the neurotic conflict with psychological symptoms and other psychosomatic problems. Rycroft (1995) in *A Critical Dictionary of Psychoanalysis* states the following: "In Freud's first formulations the mental agency responsible for dream distortion and repression was called the censor. The censor is the theoretical ancestor of the super-ego" (p. 20).

Freud spoke about censor/guardian metaphor and mental agency responsible for dream distortions. The censor/guardian mental agency was placed between the unconscious and preconscious mind, preventing the unconscious content from coming into consciousness, due to its disturbing material. Similarly, there was another censor/guardian placed between preconscious and conscious mind that was less restrictive than the first one. Therefore, what one would experience in the manifest content is only a restricted version of dream material. In the dream the censor/guardian is not as fully at work as in waking life and there is a degree of relaxation of the censorship. In that process of relaxation the unconscious thoughts come out and turn unconscious content into a dream. So one can find some way of fulfilling the wishes that in general are unacceptable to the sleeper's waking part of the self. Such unconscious wishes are generally unacceptable, because they may be in conflict with one's value system (i.e., death wishes toward loved ones) or because they are of infantile nature. In that view dreams express wishes as fulfillment, and they are guardians of sleep. The wish-fulfilling function of the dream facilitates sleep because otherwise there is too much disturbance in the unconscious mind. The wish-fulfilling dream turns the unconscious content into something less threatening and more soothing.

In Freud's view of theory of dreams, we dream in order to sleep. The manifest content of the dream is only a disguising, superfluous aspect of the dream that has no meaning with its only purpose to conceal the message coming from latent content. The psychoanalyst has to do a certain amount of investigative work in order to be able to translate the manifest content and understand the meaning of the latent level content, with its real hidden unconscious conflicts. In order to reach the meaning of the latent content there are many rules as to how to interpret the dreams. One of these essential rules is the notion of having patients' dreams associations in order to have more information about the dream latent content and its hidden message.

This process of free associations enables the patient to become more aware of the dreams latent content, so deeper psychoanalytic work can be done, on resolving neurotic conflicts, and the patient can become more aware as to what is troubling him/her. Therefore, if the psychoanalyst can penetrate the manifest content and understand the latent content there is a possibility of discovering real deep unconscious conflicts and anxieties.

Freud felt that dreams are the royal road to unconscious, because in dreams more unconscious material will have a chance to emerge (but not fully) or dreams can give important confirmation to the material that psychoanalyst may only suspect but not yet fully understand. Dreams can give a much clearer picture of the patients' internal state of affairs. For instance, if we look at the category of a patient, who feels internally psychologically dead and lives an emotionally disconnected form of life; the dream image of the skeleton with piercing eyes, gives more confirmation that such a patient does feel like a "walking dead person." Such a dream image gives certain conviction in the unconscious and conscious mind that deep down there is that real state of psychic deadness. The skeleton dream image emphasizes the inner deadness in the real and concrete way and provides important insight to patients' inner psychic reality. The understanding of such dream imagery needs to be fitted with the overall understanding of the patient. Dreams often point to new avenue that one many not have thought about and take one into a deeper unconscious content.

Current British object relations theory presents much more complicated views on dream phenomena; not just as guardians of sleep or wish-fulfilling dreaming experience as Freud pointed out. In fact, we sleep in order to dream and only a minority of dreams is manifesting wish-fulfilling needs.

In classical theory thinking, in relation to a more neurotic personality issues it is helpful to think in terms of dreams manifest/latent content and dream associations. However, when there are deeper paranoid and annihilation types of anxiety that patients are dealing with, the manifest disguise of the latent content is not an appropriate description. Such patients are actually engaging in evacuating that type of anxiety or unbearable mental states.

The manifest content disguise is a higher-level mental agency that is engaged in disguising and not evacuative function, which is related to a neurotic process. When we deal with dreams of more disturbed patients who are attacking their sense of reality and, therefore, they are losing the distinction between reality and phantasy, sleep and wakefulness, the notion of manifest content disguise is not useful. In such a patient, the inner deep nightmare is going on in the wakeful life, creating a much more chaotic situation. Such patients do not have capacity for producing proper dreams that Freud was talking about, in which there is a latent and manifest content disguise active. When there is a greater level of disturbance in a patient dealing with a psychotic type of anxiety, than such a patient may engage in the process of evacuating dreams, obliterating the mind and ability to perceive what is occurring within psychic reality and in external reality.

In his book *Dream Life*, Meltzer (2009) states the following:

> Perhaps the only psycho-analyst who has written extensively about dreams to take a quietly divergent view from Freud's has been Ella Sharpe. It must certainly have been done so quietly in her book on *Dream Analysis* that hardly any notice has been taken of it. Her central creative contrition to the theory of dreams was to point out the mountains of evidence that dreams utilize what she chose to call the "poetic diction" of lyric poetry. By this she meant that dreams employ the many devices of simile, metaphor, alliteration, onomatopoeia, etc. by which the language of poetry achieves its evocative capacity. (p. 27)

According to Meltzer, the sharp distinction between the manifest and latent dream content does not have to be so sharp. There are various ways in which one part of the self is communicating through the dream to another including metaphor, simile or "poetic diction" about which Ella Sharpe (1937) in her book *Dream Analysis: A Practical Handbook for Psychoanalysts* talks about. For instance, in a supervision session the following short dream was presented about a female patient. The presented patient stated that in her dream her psychoanalyst was sitting in his chair and there were a lot of broken #2 pencils lying close to his chair. This patient wanted to move closer to the psychoanalyst but was scared that this was "no go" territory around the psychoanalyst's chair. She remembered in her associates that in her school, there were #2 brown color pencils that she used for various drawing purposes. But in fact the broken brown #2 pencils metaphorically represented her crappy/angry feelings with her psychoanalyst even though in other ways she idealized the whole psychoanalytic situation.

We may wonder whether in her psychic reality, was the patient or psychoanalyst surrounded by crappy/angry feelings? Was there a "no go" area in the patients inner reality; her inner "crappy part" that she could not bring out in her treatment or was the psychoanalyst a broken #2 pencil creature full of crappy/angry feelings? The notion of #2 pencil could be referring to the patient using the #2 pencil in school, or the American phrase "number two" referring to crap/shit/excrement, has been picked up by the patent's unconscious as a metaphor that presents a deeper meaning of the dream. This patient was not consciously aware of the fact that the phrase "number two" applied to her crappy/angry feelings about psychoanalysis. She was afraid of getting in touch with such a disturbing content.

We can see that one of the dream functions here was to move away from what really disturbs one inside, which is the feeling of hate and anger. Generally speaking it would be very disturbing to bring such content out into the open in treatment or a life situation. The latent content of this short dream is about aggression, but the manifest content is about the #2 brown pencils used in primary school for drawing purposes. One part of the patient has disguised the inner anger, but the #2 broken brown pencils appear in the manifest content. This patient kept on repeating the phrase "number two" in her session and psychoanalyst had to judge from the entire psychoanalytic material including the types of anxieties being expressed (or not being expressed), as to what the patient was trying to convey and what was troubling this patient. The psychoanalyst had to use all this information in order to formulate tentative dream interpretation.

In this case patient's associations took her psychologically speaking to primary school and her childhood experiences of drawing with #2 pencils in her classroom. However, there was a lot of aggression in her session material and feelings of being "stuck" in useless treatment. Underneath her facade she felt that she was not going anywhere in her life and had no hope. On another level the same psychic situation of "stuckness" and anger presented itself in all of her relationships, with the similar feelings that all her relationships were not going anywhere. In reality she attacked and devalued all her relationships. In order to understand any dream material one has to scrutinize not only entire dream content but also the content of a given session, particular stage of treatment, including predominant anxiety in transference and countertransference.

According to the British object relations theory the main function of the dream is the working-through process, of underlying anxieties, and the manifest and latent dream content are not so sharply divided as in Freud's thinking. Dreams are part of working-through process in which one part is trying to communicate some difficult issues in the inner world to another part that is engaging in working-through process. Therefore, the main function of the dream is not to facilitate sleep via wish-fulfilling process, but there is also a process of working through of the underling anxieties and conflicts.

At some level as human beings we are always engaging in our internal words in the process of sorting out our conflicts and addressing our anxieties. The individuals who can't engage in the process of working things through in their dreams and are overwhelmed by life content may use dreams to evacuate their inner unbearable content. Some patients may not want to discover the meanings of their dreams. They may not have an active interest in knowing the deeper essence of their dreams. In fact, they may frequently use the dream to dispose off and eliminate some feelings and mental states. In such situations one may not get some collaborative response regarding free associations. The manifest dream content in such situations has to be put together in some metaphorical way, with other hidden dream meanings in order to give a fuller interpretation of the dream.

As already stated in British object relations thinking the manifest and latent dream content are not so sharply differentiated. In fact one has to recognize that in certain cases patients are not able to disguise dream's message with the manifest content, because the eruptions of their deeper emotional issues are such that they try to divest themselves of their feelings rather than engaging in manifest content disguise work. In *The Dream Discourse Today* (1992), we find the following statement regarding Hanna Segal's views on dreams:

> From this perspective on the dreaming function, best expressed in this volume by Hanna Segal, the power of wish fulfillment in dream or in the ego's relation to its objects is not denied, but is frequently evaluated along a continuum measuring the extremity of projective processes aimed at getting rid of, finally evacuating unacceptable or unbearable feelings. Avoiding disturbing recognition is of course, according to Freud the motive for much of the dream-work. Disguise, however, is a qualitatively different concept from the extreme projective evacuative processes observed by many Kleinians. Ultimately, these processes attack the differentiation between sleep and wakefulness, reality and phantasy, primary and secondary process, and, in psychosis, shatter the fragile boundaries which fail to contain the dream-space. (pp. 11, 12)

She points out that the nature of the evacuative dream is to dispose of psychic content rather than engaging and working through its contents.

Perhaps Freud wanted to solve the riddle of the dreams, including its meanings and as to why the censorship agency was converting the latent dream content into manifest dream content. The whole enterprise of understanding how difficult it is for the patient to become aware of certain underlying conflicts and issues, which are than given in dreams some distorted picture, or are evacuated all together was not given sufficient attention in Freud's thinking.

I treat dreams as important communications about deeply rooted feelings, inner conflicts, underlying anxieties that cannot be brought out more openly by a patient, and would not appear on a regular phantasy level. The dream brings to light in a much more dramatic way the hidden, deeply rooted anxieties and unconscious phantasies. My overall approach is to ask for dream associations. However, I arrive at my interpretations based on the whole content of a given session and evaluation of entire treatment.

The human psyche uses numerous devices including already-mentioned "poetic diction" in order to communicate dreams underlying content. We have to take into account the language of dreams where our feelings are not expressed in clear verbal thoughts. They may be expressed in metaphor or "poetic diction" and one has to be able to tune into that type of communication in order to be able to understand what the patient is trying to express through a particular type of dream. The approach of conceptualizing things into rational language related to manifest dream content in order to understand less-rational latent dream content is to facile. For instance, the phrase "number two" presented in the earlier dream, and the tentative interpretation of it, was based on full awareness, as to where the patient was in treatment, the themes that were emphasized such as attacks, and devaluations of the psychoanalyst/others. In fact, this patient's associations were leading in the wrong direction, toward her childhood and primary school benign experiences, and not toward hatred related anxiety.

Frequently patients may not have associations or their associations may lead in the wrong direction and then one may have to go beyond dream associates, and treat the entire session as associative material. Dream associations are important, but psychoanalysts still have to do much further work, that goes beyond associations in order to get to the deeper unconscious issues. Too much focus on the dream associations may, in some cases, be counterproductive. When a patient is talking about earlier, more primitive issues which are not easily available through dream associations, the dream may be an attempt to empty one's mind from such a primitive and unbearable content.

In my work with dreams I always look at the dreams latent/manifest content but my methodology to get there is not based only on simple associations to a given dream. When I give dream interpretations I work with associations when they are available. When they are not available I try to understand the dream in the context of entire psychoanalytic treatment, transference, countertransference, previous and current sessions and other multiple unconscious communications including metaphor and "poetic diction." I regard these aspects as parts of the unconscious associative process to the dream. From that point I make a tentative dream interpretation in order to get patient's cooperation, so the patient may be able to build up on my tentative ideas. I never give definitive dream explanations. I only suggest the meaning of the dream with regard to the patient's real life. Such a psychoanalytic process of gathering and putting things together can perform a holding and containing function and reduce patient anxiety.

The psychoanalyst working within classical psychoanalytic framework may put less reliance on these types of unconscious communications and might be more concerned with patient's associations. If psychoanalysts feel that they cannot interpret dreams because there are no dream associations, then the anxiety remains inside, and the patient may get an idea that his inner psychic issues cannot be understood.

The more unformed primitive anxieties are not easily captured by the dream associations in the therapeutic process. The wish-fulfilling elements are always working in all types of dreams but the wish-fulfilling terms may be expressed in a sense of trying to address the anxiety by expelling process and therefore not dealing with unbearable material. Such a dream may turn more into evacuative dream in terms of trying to expel the unbearable phenomena. However, when the patient becomes more integrated than the dreams functions will be more directed toward working through of difficult anxieties rather than just expulsion of them. The more integrated patient has more contact with what is developing in his/her dream life. It is possible that in a more integrated patient, there is more interest in accepting and working through of different types of anxieties, rather than expelling them.

The British object relations approach to interpretations of dreams goes beyond the neurotic model of the mind introduced by Freud in which there is a manifest and latent content of the dream sharply differentiated and related dream associations. In fact, in such an approach, where there is no sharp differentiation between manifest and latent dream content and dream associations are not available, the depth of understanding is not being lost but a different form of depth based on multiple unconscious communications is being looked at and addressed. The total dream has to be understood and hidden meanings as well as surface meanings in order to work out the hidden message of the dream in the context of psychoanalytic treatment, which is part of the same fabric.

According to current psychoanalytic thinking conscious mental activity is sustained and enlivened by unconscious phantasies which began in early childhood. The psychoanalytic concept of phantasy plays a very central role in British object relations theory and thinking. In British theoretical writing the spelling "phantasy" was adapted, where in American writing the spelling fantasy is mostly used. In *Journeys in Psychoanalysis* (2015), Spillius states:

> Isaacs, like Klein particularly emphasises the idea that everyone has a continual stream of unconscious phantasy, and, further, that abnormality or normality rests not on the presence or absence of unconscious phantasy but on how it is expressed, modified and related to external reality She distinguishes between conscious and unconscious phantasy and suggests the *ph* spelling to distinguish the latter.
>
> Isaacs' and Klein's definition of phantasy is thus much wider than Freud's central usage. In the Kleinian view, unconscious phantasy is the mainspring, the original and essential content of the unconscious mind. It includes very early forms of infantile thought, but it also includes other forms that emerge later on in development through change in the original phantasies. (p. 116)

According to Spillius (2015), currently most British analysts use the *ph* spelling for all types of phantasies, which may be a reflection of frequent difficulties in distinguishing whether phantasies are conscious or unconscious.

Throughout this book I use *ph* spelling of phantasy that refers much more to the unconscious level of phantasy. The fantasy concept and its spelling with "*f*" often used in American writing refers more to conscious and preconscious fantasy which is much more related to daydreaming or having a wish for something good to happen. The concept of phantasy has important meanings and often refers to the imaginative activity that is underneath our thoughts and feelings. The more conscious and preconscious phantasy is a higher level phenomenon (than unconscious phantasy) that develops later in life when verbalization has been achieved. Behind every conscious and preconscious phantasy there is a series of unconscious phantasies. In British object relations view when a psychoanalyst is listening to a patient's material he/she is always tuning into the unconscious-level phantasies that is beyond verbal content of what the patient is expressing. The unconscious is present all the time in the patient's material, but it has to be decoded by a psychoanalyst.

In contrast, classical psychoanalysts give more credence to verbal content and they feel that unconscious material appears with great difficulties. For example, in classical thinking, in dreams the manifest content must be removed first in order to have access to latent unconscious dream content. Generally classical thinkers tend to believe that such unconscious phantasy interpretations are likely to produce wild analysis because the unconscious phantasy-based interpretations such as wishing to attack breast/penis do not make too much sense to the adult ego.

The Kleinian theory uses unconscious phantasy as a linking concept between thoughts and instincts. In *Clinical Lectures on Klein and Bion* (Anderson, 1992) Juliet Mitchell (1986) states the following about Klein' concept of phantasy:

> phantasy emanates from within and imagines what is without, it offers an unconscious commentary on instinctual life and links feelings to objects and creates a new amalgam: the world of imagination. Through its ability to phantasize, the baby tests out, primary "thinks" about its experiences of inside and outside. External reality can gradually affect and modify the crude hypothesis phantasy sets up. Phantasy is both the activity and its products. (Anderson, 1992, p. 21)

According to Kleinian psychoanalytic theory, there cannot be instinctual experience that does not have mental representation. This is in contrast to the classical theory of Freud who felt that an infant is purely driven by instincts and it takes a considerable amount of time before mental representations begin to develop. Klein felt that as soon as we have an instinct of any form, there must be some very initial preliminary metal representations. There cannot be instinctual experience that does not have mental representations. For instance, by definition the infant feeding on the mother's breast does not represent just a mechanical instinct feeding that is occurring. There will be some mental meaning connected to the breast-feeding experience, about mother's world, the experience of taking in the breast, in a very preliminary way. There is a mind that gets activated from the start of an infant's life and no instinctual experience can exist without mental representation of the phantasy. According to *A Critical Dictionary of Psychoanalysis*, Kleinian theory uses "unconscious phantasy" as a bridge concept between instinct and thought:

> On the views here developed: (a) Phantasies are the primary content of unconscious mental processes. (b) Unconscious phantasies are primarily about bodies, and represent instinctual aims towards objects. (c) These phantasies are, in the first instance, the psychic representatives of *libidinal* and destructive instincts. (p. 132)

According to Klein all phantasies are object related, and the object exists in the mind. For example, when the infant is sucking on the mother's breast, there is an object present which is a breast and there is a phantasy about the object/breast. The object is present from the beginning of the infant's life and so is the phantasy about the object. The object is seen and perceived as a mixture of reality and phantasy. Klein emphasized the centrality of the object seen through a mixture of reality and phantasy. She introduced a more interconnected way of living where individuals are not so distinctly separated. One could see her theory as corrective to Freud's classical theory with its great emphasis on individualism.

In this book my level of focus is different from classical psychoanalytic theory point of focus. I am more concerned with unconscious and conscious phantasies and such psychological defensive processes as splitting, projective identification, internal envy and others. For instance, a patient presented in a supervisory session was concerned about her two sons, the successful son and the unsuccessful one. She was also concerned about her own level of professional success in her life, and her conflicts about that. I understood the above material in terms of inner conflict between two split-off parts of herself. The conflict was between her own successful part and the unsuccessful part, and as to how to manage the unsuccessful part that was pulling back the successful one, undermining movement forward. The unsuccessful part was holding her back and tearing her apart. In fact, the unsuccessful one was envious of the success of the healthier part of her. This patient functioned well in the real world but with the degree of false self structure. Her underlying issue was not a fear of success and a neurotic type of Oedipus complex conflict, where she was not permitted to be better than her parents. She was dealing with inner splits of herself where one part of her was not allowing the other part to move forward out of envy.

In summary, the important aspect of my psychoanalytic methodology is working with unconscious and conscious phantasies and dreams as deep unconscious communications. In my clinical work I always have in mind the underlying issues at the level of Klein's descriptions of phantasies. I chose to emphasize the notion of unconscious phantasy in order to illustrate the differences between classical theory thinking and British object relations theory thinking informing this book. The Kleinian school of psychoanalysis exists within the Freudian fold, but its theories differ in several fundamental ways from classical theory. Kleinian analysis attributes greater importance to the first years of an infant's life rather than the childhood experiences as a whole. Phantasies are regarded as psychic representations of libidinal and destructive instincts. It assumes that the infant has vivid often violent phantasy life. The main task of the psychoanalyst is to interpret unconscious phantasies rather than interpret defenses against unconscious phantasies and impulses. The Kleinian school of psychoanalysis rejected the concepts of Freud's stages of development in favor of theory of structural states of mind called the paranoid-schizoid and depressive positions. For further elaboration of Kleinian and British object relations theory see *Introduction to the Work of Melanie Klein* (1964) by H. Segal and *A Dictionary of Kleinian Thought*, by R. D. Hinshelwood (1989).

There are fundamental differences related to the origins of mental life in Klein compared to Freud's thinking. Freud did not assume that mental life is in existence at the very beginning of life. However, Klein introduced the whole area of mental life that was not perceived by classical thinkers. The concept of unconscious phantasy was considered in Klein's theory to be essential because it is pointing toward the whole terrain of mental life that was not acknowledged in classical thinking.

In my clinical work I am more aware of that psychic terrain of mental life which classical analysis may not take into account. In my way of thinking (as pointed out by Klein) psychic life is present in the form of unconscious phantasies from the earliest stages of life in comparison to classical thinking where psychic life develops much later in an infant's life. I have highlighted one important feature of British object relations methodology which is unconscious phantasy in order to indicate how psychoanalysts try to listen to clinical phenomena that goes back to very early stages of development. The unconscious phantasy concept indicates that mental life is emanating from the instinctual origins of life rather than in later stages of psychic development. In my clinical work I am listening to a patient from the frame of mind that takes into account the existence of the very early unconscious phantasies with its particular anxiety contents and defensive set ups. This creates a significantly different form of clinical listing than the classical form of listing where there is no awareness of unconscious phantasies at a very early psychic level.

Chapter 2

Development of the Authentic Psychological Home and the False Psychic Home Structure

What is the authentic emotional and psychological home, and what is the false psychic home structure? Donald Winnicott has written about the true/false self and states that we all have the inherent potential to truly *be* and out of this *being* comes the capacity to live creatively and play. The true self (Winnicott, 1971) and our authentic emotional home develop out of this deeper being.

Winnicott suggests that the alternative to *being* is reacting, which interrupts and annihilates the *being*. I think this leads to alienation and the construction of a temporary false psychic home structure. The true self is an aspect and, ideally, an expression of *being*, and has the particular functions of organizing, synthesizing, and so forth.

The *being* gets interrupted and cannot "go on being" due to "impingements of the environment" which lead to the development of a false self (Winnicott, 1971) and therefore, a false psychic home. Winnicott (1971) goes on to suggest that we discover the *true self* and therefore our true psychic home only in play and in creativity, but the artistic product itself does not heal the underlying deficient empty sense of self. The more the environment provides what the developing human being needs, the more the human being can be the *true self* or *being* which, according to Winnicott, becomes the continuity of "going on *being*" and truly living in our emotional home.

According to Winnicott (1971), the ability to *be* in our true psychic home derives from the experience of a holding environment. From the experience of *being*, the individual can develop the capacity to live creatively and to play, both of which are aspects of integration and lead to doing, and authentically living in one's psychic home. In the paper "Group Influences and the Maladjusted Child" (1955), Winnicott writes about his theory of holding where his emphasis was on the psychological holding of the baby in the mind of the mother:

> the infant is held by the mother and only understands love that is expressed in physical terms . . . by the human holding. . . . failure at this early stage can not be defended against, except by a hold-up of the developmental process. . . . (pp. 147–48)

Winnicott claims that the self is in existence as an inherited potential from the beginning, and develops into a whole integrated self if given a "good enough" environment. Winnicott's use of the "good enough" environment relates to the mother's (caretaker's) adaptation to the infant's different needs, at different stages of development, and provision of an emotionally holding and containing maternal matrix. He further states that the *ego* is the aspect of the self whose function is to organize and integrate. Alternatively, if the environment is deficient and does not provide what is needed, then there is a disconnection from the *being* and deficient emptiness is filled up with the form of the *false self structure*. The false self structure comes into place to fill in what is missing, and underneath that structure is deficient emptiness that often is covered by the false structure.

Winnicott asserts that the infant is born with the nucleus of an unintegrated self. It is only through provision by the mother (or caregiver) of the right "holding environment" that gradually some integration can take place. The split of the self into a good/bad dichotomy comes about from the environmental failure of this "holding environment." That normal unintegrated self comprises components coexisting (not split parts) that need to coalesce through the mother's holding function that leads to integration. In such an integrated self (a higher level self), hateful feelings are not split off from loving feelings.

Generally speaking, according to object relations theory, the psychic structure called the *self* is a construct that needs to be seen as a complex, alive, adaptive, resilient, and dynamic entity that is by no means a dry static image of a scientific psychoanalytic concept. The psychic structure of self develops through the integration of the many impressions, images, and beliefs reflected back to us by our environment. According to object relations theory, the sense of self develops in conjunction with the other, usually the mother (or the caretaker).

At this point, there is no unified definition of the *self* within psychoanalytic theory. Within object relations theory itself, there are various developmental frameworks for self-structure and development. Therefore, I have used definitions of the self, mostly with emphasis on the object relations theory conceptualizations of Winnicott and of Klein and some self-psychology of Kohut (conceptualization of selfobject) and others.

Winnicott, a major contributor to object relations theory, suggests the existence of three selves in his 1950 paper "Aggression in Relation to Emotional Development":

> The personality comprises three parts: a true self, with Me and Not-me clearly established, and with some fusion of the aggressive and erotic elements; a self that is easily seduced along lines of erotic experience, but with the result of a loss of sense of real; a self that is entirely and ruthlessly given over to aggression. (p. 217)

In this paper he refers to the true self that has already-established boundaries and the two types of the false self that could be in existence in the same person. The concept of the different parts of the self implies the existence of the multiple selves.

Winnicott suggests in his 1960 paper "Ego Distortion in Terms of True and False Self" the existence of a true self in order to balance the concept of the false self:

> The spontaneous gesture is the True Self in action. Only the True Self can be creative and only the True Self can feel real. Whereas a True Self feels real, the existence of a False Self results in a feeling unreal or a sense of futility. (p. 148)

Winnicott felt that the false-self-organization which he called a "caretaker self" is a structure that is there in order to defend the true self, which appears as soon as there is any mental organization of the human being.

We all are searching for the deepest connection within, which we may call (our) psychological home and self, and for a sense of belonging. The awareness of home means an awareness of experiencing a psychological and emotional home, not merely awareness of a physical place. What is that experience called "psychic and emotional home"?[1]

Awareness of the *psychic* or *psychological home* means experiencing within oneself emotions, components of personality, that feel authentic, genuine, alive, and have an element of coherence and continuity. To have a psychic home is (1) to have an authentic sense of the self, which in turn is related (2) to taking responsibility for components of personality, and living fully within one's *body home,* and authentically relating to others. The psychic structure of the internal self, consisting of many different parts, could be called or considered our emotional and psychological home. One can experience life genuinely only if living in one's psychological home.

---

1. Psychological, Emotional Home—This term was coined by Nasir Ilahi, LLM in 2003 (personal communication). To have a psychic home means to have an authentic, well-integrated sense of self from which one can experience life fully and meaningfully.

We often leave the emotional home when it contains too much pain and suffering, due to painful psychological traumas. When we are not living in the psychological home, then we are psychologically homeless, defenseless, split off, dissociated, and therefore unable to relate fully to our own internal and external life and reality.

One such painful psychological trauma is migration from one country to another. The process of migration may be seen in terms of trauma stemming from the multiple losses of one's culture, language, country, value systems, home base, and so forth. Severe trauma can awaken multiple fears, phantasies, and defenses. What does it take to overcome and work through such huge anxieties and fears related to the old and the new world? Is it possible to recover from often severe culture shock and retain a sense of identity, and discover or rediscover a psychological home within oneself?

QUALITIES OF THE AUTHENTIC EMOTIONAL HOME VERSUS FALSE HOME

What then are the experiential and structural qualities and elements of an authentic emotional home? What leads to the construction of the false home and what are the structural elements and experiential qualities of such a home?

According to object relations psychoanalytic theory, ideally, *being* manifests itself in two modes, the subject and the object (the mother and infant relationship becomes internalized), which is a natural extension of the *being* and thus *being* capacities become the self-capacities and functions. Therefore, true thinking (organic, intuitive, less intellectual thinking), doing, speaking, and even suffering come from our *being*. This kind of dynamic self, which may be called our psychic home and which is an expression of our *being*, is a locus of living experience, awareness, consciousness, perception, thought, feeling, and action.

Nasir Ilahi, LLM,[2] maintains that if there is an internal true functioning going on, and the integration of the self has taken place, then there is capacity to express the deeper emotional states such as love, sorrow, and so forth, in a most fundamental way, in which the whole sense of self is engaged. If there is no well integrated sense of self, the individual cannot have deeper emotional and authentic experience.

How does culture impact the growing child and how does it come into play? Culture is something that the mother carries within herself. Given that the mother's way of dealing with the child may reflect different cultural

2. Personal communication.

beliefs about child rearing practices, culture comes into play right from the beginning of the child's development. Loving and caring for the baby may be a universal maternal response; certain cultures may encourage particular responses more than others, and therefore communicate to the infant different cultural beliefs and culture.

The early infantile sense of self develops as a result of the caretaking by the nurturant figure, usually the mother, who therefore plays a fundamental role in the development of the infant and is contributing to this development. If there are difficulties of some sort in the early maternal holding and containing environment that is provided by the parents, and the infant's basic needs are not met or there is difficulty in the inherited infant potential, then we have a trauma situation. In such a situation the false self sometimes takes over and constricts the more authentic sense of self; such a false self structure controls to some degree the emerging authentic sense of self. False self structures are put into place and they overpower the true self potential and "as if" (Deutsch, 1965) structures may develop. Such a particular defensive organization comes into place and undermines any healthy parts of the self.

In "Some Forms of Emotional Disturbance and Their Relationship to Schizophrenia," in *Neurosis and Character Types*, "as if" personality was introduced by H. Deutsch in 1965. By "as if" personality type she was referring to a schizoid character who behaves as though she/he had normal emotional responses to situations. In such a person there is a split between the intellectual and emotional functions. Schizoid individuals tend to be withdrawn, with an often vivid phantasy life. Broadly speaking I have also applied this term to mean a false structure.

The *being* (that perhaps might also be called *consciousness*, which would include conscious and unconscious mind) has the capacity to manifest from the bottom up such fundamental emotional states as love, sorrow, and so forth. It seems that the basic matrix of our true emotional home and our *psyche* is a field of energy called *consciousness*, including the conscious and unconscious dimensions, that is vulnerable to being conditioned and impressed by our environment and culture. If the environmental and cultural conditioning and imprinting are too strong, due to various trauma, then the *being/true self* is constricted and unable to fully manifest itself, but is stuck in a hollow imprinted mold or shell or false self/home. By this process of conditioning, we put the images over the being. If the image is good/bad, then the *being* starts manifesting as such, then we become disconnected from our deeper authentic home that in turn becomes an alienated refugee home, a temporary shelter for the homeless person waiting to return home (inauthentic way of being).

If due to traumas a self/object psychic structure is too rigid, then such a structure blocks the dynamism of being/true self and the life force energy of consciousness is trapped within and the individual is stuck in some form of temporary psychic home. In order to live in our true psychic home, we need to allow ourselves to be formed more by innate potential and less by outside conditioning, where our ego/self is more of a permeable protective cover.

Bion (1970) has called the deepest ultimate, unknowable reality and the absolute truth *O* reality. Bion (1970) notes that:

> transformations into "O" are those that effectively promote change, growth, and the search for truth and the achievement of insight. O represents ultimate, unknowable reality, the absolute truth contained and inherent in any object. . . . The transformation into O is like "being what one is" or embodying one's own truth. For this reason transformation is feared and resisted. (p. 66)

What Bion states could be further developed and applied to the situation of migration. There is a big difference between intellectually *knowing* that one is an immigrant and it is a different experience of *being* an immigrant and, working through the internal and emotional issues related to immigration. Temporary psychic homes are often created by immigrants who have to go through the various psychological processes (about which Bion writes), in order to be able to integrate these temporary homes into something more authentic and therefore to grow and develop.

From the immigrant point of view, the immigration situation represents yet another challenge in the individual's life, the challenge of how to integrate new situations emotionally and psychologically, and how to incorporate them emotionally into the person's life in a meaningful way. On the other hand, one could not work through this new immigration situation and be in denial and then the experience of immigration cannot be worked through, and the individual feels psychologically blocked, stuck with an un-metabolized experience and in a state of denial. Migration presents the individual with a huge psychological challenge, but also insight, because the individual must, to some degree at least, take in the new culture and the experience of being in a new culture. The situation of immigration could be worked through different stages and the creation of temporary psychic homes may be a necessary part of the process. In some situations, the challenge of immigration cannot be worked through, and immigrants may go into a state of denial and some sort of dissociated state, and psychologically and emotionally feel that they are still living in the home country (of course outwardly knowing that they are in a different country) because it is too threatening to work through the new experience. In other cases, immigrants are able to create temporary psychic homes and go through the process of intense gradual integration that leads to the creation of a more authentic home.

We create many forms of temporary psychic home, with many degrees of authenticity and falseness, before we are really ready to embrace the depth, fullness, aliveness, and dynamism of our authentic psychic home. We often leave our emotional body home due to too much pain and suffering related to psychological trauma (such as migration). The more unbearable the pain and suffering, the more the individual becomes disconnected from the emotional home and lives in a temporary structure that may be called a false home psychic structure. Thus, for example, the temporary psychic home of a psychotic patient is going to be quite different from the home of a neurotic or even borderline patient. In order to return to the true psychic home and to live fully within one's body home, one needs to fully own up to all feelings (good/bad), affects, and components of personality, while rejecting nothing.

In this work I have explored my immigrant patients' different temporary psychic homes, such as psychotic, borderline, narcissistic refuge home, and so forth. I have illustrated the often slow process of psychological migration to more integrated and authentic types of psychic homes.

If the individual is unable to take responsibility to own up to hateful or needy aspects of the self/psychic home, then the internal emotional home becomes impoverished, divided, and no longer safe. The psychic home becomes impoverished because the individual is unable to connect with something genuine (good/bad) within him or herself, and has to engage in defensive maneuvers of denial, splitting, projections, etc. The use of these types of defenses will make the individual impoverished because she/he is not authentically in touch with his or her sense of self. The ego is left impoverished although it needs these defenses to survive psychologically, but the consequence is that the individual is left out of touch with reality, and the sense of self and sense of reality are impoverished. This process of splitting and projection (when the individual cannot bear difficult feelings) leads to parts of the self being projected onto others (housed in others), which leaves the individual in a state of deficiency.

When running away from painful aspects of the self, other areas of the emotional home need to be pushed away and disowned. Anything that comes close to the needy/hateful parts must be denied and disowned. Therefore, there is no psychic depth and no deeper feelings in the psychic home.

A well-integrated self is needed in order to function well in society, but this true psychic home must develop according to the deeper reality of the "inherent potential" to truly be. Such a self/psychic home (self/ego structure) must be a permeable and transparent membrane acted upon by the being (the inherent potential) which is the source of creativity. I agree with Nasir Ilahi, LLM,[3] that such a self/psychic home, in order to be authentic, must be touched from the bottom up by the fundamental states of existence such as creativity, love, will, compassion, etc. The fundamental states of

3. Personal communication.

existence (such as love) do not come from the external past conditioning but from the states of being. If we try to control the internal organic experience, we get disconnected from *being* and the spontaneity of the creative process.

Reactivity and a need to control the experience (due to lack of a proper holding environment) lead to the development of the false self/psychic home. Such a false self-identity tries to be good/bad in order to get what it needs. Such a self-structure/temporary home is alienated from *being*. Psychic pain makes one react and creates a degree of disconnection from the *being* in order not to feel pain. This creates a void between the true self/being and the false self/psychic home. In order to reconnect with the true psychic home and our being, it is necessary to go through the pain that underlies the false self-image.

Hinshelwood (1989), in *A Dictionary of Kleinian Thought*, states that for Klein:

> The term Self would seem to suggest the experience of the subject, his phantasies about himself . . . Self tends to stand for the subject in his own phantasies . . . from a subjective point of view. (p. 285)

Klein (1957) often uses the term *self* (the psychic home) synonymously with ego. She asserts that the self exists from birth, and has boundaries and the capacity to identify with objects. Klein further states that, from the start, this self performs primitive functions such as discriminating good from bad sensations, separating *me* from *not-me*, and has the capacity for primitive innate phantasies of incorporation, expulsion, and the mating of preconceptions and realizations. Klein believes that the early self alternates between states of integration and disintegration and falling to bits. She further discusses the self/ego in terms of phantasies the self has in struggling with fears in its relations with objects that are perceived by the self/ego through instinctual phantasies.

Klein describes parts of the self as being projected out (from birth) and located in the external world by means of psychic phantasy, where parts of the self are projected into an other in order to take over its contents and therefore to control the other. The above process is based on a primitive kind of phantasy, based on the belief that certain aspects of the self are being located elsewhere, which leads to a degree of self-depletion, depersonalization, feelings of being lost, a sense of imprisonment, distortion of identity, a weakened sense of self, and feelings of homelessness and loss of the psychic home.

As already stated, in order to return to the psychic home, to have an authentic sense of self, and to be able fully to experience life in the psychological home, the individual needs to develop the capacity to be able to bare his/her true feelings, emotions, and split-off and projected components of his/her personality. The process of splitting and projection leads to consciousness being divided in bits and the consequent inability to tolerate the authenticity of feelings and to achieve integration. This in turn affects the ability to experience life fully, to be authentic, and to have the capacities for concern and love. One can experience life fully and genuinely only if one is living in the psychological home, and only in our emotional home can we appreciate our life.

To be authentic and real implies self-integration and the capacity to experience things in an authentic way, rather than those things (feelings, emotions, conflicts, etc.) being denied and split off, which introduces unreality in the individual's life, even though it may make the individual temporarily safe but not fully authentic, alive, and present.

The process of integration of different parts of the self is about tolerating and containing loving/hateful, needy, and vulnerable elements of the psychic home. When the individual denies his/her emotions and needs, and does not acknowledge these parts of the self, then we have feelings of homelessness, lack of trust, greed, and envy. Such individuals are unable to trust that rationality and fairness will be available for them when necessary, and have a general mistrust that emotional supplies will not be accessible.

Such patients may try to dissociate good/bad feelings and then fill the internal emptiness and sense of homelessness with all sorts of internal phantasies, obsessional illusions, or external things such as alcohol, food, and so forth. The endless deficient psychic void will never be filled with more external (or internal) things. Such a person is without peace and well-being, and therefore without an emotional home. He or she is unable to take in emotional nourishment (such as psychological insights) and is always searching for those lost external nourishing objects (originally parents) that are never assimilated due to constant internal (psychic) criticism. Such an individual can feel constantly homeless and without any emotional home due to painful trauma (such as immigration).

According to Grinberg and Grinberg (1989), the immigrant may dissociate:

> for the sake of protecting himself from painful effects of these often intolerable emotions, that the immigrant make use of dissociation so as not to evoke in a hopeless form the losses he has suffered. . . . By belittling his losses, denigrating all that is known and familiar, and exaggerating his admiration for the new and unknown, he tends to regulate his anxiety and guilt, feelings that are nearly inevitable in every experience of migration. (p. 9)

Therefore, true psychic freedom comes with the ability to experience the full spectrum of feelings, emotions, and the capacity to tolerate internal conflicts and vulnerabilities. The true internal connection to the psychic home is possible only when we accept all our needs, feelings, and vulnerabilities of the self. Individuals who have basic trust can be vulnerable to pain but can also be truly open to the deeper underlying nature that can hold, contain, and create the true home. True psychological freedom comes about when we are open, trusting, and accept our vulnerabilities. False and illusionary psychological freedom is created through splitting, dissociating, and denial, all of which lead to homelessness. Grinberg and Grinberg (1989) have suggested that:

> To the extent that the individual can assimilate the experience of his migration . . . integrating derived and dissociated aspects and feeling, he will grow enough to be able to feel pain. . . . He will then have a greater knowledge of the experiences he has lived through. It will not be mere intellectual knowledge but what Bion (1970) has termed the more experiential "becoming O." He will not only "know" that he is emigrating, he will be an emigrant. (p. 65)

THE MOST AUTHENTIC PSYCHIC HOME "O"

According to Bion (1977), the *O* reality is the core of our being. Bion was dissatisfied with Freud's drive theory and Klein's extension of drives as unconscious phantasies. Bion speaks of *O* reality as transcendent *a priori* considerations beyond drives. He contends that intuition is the instrument of apprehending and resonating with *O* reality. Bion further contends that mental concepts are based on the original concepts that are part of the *O* reality and are encapsulated by our minds into concepts. *O* reality is home for the unconscious mind, and perhaps in the deepest sense it is our most fundamental and authentic psychological home. It is a parallel reality without categories and beyond phantasy and symbol formation. It is an unmetabolized emotional experience of the unrepressed unconsciousness that is home for our preconceptions and the drives that are modifiers for the ultimate *O* reality. According to Bion, as we evolve to one with the *O* reality, the need for the image vanishes, and we are faced with the void of creation, *O* reality, and our true home. The ultimate state of consciousness is to become *O* reality.

I believe that psychoanalytic theory, in the deepest sense, is a doorway to Bion's *O* reality. The theory and concepts of psychoanalysis cover and reveal the boundless parallel *O* reality that is our most authentic home. However, to be able to live and be in such a home implies that one first has to fully, deeply, experience the painful (or pleasurable) mental and emotional states related to human existence, and to be fully in touch with all parts of one's psychic home. We all could only aspire to be able to someday live in such a most authentic home as *O* reality.

According to Grinberg and Grinberg (1989):

> To be an emigrant, then, is very different from "knowing" that one is emigrating. Being implies assuming fully and deeply the absolute responsibilities that go with being an emigrant. To achieve this, one must inhabit mental and emotional states that are not easy to endure. Thus people need to resort to various defensive devices in order to commit themselves to knowing they are, without being, emigrants. (p. 66)

All psychoanalytic theories address the question of the transformation of consciousness. Our conscious and unconscious histories are represented by internal dynamic images, and our unconscious surrounds us due to the projective/introjective psychic processes of the human psyche. In this study I hoped to be able to raise the level of consciousness related to immigrant cultural consciousness and identity.

I believe that a given culture is a very important aspect of the conscious and unconscious psyche and therefore needs to be understood, respected, and valued. I further believe that it is important to capture both cultural variability and the universality of human nature across different cultures. The *cultural self* across other civilizations needs to be regarded and therefore the variability of human nature acknowledged. The universal essence needs to be integrated or realized in individual human beings, in order for them to become more fully integrated, complete, real, and living in the authentic psychic home.

I agree with Roland (1996) that there is a need for culturally comparative psychoanalysis, a new theoretical approach, and the creation of broad universal psychoanalytic symbols and categories that can cut across different cultures. Roland believes that universal psychoanalytic categories such as ego, superego, and self/object, boundaries must be decontextualized of the content related to the culture of individualism and recontextualized with clinical content from other cultures. This would expand the universal psychoanalytic language by adding new universal psychoanalytic categories of consciousness (from radically different cultures) such as *we-self, inner ego boundaries, private self, bicultural self, cultural self, elemental self,* and so forth.

As already stated, migration from one culture to another could be seen as a trauma of loss of one's culture, home, value system, language, family, country, and so on. However, migration involves more than simply trauma related to the loss of external things and home. What is even more painful is that the immigrant's internal emotional home often (to a different degree) is abandoned, disowned, broken to pieces, denied, and discarded due to too much psychological pain related to such overwhelming losses. The new temporary refuge home may be created until the time one may or may not feel emotionally stronger and able to come back and reconnect with the more authentic, emotional home. It is possible, on the other hand, that one may never be able to reconnect with the emotional self due to too much trauma.

Immigrants who function well in their own home country may nonetheless go through psychological and culture shock in the new country. Often, as a result of great stress, themes from very early childhood get stirred up and revived. Most likely, these issues would not be revived in a home base country. In such circumstances, feelings, fears, and phantasies are stirred up in the foundation of the personality, with the result that some immigrants may experience great problems and often develop even psychotic issues. They move to a psychotic temporary refuge home that provides the illusion of control and, paradoxically, some illusionary measure of safety and escape from painful external realities.

Grinberg and Grinberg (1989) have stated that:

> an immigrant also suffers losses and the absence of protective, containing objects and for that reason may become exposed to states of psychotic decompensation. In short, migrant [*sic.*—migration] tends to touch off psychotic aspects of the personality on the basis of the person's inner disposition; the discontinuity of context and breakdown in communication also may play a role. (p. 141)

Losing the connection to the native culture and country home base and the stress of adaptation can trigger neurotic, borderline, and, as stated above, even psychotic breakdown of the internal emotional home. However, for more integrated immigrants, the mourning process (due to loss of culture and value system, etc.) is ongoing, and immigrants need to find a way to live with it. On the other hand, often immigrants do not want to accept the painful effects of migration and to give up their culture, language, and so forth, and there is enormous ambivalence about it.

The coming together and the integration of the old world (culture) and the new world may never be completed and there may always be issues that do not get worked through. It is possible in most circumstances, that over time, elements of the new culture are incorporated into the creation of a more integrated and expanded cultural identity. Such a self becomes expanded in many ways but also impoverished by not being able to cultivate parts that cannot be further developed in the new culture, but only in the culture of origin. Perhaps emotional links and bridges between the old and the new worlds inside the self must be built as the individual decides just how much of the "old world" must be kept alive.

On the other hand, some may choose to close off the connection to the "old world" and either do not remember or do not want to remember because to keep both "old world" and "new world" alive and both identities functioning internally is too difficult. However, closing off the past and the old world is always at some cost. When emotional roots are cut off, then a more artificial psychic home and a more intellectual identity is developed. Perhaps it is best, even though more painful, to keep both the old and the new world and identities alive. Those who do not want to remember the old past world and history nonetheless reenact, albeit unconsciously, their forgotten past history.

Migration Proper

In this section, I present, discuss, and define such pivotal concepts to this study as migration and identity. For the purpose of this exploration I intent to use the well-phrased definition of migration by Grinberg and Grinberg (1989):

> Migration proper—that is, a migration in which people come to be called emigrants or migrants—occurs when the movement takes place from one country to another, or from one region to another, where the second is sufficiently distant and different from the first, for a sufficiently prolonged period of time, such that one would consider the person as living in another country, there taking up the activities of daily life. This idea forms the basis for the definitions found in most studies of migration: the action and effect of moving from one country to another for the purpose of settling there. . . . (p. 17)

The migration phenomenon despite its ubiquitous nature is difficult to penetrate. There are multiple reasons for migrations which are conscious and unconscious. The conscious and external reasons for migration may be related to poverty, wars, difficult political conditions, and many other economic, religious, political, and psychological reasons.

There are also all kinds of unconscious reasons and phantasies such as a desire to find a new, safe, and nurturing home (symbolically the mother womb) or the phantasy of finding a potent father in the form of a plentiful new promised land.

There are voluntary and involuntary migrations/exiles due to political, religious or ideological reasons where returning to the homeland may no longer be possible. The term migration may also be applied to all kinds of relocations: from a village to a city, from one city to another, or from one country to another.

In any event the migration process, as any major event in a person's life, implies a major challenge to one's sense of self. In the face of multiple losses and changes related to the migration process different types of fears and phantasies get awakened. These fears and phantasies may produce what Grinberg and Grinberg (1989) called "psychopathology of migration."

The ability to work through these fears and phantasies promotes one's development of a more mature sense of self and identity. The migratory process may be seen in various stages, as stated by Grinberg and Grinberg (1989):

1. In the first stage, the predominant feelings are intense pain for all that one has left behind or lost, fear of the unknown, deep-rooted loneliness, need and helplessness. Paranoid, disorienting, and depressive anxieties may alternate with one another, leaving the person prone to periods of total disorganization.
2. After a period of varying length, the feelings that arise are sorrow for the lost world and nostalgia; the migrant begins to recognize feelings that were previously dissociated or denied because they were unbearable. . .
3. In the third stage, the migrant rediscovers the pleasures of thinking and wanting and recovers the ability to plan for the future, in relation to which the past is felt to be past, not a "lost paradise" to which he constantly yearns to return (pp. 97–98).

Migration at times may be seen as Bion's "catastrophic change" with the outcomes that can lead to real catastrophes or the opposite, the psychological rebirth and creative development. Every migrant experiences and carries inside of him/her a mixture of fears, sadness, guilt, pain, nostalgia, hopes, and expectations for a better future.

The quality and outcome of the migration process will be influenced by such factors as the migrants' personality, age, prior object relationships, and the quality of new relationships, the receptivity of the new environment, the reason for leaving (voluntary or involuntary), and the capacity of the uprooted person to work through his/her fears and assimilate the experience of migration. In short, we always react to current life events according to our past history and in particular our experiences having to do with separations and losses of others.

Migration as a form of massive change and multiple losses exposes migrants to states of disorganization and the need for internal and external reorganization that may not always be possible. The migrant's capacity to reorganize internally and externally after a temporary disorganization (due to migration) to some degree will predict the success or failure of migration. The sufficient capacity to work through the fears due to a crisis of migration may lead to some form of recovery, rebirth, and development of creative potential.

On the other hand, some migrants are not able to deal with massive social changes and the fears related to such changes and losses. Such migrants often attempt to recreate the old and familiar world in order not to feel the pain of loss and change and they remain—psychologically speaking—in the same "old world" even though physically they are in a "new world" and culture.

Due to intolerable emotions migrants make use of splitting and dissociation, and by belittling the losses, and admiring the new world (or vice versa) they try to negate the fears, guilt, and pain of migration. The breakdown of dissociation leads to confusion (between good and bad, love and hate, etc.) which migrants often experience as punishment for leaving the old world and desiring to know the new world.

The migrant, due to the loss of reliable others and his/her cultural environment, often suffers from diminished creative capacity. The cultural inheritance can be seen as an extension of the "potential space" between the migrant and the new environment ("environmental mother"). Migrants need such a cultural-potential space that can be used as a "transitional place" (D. W. Winnicott) between the "old world" (mother/culture) and the "new world" (mother/culture).

If a migrant fails to create such a cultural-potential space between self and the new culture (mother) then he loses the capacity to play and symbolize. Such a migrant will exhibit impoverished development of creative potential and cultural awareness.

The migrant's ability to recover and regain his/her capacities will depend on his/her ability to work through his/her fears and overcome deprivation. Metaphorically, the human development with its different stages of maturation can be compared to multiple psychological migrations. In human development there are also times of great change, deprivation, loss, and crisis during transitional periods such as birth, weaning or adolescence, and so forth. Such psychological migrations also represent the potential for growth or the danger of mental disturbance.

Similarly, the physical migrations due to changes and losses that they imply represent on the one hand a trauma and crisis, and on the other hand the potential for growth, development, and identity transformation.

Identity

In 1919 Victor Tausk introduced the term "identity" into psychoanalytic literature. He examined how the child discovers his/her own self and his/her objects. He maintained that similarly an adult (throughout life), in his/her efforts for self-preservation, often repeats the experience of "finding him/herself."

In psychoanalysis, the identity is defined by Rycroft (1968) as follows:

> The sense of one's continuous being as an entity distinguishable from all others. According to Erikson (1953), many aspects of ego development can be formulated in terms of the growth of the sense of identity, an "identity-crisis" of greater or lesser severity being characteristic of late adolescence and early

> adulthood. The sense of identity is lost in fugues and perverted in schizophrenic delusions of identity in which, typically, an underlying sense of nonentity is compensated for by delusions of grandeur. . . . Failure to identify with parents, particularly the parent of one's own sex, during childhood is held to diminish the sense of identity, but failure to disidentify with them in adolescence has a similar effect. (pp. 76–77)

In my discussion about identity I will be using the above dictionary definition that is based on the original ideas of S. Freud, M. Klein, D. Winnicott, W. Bion and others. There are different views on the subject of identity and competing theories of the development of the self. According to one developmental theory (Fairbairn, Winnicott), infants are born with a rudimentary sense of self, which goes through various developmental stages, a process which is facilitated by the environment or could be impeded by it.

On the other hand, according to Freud, infants at birth lack any sense of ego (there is only id) and they gain one by the introjection of parental objects. M. Klein often used the term "self" interchangeably with ego and she felt there is ego at the beginning but dispersed and with only fragmentary awareness of an object. According to Klein (1946), the "early ego largely lacks cohesion, and a tendency towards integration alternates with a tendency towards disintegration, a falling to bits" (p. 4).

She saw the ego as the experience it has of itself, and thought about it in terms of phantasies the ego has in struggling with fears in relations with objects. The perception by the ego through instinctual phantasies creates a vivid world of anxieties, and love/hate experiences.

D. Winnicott felt that an infant is born with the unintegrated self nucleus, and only through the mother's provision of the right "holding environment" that gradually some integration takes place. The self starts off as the potential in the newborn infant. The ego is the aspect of the self (the subjective sense of being) that has a particular function to organize and integrate.

An individual with a well-established identity will have the capacity to remain emotionally and psychologically oneself and maintain internal stability during periods of change such as migration processes or changing life cycles. The establishment of one's sense of identity depends on one's capacity to authentically (not manically) assimilate, internalize, and introject object relations by the ego. The acquisition of the sense of identity is a long and very complex process.

According to Rycroft (1968), the capacity for introjection is "the process by which the functions of an external object (see also externalization) are taken over by its mental representation, by which the relationship with an object 'out there' is replaced by one with an imagined object 'inside.' The resulting mental structure is variously called an introject, an introjected object, or an internal object" (p. 87).

The sense of identity always develops through one's connection and links to others. Object relations are critical to identity formation, because they are repositories of various fears and they are also the source of various identifications which are necessary to identity formation and differentiation.

The sense of identity expresses a series of unconscious phantasies which when integrated constitute what could be called the unconscious phantasy of the self. The frequently used expression "pieces of the self" is a metaphor describing such unconscious phantasies of the self in a diffused type of identity. The "pieces of the self" are split off and dissociated parts of the ego with underlying phantasies; and they form a diffused identity type.

Migration processes which cause multiple losses and drastic changes in a migrant's life can pose a real threat to one's sense of identity. In the early period of the migratory process states of disorganization are frequent and various fears including primitive phantasies of being swallowed or torn apart by the new culture (symbolic mother) may be reactivated (with different degrees of anxiety).

These states are related to conflicts between the desire to assimilate with others and the opposite desire to be different. These conflicts of subjective desire and other ambivalent feelings about the new culture may cause confusion and depersonalization. A migrant, in his/her struggle for identity preservation, may need to some degree to hold on to his/her native familiar culture, other nationals, music, memories, food, and so forth in order to be able to feel like him or herself.

Migrants often need such familiar cultural objects (of emotional significance) in order to create through them the links to the past and to create an anchor for one's sense of identity. Such cultural objects emphasize the difference between the migrant and the new culture, introduce the evidence of the "old world" that has been left behind, and help the migrant bear the sorrow of being a stranger without roots in the new world.

In some situations the tendency to cling to such cultural objects may prevent the migrant from assimilating the new culture and accepting the past as part of one's evolving history. The surrounding environment is where the most visible change happens. The migrant loses most of his/her social, professional, and family roles that he/she played in the "old culture." The fears and phantasies that appear in the initial stages of the migration process are of the persecutory, depressive, and confusional nature, and they are in various degrees a constant feature of any migratory process. They differ in intensity, duration, and their evolution.

Persecutory anxieties are activated in the face of the unknown and the desire to transform the unknown into something familiar. The paranoid fears escalate into panic when the demands the migrant faces are too powerful. The confusional and disorienting fears are linked to difficulties in differentiating feelings about two subjects of interest, desire, and conflict which is the old culture and the new culture.

Migrants frequently set up triangular Oedipal situations as if each world/culture represents one of two parents in relation to whom they experience ambivalence, conflicts of loyalties, and various other phantasies. The depressive anxieties are created by the experience of multiple losses and the fear of never being able to recover all that has been lost.

When the migrant is not able to go through the required process of mourning, and feel, recognize, and express his/her losses, then the mourning process takes on pathological qualities.

Different types of fears in a person with a fragile sense of identity can develop into psychotic anxiety and a person may lose his/her sense of identity and become disoriented in time and space. In migrants with latent pathology and a fragile self, migration can promote the outbreak of psychotic anxiety.

Winnicott's paper (1974) "The Fear of Breakdown" examines the environmental factors and experiences in the early stages of development that had failed to provide a good-enough facilitating environment and support for the individual:

> Fear of breakdown is a feature of significance in some of our patients, but not in others. From this observation, if it be a correct one, the conclusion can be drawn that fear of breakdown is related to the individual's past experience, and to environmental vagaries. ("Fear of Breakdown," p. 87)

The migrant with a fragile self may experience the "fear of breakdown" of the self (Winnicott, 1974) and disintegration at the time when the support is lacking in the new culture. Such a migrant may feel like a child who suffers a prolonged separation from his mother/culture, when the new mother/culture cannot always offer the needed support and containment. The separation from familiar objects of containment and poor communication (due to a new language, customs, etc.) may permit the psychotic aspects of the migrant's personality to gain control over the psyche and lead to a breakdown that has already happened in the past.

According to psychoanalysts:

> Among the major sources of psychotic organization one finds the traumatic experience of separation, the child's loss of important objects, such as the mother or mother-substitute, at precocious stages of his development, or the mother's failure or inability to alleviate the child's anxieties. The child experiences great distress and in his desperation feels that he is "failing into the void." (Grinberg & Grinberg, 1989, pp. 135–36)

Therefore the key role played in psychosis is related to object loss, prolonged absence of the mother/container, and the subsequent inner void. Such a deprived migrant will have a very limited capacity to use his/her "cultural-potential space" in order to promote an imagination and a degree of creative attitude toward the process of assimilation into the new world.

In short, migration may touch off psychotic anxiety on the basis of the person's inner identity, rapture of environmental context, complexity of his/her new circumstances, and intensity of his/her feelings of loneliness and helplessness, and so forth. In some cases, psychotic disintegration takes place shortly after arrival in the new world that cannot be assimilated.

Others who apparently function normally may experience some form of identity collapse in the form of delayed psychotic state, depression or psychosomatic illness a few years later. (See cases of Ela and Zbyszek.) The delayed reaction often appears when the person loses the phantasy of the possible return to the old world and realizes that the change and loss are permanent. Psychosomatic disorder is frequently common in migrants who have fragile identity with latent psychotic anxiety.

Some migrants may react with manic pseudo-adjustment to a new culture. Others may cling to the old culture and be part of their own ethnic group only. Such a migrant may fail to become assimilated into the new culture.

According to Grinberg and Grinberg (1989) the postponed depressions in migrations, when the manic defenses become exhausted, may develop into somatic symptoms. In such cases emotional conflicts and difficulties become displaced to the body level and there is a development of psychosomatic disturbances such as digestive symptoms (one cannot digest migration), respiratory (being suffocated by the new world) or circulatory (the new world produces too much pressure).

In "Migration and Exile" (Grinberg & Grinberg, 1989), the psychoanalysts state:

> At times, the price of the effort to overcome a problem at the emotional level is displacement of the conflict to the body. It is then that psychosomatic disturbances appear. . . . The person may have a greater propensity to accidents, disguised suicide attempts. Instead of somatic symptoms, some immigrants display phantasies and hypochondriacal fears. (p. 94)

Had they not migrated, migrants with such a fragile identity may have been able to continue to maintain some level of precarious psychological balance (existence) in the old world.

In such situations the migration may take on pathological development due to unresolved identity problems and other conflicts. Such an experience of migration must be differentiated from migration in its healthy development in which one experiences nonetheless a sense of discomfort and uneasiness about one's identity in a new culture.

Migrations, like any major life event, are always a challenge to one's identity. A migrant with a stable sense of identity has to, to some degree, reorganize and resolve some of his/her internal conflicts and issues which are underpinning his/her sense of self and identity. Migration represents such a challenge to one's identity, and an opportunity to work through old conflicts and achieve new integrations.

When one migrates, one is no longer quite the same person one was in the old world and its culture. One enters a different place, time and culture, and the external changes have bearings on the internal adjustments one has to make. There is a need for reorganization of one's internal state of affairs that is called for in everybody who has the experience of migration.

Those who have problems in the area of identity to begin with may have difficulties navigating this type of move. In such a situation normal things that go on due to migration trauma for such people will be much more problematic and cause a greater challenge to one's identity. Some may put on a false/image (identity) in order to cope with it. Others may go back to traditional ways of being in order to cope with the challenges that the new world presents, creating their own ethnic neighborhoods where they can speak the same language, and be part of the old culture. Migrants often congregate together as a way to have a better sense of who they are, rather than being lost in an alien way of living which is what the rest of the world outside represents for that group.

Finally, migration may not always destabilize one's sense of identity. There are times when migrations are made to places of one's ancestors, in order to connect more deeply with one's long lost native identity roots and to anchor one's identity more securely. The prominent artists and other professionals whose work is already known in the new world can be seen as a special group because they can maintain their professional status and sense of identity with greater freedom and flexibility.

No matter what the circumstances, however, it seems that migration inevitably presents a challenge to one's sense of psychic and emotional equilibrium and makes life more complex.

Chapter 3

Migration Composite Case Stories

Treatment of Patients with a Precarious Sense of Identity and Self-Integration from which Composite Cases Were Developed

As already stated in my introduction, in each of the three presented migration stories only relevant material to the themes of migration, identity and culture has been abstracted from various clinical case histories and treatments. Therefore, the composite case studies are not presented as usual clinical case studies with the particular unfolding course of treatment and its outcomes. They are composite cases created in the interest of illustrating the phenomena of migration, identity, and culture, consisting of two but not more than three migrants composite being. The circumstances that are described are collected from a few clinical cases. All of the elements of each composite case come from direct observations and each composite case study shows some level of the progression in treatment.

The three composite case studies were selected due to their unique situation of being immigrants from Eastern European countries who are in the ongoing, intense, and often difficult to manage process of integration into American culture. All three composite case studies are rich in personal, cultural, and historical information about the topic of migration, identity and culture. Each case illustrates a different level of psychological development, a different age at the time of migration, and different capacities to deal with the process of migration. Hence, much can be learned about the phenomena in question from this small sample.

In my approach to these composite patients I paid close attention to their fears and anxieties at all sorts of levels, including very primitive anxieties that may have a basis in early mother/child infancy relationship, and issues related to separations. In all three composite cases the intensity and nature of the fears and conflicts were such that one had to pay particular attention and consider the early nature of the problems.

This kind of early anxiety often seems to be overwhelming in its nature and is suggestive of early problems in development rather than something from the later period. These early primitive anxieties in each case study were extremely important to consider, think about, and to engage with each composite patient on this level. Furthermore, these early primitive anxieties were present and re-experienced in these patients' lives but in much more disowned and disguised ways. In clinical work with these patients one had to be attuned to that level of anxiety in order to be able to address the fears and recognize where these patients lived psychologically.

In each composite case study, as treatment progressed, different disowned fears and anxieties had opened up and become more explicit and dealt with. As one goes deeper into the treatment one begins to see the themes and fears manifesting in their deeper forms as they continue to unfold.

By the very fact that these fears become more explicit when brought into treatment, their forms become better understood, leading to some conflict resolution as well as new integration and ongoing nonlinear development in treatment. The basic idea of treatment is to be able to provide space where patients can feel comfortable to bring out more aspects of themselves, in ways that were previously unbearable and unthinkable.

In this book I have presented many different dreams of my migrant patients. My approach to interpreting and understanding dreams is to seek associative material. However, often with the composite cases presented in this study, the associative material was not always available. Patients with a more precarious sense of identity often are not able to give dream associations, and their dreams often take the form of an expelling and evacuative-like experience (see Chapter 1 for further elaboration).

When associative material is not available I treat the given therapy session and the entire context of what is developing in the treatment as a part of the associative process. Therefore my dream interpretations are based on a patient's entire presented material, which could include the dream associations. Hence, in the composite cases presented in this study I may not have provided the given dream associations (in each instance), but my interpretations were based on the associative material (when available).

Furthermore, in this study I have not gone into the full description of the possible, expected transference, and countertransference developments, even though they were operative in my work all the time. In order to understand a patient's transference, I utilize my own countertransference experience in conjunction with the rest of the patient's presented material.

In each composite case the process of unfolding themes and working things through lead to anxiety reduction and a better capacity to manage life, work through situations, and be part of the new world. In each case the migration had a profound impact and working through its effects maybe an ongoing process.

A COMPOSITE CASE OF ELA: A FIGURE SKATER

Introductory Remarks

The composite case of Ela migrated to the United States (the "new world") as a teenager with her immediate family. It is clear that migration presents different challenges when a migrant comes to the new world at the stage of adolescence with the family members.

In such a migrant the sense of self-identity and their Eastern European self is already well developed and they often strongly identify with the native world and culture, as the composite being Ela had. The presence of the immediate family in such a migrant's life could be a protective force but, also, the force that can stifle the separation-individuation process.

In migration situations (the environment) where the entire immediate family is involved offers many interesting aspects to observe. Such families may often cling to the old native world and view the outside new world as a dangerous environment.

In Ela's composite case her family had gone through several migrations together, having lived in other countries before settling in the United States. Such a migration offers unique dimensions to the process of studying individuals with more complicated migration histories. I felt that it would be useful to study this category of migrant patients with complex migrant experiences. In today's age of global economy it is not uncommon for people to experience multiple migrations before settling in one location. Therefore this composite case has other features and dimensions to it, which may be of interest considering the global nature of our era.

Each composite case in this study presents different aspects of migration and additional unique features to each case are explored in detail, so the reader can consider the different dimensions of migration.

For instance, in the following case of Bruno, the childhood aspects of migration without the most immediate family are emphasized. Whereas, in Ela's composite being, the adolescent aspect of migration with the immediate family is a unique feature explored in detail in subsequent clinical discussions. All of the presented cases have childhood traumas. The age of the migrant was one of the important selection criteria but also a particular migration situation was of great interest.

Ela's composite being represents an adolescent migrant with anxiety of a rather severe nature, where she had to reinvent herself over time. The premigration history includes several other migrations. The particular issues in this composite case are centered around Ela's separations from her early objects (caretakers). Her mother was a constant overwhelming presence in her life and this migrant's obsessions related to "jumping from airplanes" is clinically understood as her manic attempts to jump out of the mother's body and separate from her psychologically but through physical ways.

However, this obsessive process of jumping from airplanes would not resolve her fear of being taken over by the mother figures. The separation from her early objects was particularly problematic in this case.

Background and Family History

In her first psychoanalytic therapy contact Ela presented a neat and well put together picture of herself. She appeared confident, self-assured, and well spoken. She was in her early 30s when she began her treatment. She worked in the field of artificial intelligence as a researcher.

Ela was seeking help because she felt intense anxiety about her upcoming engagement party. Ela stated that she had "run away" from her first engagement to another man. She did not know why she had escaped her first "wedding-like situation" and wanted to find out why she had done so. She was now in another intimate relationship facing similar feelings and phantasies of wanting to run away again, from her upcoming wedding party.

Back in Eastern Europe where Ela was born she was an accomplished figure skater and dancer. She migrated to the United States with her immediate family when she was in her adolescence. In the United States she became part of a well-known dance company.

She presented a striking image of herself. On the one hand, she dressed in a very feminine way, had long, straight, light hair, and very blue eyes. On the other hand, she was very athletic and addicted to all kinds of very dangerous sports like sky diving, rock climbing, and scuba diving.

She was very modest about her considerable achievement as a figure skater back in Eastern Europe and was rather reluctant to talk about that time of her life. Ela stated that she had many intimate relationships but all of them did not last longer than two years. In fact, every two years she had to reinvent her identity, self-image, and her life style. The images of dangerous sky diving, travel to exotic foreign places were themes that appeared regularly in her treatment. She often stated with an air of superiority that she had traveled to 47 countries around the world and frequently by herself.

However, underneath this idealized picture of a cultured, well-traveled, and very accomplished figure skater Ela had all kinds of paranoid fears and phantasies about intimate relationships and her basic sense of identity which felt to her very incomplete and often empty.

She presented a very exciting and idealized image of a person in constant search of new exciting experiences which was covering up her underlying fundamental depression.

Ela came from a well-established family of lawyers who lived in the Northern part of Eastern Europe. Her father was a lawyer and an engineer, who was often away from home due to his work on contracts abroad. The mother came from a less professionally invested background. She stopped working when Ela's two younger sisters were born in order to take care of the family and home.

When Ela was in her early adolescence, due to her father's various work possibilities, the whole family migrated and lived in different Arabic countries for several years. The family as a whole moved permanently to America when Ela was in her late adolescence. Even though the family did well economically, they found the integration to a new world and new culture emotionally and psychologically very difficult. The mother became depressed and chronically anxious and the father developed a serious drinking problem due to his own depression. Ela became a central family figure mediating between her parents' frequent conflicts and between the family and the new culture.

As a teenager Ela was more of a tomboy-like personality and interested in various sports. She idealized her father who was frequently physically and emotionally absent throughout Ela's childhood and later life due to his work abroad.

From a very early age she became involved in figure skating and ultimately became a part of her nation's international team, which offered her an opportunity to travel the world at a young age.

In the face of Ela's father's frequent physical and emotional absences she developed an intensely close and adversarial relationship with her mother. Ela described her mother as very emotional, intrusive, anxious, and too needy of her husband's approval and recognition.

In America the family as a whole was trying to recreate with some modifications the old world and familiar culture in order to remain in phantasy and psychologically speaking in the similar Eastern European old world. The family had bought a home in a very Eastern European part of the city, which they decorated according to their native country's standards. They had great preference for mostly Eastern European food, music, films, and so forth. Due to the family's difficulties in adapting to the new world, the family members became more enmeshed and detached from the "dangerous" mainstream American world.

RELEVANT THEMES RELATED TO MIGRATION, IDENTITY, AND CULTURE (WHICH AROSE IN THE TREATMENT OF ELA COMPOSITE CASE STUDY)

The Subtle Sybil Phenomenon

Henri Rey (1979), who writes about the claustro-agoraphobic dilemma states:

> Claustrophobic persons are afraid to be in an enclosed situation so they develop extreme anxiety or panic and want to get out. The "situation" may be a room, a traffic jam, a marriage. When they are not contained they become agoraphobic and develop anxiety or panic. Thus they may be housebound or may only travel so far alone from the place of safety and no further, or have to be accompanied . . . this condition is a really basic one in schizoid states and schizophrenic patients. (p. 218)

Rey emphasized that such a person feels engulfed by the emotional contact in closer relationships and, in many situations, this is experienced as a claustrophobic anxiety and fears of being imprisoned or suffocated. On the other hand if the person moves away from his objects there are fears of confusion and fragmentation which are often experienced as agoraphobia.

Rey stresses that the schizoid personality is caught in a claustro-agoraphobic dilemma. Due to such a person's projections, the space around them seems very hostile and harmful but to leave this dangerous space leaves such a person in a state of fragmentation, confusion, and with no containing structures and space.

Steiner (1987) speaks about the manic position pathological organizations that seems to offer a solution to the claustro-agoraphobic dilemma:

> If the patient attempts to emerge from it and moves towards his objects he will often retreat and argue that he cannot afford to experience the emotional contact which closer relationships entail. In many cases this is experienced as a claustrophobic anxiety and the object is felt to threaten the ego by imprisoning it, by suffocating or by making too many demands on it. On the other hand there is also a fear that a relinquishing of the defenses will plunge the patient into schizoid anxieties, especially confusion, and fragmentation which are often experienced as agoraphobia. If he moves towards his objects he becomes claustrophobic, while if he moves away from them he is agoraphobic. The pathological organization often appears to be the only way out since in it objects are bound in an organized structure, where the emotional distance to them can be controlled. . . . (p. 337)

Such a pathological organization(s) in phantasy can be represented in many ways described by Rosenfeld (1971) as gang, or mafia. Possibly Ela's constant need to reinvent her sense of identity every two years and her constant search for new exciting experiences, relationships, and places is an example of such a manic and schizoid type of personality who uses migrations and different types of physical travel/journeys as an escape from the internal tormenting feelings and threatening internal presences.

This may create great obstacles to the process of true integration into the new world and culture. The migrant's capacity to cope with difficult and often tormenting feelings of loneliness, hatred, shame, guilt, and so forth require some level of emotional development and "capacity to be alone" (Winnicott, 1958) that one develops in childhood, which Ela has never developed.

On the one hand Ela would idealize her father and all men but, on the other hand, she was terrified of intimate relationships and she would drop her partner unexpectedly and at the last minute before making some major commitment.

> In the initial stages of treatment Ela presented the following dream: "I was in a big house. I wanted to take a shower. I closed all the curtains, doors and windows. I spend a long time making certain that there was nobody around. I took my clothing off and I got into the bathtub. But when I looked in the mirror behind me I saw a South American man that wanted to kill me. I could not believe how he got there. I was feeling panic and terrors."

In the interest of space and time I will not be presenting detail clinical material and detail associations since my focus here is related to the particular themes connected to migration, identity, culture. After presenting the above dream Ela had the following memory. She spoke about her trip to Columbia and the incident when was attacked by an unknown man while she was wandering and exploring the remote parts of the countryside. The man wanted her passport and money but she was able to fight him off. The man reminded her of her ex-boyfriend. The dream expressed her fears of treatment and in transference her fears that I would rob her and take her identity away. On the other hand, this patient has a fear that if she exposes herself and lets down her defenses—essentially undressing herself psychologically, in the mirror of psychotherapy—she will find a murderous South American man who is also a part of herself. The lethal man is hidden inside of her body and this brutal alien creature inside of her is very deceptive.

Possibly this is one of the reasons why she had to run away every two years from her partnerships and reinvent herself. Part of her wants to run away from this alien part of herself but this part of her shows up in the mirror of psyche in her dream. Every two years part of her kills something essential in herself in order not to see and become aware of a murderous part of herself. She constantly runs away from this part of herself and pretends that this other part is not there. She migrates every two years into a new identity and reality. She is cutting off all her emotional, psychological, and physical links and makes herself up into a new part of herself and, seemingly a new person. Her more authentic sense of self is well hidden behind her heavy psychological makeup and therefore she constantly fears what will be discovered in the mirror of her life and of her psychotherapy.

In yet another dream which Ela called the "subtle Sybil dream" she states:

> The world outside is very dangerous for women. If you step out of the house you get murdered, raped, or attacked. I am living in the house with other women. The first one is Olga who is smart and attractive. She met this ugly man who took her all over the place, kidnapped her, and raped her. She was his slave and he would not let her go. Now she is living with me. She can go out by herself, be free, and live like a man, even though she is ruined by that man. I can go out only with my boyfriend. The other woman Ula is very slim, beautiful with long blond hair. She emits light. I want to be like her. She is just sitting there not concerned about anything and very mysterious. The next woman Ana is in her 40's and she is barren with no family of her own, lonely. She is a tragic figure. The other woman Eva has black hair and blue eyes; young, child-like. She has nothing to offer. All these women know me and we all go to the same psychologist. This is my life in this home and I cannot get out by myself. I am the sanest one. They all listen to me, but I do not care about listening to their painful traumas. I am the central roommate. . .
>
> The evil man that was with the first woman, Olga, got caught and they took him away. I do not know if he was going to kill her. He had two faces of Mr. Bean and big, handsome Al. She was the captured slave. . .

After this dream she said, I feel these women represent different aspects of me. The one that is most scary is the barren one who is over forty years old, not able to get married and have children.

Possibly the different women in Ela's dream are different identities that she takes on. There is a dangerous phallic element in her and also a terrified woman who needs her boyfriend to sustain her. She is scared of a murderous man part of herself and of other less sane identities that she refuses to pay attention to and disregards them. She presents the sanest part of herself and does not recognize the rapist inside of her that is covered up by her nervous Mr. Bean image. She wants to banish the less sane and psychotic parts of herself and pretend that they do not exist.

Part of her believes that she has to move and change her identity every two years in order to keep her emotional and psychological distance from the "psychotic" parts of herself. Possibly she is afraid that the "psychotic" part of her will emerge from hiding in the depth of her unconscious mind and the myth of her exciting, good, and happy life may be destroyed. Will the dangerous man kill her or will she kill the brutal man and therefore a part of her own personality.

For this patient, any experience where there is any emotional involvement becomes a prison-like situation from which she has to escape. Ela's reinvention of herself every two years was her manic attempt to become a new and "free person" because on the deeper level she felt that she could never become an authentic person in her own right. She had to engage in this external reinvention because otherwise she felt "stuck" in her emotional internal prison. The only way out was via her identity reinvention and magical migrations into new, exciting situations, and places.

Food Recipe

Ela is the child of a migrant father who was away abroad on his work contracts for long periods of time. The father was an idealized but also scary, god-like figure. Ela was left with her mother and younger siblings without the father to help her with the process of emotional and psychological separation and individuation from the mother.

Possibly the absent "migrant" father may have to some degree prevented the separation process between Ela and her "emotional" and controlling mother. However, the relationship between the mother and this child was problematic as well. Ela's mother would try to take over Ela's thinking and feelings. The mother often expressed her interest in coming to Ela's therapy and participating in her treatment.

Ela presented the following dream: "I am in the kitchen with my grandmother. She pours me a large glass of water. I drink the whole thing. She pours water again and I drink it again, and again, and again. My grandmother calls everybody and tells them . . . look how much she can drink!"

This patient also had frequent dreams about the "stolen dog" which she associated with the stolen child part of herself. Ela felt that her mother, the analyst, and everybody else do not give her anything of value. Her thirst and her needs are so powerful that whatever is given to her will never fulfill her needs and the other would give her only water instead of nourishing milk.

In the transference she sees the analyst through the images of her parents, whom she feels have never given her anything of value but useless promises. In this patient's deep unconscious phantasy there is a powerful needy and deprived infant part of her that is projected into other people and situations. The needs of that infant are so powerful that they have to be disowned.

All the needy and greedy people around her are projected parts of herself. She sets up this reality with others, and then colludes with this reality, and feels that others want to empty her and exploit her. She surrounds herself with deprived and needy people so they can carry her own disowned parts for her.

Therefore she does not have to feel the neediness and her own sense of impoverishment. She can place herself in a powerful manic position of a champion figure skater who can do sky diving, rock climbing, and so forth, and in this way she creates an illusionary sense of freedom and power based on disowning the deprived child part of herself.

As long as she projects the deprived baby part of herself she will feel exploited, invaded, and used by others. The analyst, her parents, and so forth, in her phantasy are devouring and hungry parts of herself (placed in others) that will empty her out. In her phantasy she has no needs and her losses and deprivations are manically denied. However, without this child part of herself, she is just a stage actress who reinvents herself every two years.

There is something essential about her adult self that is gone and missing. The other becomes just the projections of the unwanted parts of herself. She has no connection to the real other but connections only to projections of herself. She becomes an "adult stage actress" at the expense of the getting rid of the child parts of herself. The psychological migration into an authentic adulthood due to these issues may not be fully possible in this composite case.

Ela had frequent dreams about being buried in mud, with the exception of her head. She had buried all of her feelings with the exception of her intellectual self (head). Part of her feels stuck in the mud which is a messy, dirty, and humiliating unconscious situation.

Part of her wants to deny this painful psychic reality and feels that she could get out via her manic travels and identity reinvention. She is denying her own dependencies because in her phantasy she fears that she will be "eaten alive by others" (due to the projection of her oral rage.)

As long as she is not able to own up to these "mud-like" parts of herself, by recognizing and feeling these parts, she will be stuck in psychic mud forever, unable to grow and develop.

Midway through her treatment Ela presented the following "recipe dream":

> I am cooking my godchild Lola like I was cooking a rabbit. I was chatting to my partner and chopping up Lola. Her head looked like (a) potato and I was peeling off the top of her hair. I had to make the recipe. But then I noticed that it was Lola's head and that I had chopped her up into pieces. Now I feel very upset that I will never find another goddaughter like Lola.

In her dream associations Ela felt that she destroys everything in her life including her work partnerships and educational possibilities. This patient's unconscious recipe is to destroy everything; Ela has fears about destroying her intimate relationships. She feels murderous feelings toward her goddaughter Lola, which represents her own internal child. Part of her feels that everything is dispensable, including the internal child part of herself.

However, the other part of her has some awareness that Lola, her goddaughter, and her internal child self is not dispensable, but in her unconscious phantasy she fears that if she acknowledges her needs she will be eaten alive or chopped up into pieces and cooked up.

On the more fundamental level she fears her own projected out into other, oral rage. She fears that if she acknowledges her needs she will lose the illusionary freedom based on disowning huge parts of herself. But if she does not accept her dependency needs then she is really in a prison of her own projected outrage.

Ela seems to be caught in what Ray (1979) called a claustro-agoraphobic dilemma where the external situations and people overwhelm her. The needy and desperate parts of her are put out and projected into these external situations. The result is that now external situations, things and people control, monitor, and take her over due to her own denial of her needy side. This patient's parents could not respond and accept her need for them, but they needed her for their own emotional and psychological needs.

She is not able to symbolize her wishes and needs for others. Her needy feelings and angry impulses are put out into others, and then she loses the conscious connections with these parts of herself that are carried by others. This process leads to internal impoverishment, confusion about one's sense of identity, and loss of one's psychic home.

In order to become an authentic adult with a real sense of identity Ela needs to own up to her infantile early needs and vulnerabilities, so she can be in touch with who she really is.

El Diablo Sky Diving

According to Rycroft (1968), who writes in his "A Critical Dictionary of Psychoanalysis":

> the idea that much psychiatric illness is due to separation from the mother during infancy and childhood has achieved considerable currency. The hypothesis is not simply that separation causes distress at the time, or even unhappiness later, but that it is the cause of specific mental illnesses, notably psychopathy, phobia and depression. Explorations of how separation produces these effects vary in sophistication and complexity, e.g. (a) it causes insecurity, (b) it increases hostility and ambivalence, (c) it interferes with (the) introjective and identificatory process(es), and thereby interferes with ego development, and (d) it institutes mourning process at an age when the child is too immature to complete them, leaving him, as it were, "stuck" in the phase of despair or depression. . . . (p. 168)

As already stated, Ela, as a child of an "absent migrant" father, was left in the care of her mother. Possibly the absence of the father had to a great degree prevented the process of Ela's separation from a symbiotic relationship with her mother, who suffered from her own depressions and anxiety disorder.

The images of sky diving and topics related to this sport were regular themes in Ela's treatment. The red sky diving equipment bag and her sky diving garment suit had the name "El Diablo" inscribed in big letters on it.

In one therapy session just before Ela's upcoming weekend of sky diving she said:

> I feel excitement about sky diving this weekend. It makes me feel alive more than sex and travel. I feel volatile about this topic. I know I will jump, but I feel edgy and jumpy about it. It's a dangerous sport. I read about all new deaths in sky diving and the reasons for them. The most dangerous malfunction is when two parachutes that are in the bag (become) entangled. Just before jumping, part of me is paralyzed and feels emotional turmoil. But another part (of me) wants to go and do it anyhow. It brings out El Diablo/Devil woman in me. You do it for the "high" that you feel afterwards. You cannot feel this kind of high and rush after anything . . . you feel happy . . . satisfied . . . great vibes . . . Then you hang out with other sky divers . . . you feel like you belong somewhere . . . like you are finally at home. . .

We may wonder about the psychological and emotional meaning of this addictive activity (sky diving). On a psychological level Ela has never properly sufficiently emotionally separated from her mother. The basic psychological and emotional theme of psychologically migrating out of her mother's body has never been worked through in her life. She is constantly trying to separate from her internal mother via manic and magical types of separations.

On the most regressive phantasy level for Ela, jumping out of planes is like jumping out of her mother's body through a hole in a plane to the safety of some other place. Ela's jumping out of planes and trying to magically chop the "umbilical cord" connecting her to a plane are her desperate attempts to separate herself from her internal mother.

However, on the phantasy level being inside her mother's body feels terrifying and claustrophobic to another part of her. Then she has to jump out and reinvent herself again in the new life situation. In fact, being in any emotionally involving relationship or situation is terrifying and she has to "jump out" every two years and create a new identity for herself.

When marriage is about to take place in Ela's life she fears that she will be consumed and taken over by it so she runs away into another relationship, which again becomes consuming. She is caught in the constant process of expelling herself from the mother body/planes, or engaging in fussing with others. She cannot make proper separation from her internal mother and she is caught up in manic attempts to separate (jumping out of planes) which are very scary.

As previously stated, this composite case study illustrates what Ray (1979) has called the claustro-agoraphobic dilemma, where another person or some emotionally involving situation is felt to threaten the self by imprisoning it, suffocating it, or threatening it in some other way. On the other hand there is a fear of coming out of the dangerous space or situation due to lack of containment and fears of fragmentation. Ela has powerful fears of being trapped and suffocated in any close encounter situation, such as marriage or treatment, and therefore has an uncontrollable impulse to "jump out" because getting in touch with these feelings is unbearable.

It is possible that the dangerous, perverse addiction to very dangerous sports is a way of running away from her unbearable depressed side that she fears may come out and destroy her chance for having a home of her own. The sky diving is another manic attempt to convince herself that she is an exciting person that has found her psychological home and belongs somewhere.

But underneath these fragile defensive manic maneuvers there is a fear of being El Diablo, a depressed woman who is condemned to sky diving, exotic migration, and endless recreating of her identities. Ela is caught in the process of continuous running away from herself and, ironically, in search of herself. She runs away (via sex, dangerous sports, identity reinventing, physical migrations like trips to exotic countries) from her underlying depression.

The psychological birth and migration from her mother('s) body is dangerous for her because it would require her to get in touch with her unbearable feelings, conflicts, and emotions. Part of her wants to be unborn, because to feel these feelings and be psychologically alive feels like hell to her.

Possibly the real physical migration to the United States has reinforced her claustro-agoraphobic problems and her tendency to jump out of planes/mother body, and then becoming scared of new situations and in her phantasy going back and fussing with the mother's body again. Part of her keeps on jumping back and forth from different situations and keeps reinventing herself. The physical migration into the new and unknown world and culture has reinforced these themes because the fear of the outside unknown and dangerous world becomes more real.

47 EXOTIC COUNTRIES

According to Balint (1959) there are two types of individuals: an ocnophilic with the tendency to hold and cling on to familiar and stable places and people, and they cannot be alone; and the "philobatic" with a tendency to seek out exciting places, people, situations, and mostly new emotions.

Philobatics tend to migrate in search of new experiences with some degree of risk-taking and an often omnipotent desire to overcome the danger. Ocnophiles are characterized by a great need to hold on to people, places, and objects. They are more rooted in their world of origin and have difficulties leaving for new places.

The extreme acting out in either of these two modes of functioning indicates some level of anxiety related to agoraphobia and claustrophobia. Victims of agoraphobic anxiety have a great need to cling to the known places, people, and situations. People with claustrophobic anxiety are often in the grips of a compulsive and uncontrollable desire for new, exciting people, experiences, risky sports, risky enterprises, and constant unrealistic manic migrations.

What would constitute a degree of mental health is the integration of these two modes of functioning, where one can choose and act according to ocnophilic or philobatic tendencies, depending on what is most suitable to circumstances. The integration of these two modes of functioning constitutes a degree of mental maturity, development, and emotional health.

Since the early years of her life Ela as an international figure skater had traveled to many countries around the globe. Due to her father's work contracts, Ela and the rest of her family also migrated to several Arabic countries.

In one of Ela's therapy sessions she stated:

> I love good adventure, risky sports, and going to exotic places. I traveled to 47 different countries around the world and quite a few times by myself. I went to Vietnam, Colombia, Haiti, Ethiopia, Jordan, Iran, etc. In Africa everything felt shocking to me, and my European sensibility. The music, the poverty, naked children, holy temples, the wildlife of tigers, elephants, eating food with your hands, sleeping on the floor. . . . I felt so free there. America seems so cleansed, materialistic, rigid, and less alive. Africa is more real and more alive.
>
> In Colombia I saw the Guerilla troops with AK47's ready to attack our bus full of Western tourists. . .

It is possible that in Ela's divided psyche different and completely opposite internal realities are externally represented by different countries and continents. The great Africa is the complete opposite of the cleansed, rigid, and materialistic America. The "messy" Africa is an emotionally and psychologically messy and anal place inside of Ela. The opposite of the messy part represented by Africa, there is a sterile part of Ela's internal place represented by America.

The "messy African-like" internal psychic space is a complete opposite of the "sterile American" internal psychic space. The emotionally messy and psychologically sterile psychic places are the opposite and fragmented parts of Ela's psyche that she cannot tolerate and therefore disowns them.

She tries to get away from her psychic messy places called Africa and Colombia by going physically (migrating) to these countries and imagining that the mess (her internal emotional mess) is out there and can be controlled via physical, concrete journeys/migrations. She runs from herself and her messy and murderous emotional parts represented by Africa/Colombia hoping to cleanse herself from this otherwise unbearable feelings. In her phantasy the unwanted parts of her are in other countries and are not in her. The AK-47 represents Ela's internal psychic place of murderous feelings, fears, and conflicts. Part of her does not want to see her psychic divisions represented by the AK-47s, Africa, Colombia, etc. and experience the unbearable feelings and fears located there.

She hopes to cleanse herself from these feelings and create a sterile and neat image of herself. The neat and idealized presentation of Ela's travels to exotic paradise-like places is on another level a cover up for her paranoid fears and phantasies, and the AK-47 murderous-like psychic places.

Similarly, on the one hand Ela idealizes Eastern European cultures as more warm, earthly, alive, hospitable, and less sterile. However, on the other hand, she feels that Eastern Europe is too oppressive, harsh, rigid, and therefore unsafe as well. She seems to be partly cut off from that internal old world reality as well.

This composite case study Ela uses, to a great degree, the physical journeys/ migrations to these exotic places in service of her internal splitting and fragmentation. She needs to go to 47 exotic places in order to psychologically run away from her unbearable internal places called Africa, Eastern Europe, or AK-47. The migrations and travel to these exotic places in this situation is a defensive maneuver and manic running away from her fears, emotional dependency, and attachments.

Ela's feelings, emotions, fears, and desires are massively projected and put out into the images of exotic countries, dangerous sports situations, etc. which in turn leads to emotional emptiness and need for more manic excitement.

Possibly Ela's early life migrations to other countries have contributed further to her already fragmented basic sense of personality and her tendency to split her experiences into different areas of her psyche. Perhaps, to some degree, she became a new person in every new culture she went to. However, even though she went to 47 exotic countries to overcome her phobia, it seems like Ela does not belong anywhere.

The idealized Eastern Europe is too oppressive and rigid, while America is too sterile and materialistic for Ela. A large part of Ela does not belong anywhere and is caught in a "no man's land" between the old and the new worlds.

We may wonder (and hope) that via her psychological migration within and via her psychotherapy she may be able to find herself (at least to some degree), and move out from the unreal, idealized internal wasteland, and idealized home of her parents, into a psychic home of her own. Perhaps to some degree her opposite internal parts can be brought more together and she may be able to tolerate the messy anal parts and not have to cleanse it all.

Possibly someday, by her enduring travels to all these places, she may be able to find herself and her own real psychological home where her internal psychic spaces represented by Africa and the AK-47 are recognized, accepted, and valued.

Therapeutic Process

Any movement in life including migration could be used constructively, destructively, or as a mixture of both for defensive or creative reasons. Some migrants may use migration as a defense against underlying trauma, and as a way of psychologically and physically escaping the fundamental psychic issues. If migration is primarily used for defensive reasons, than the migrant's capacity to address the deeper underlying issues would be greatly compromised because such a migrant will be dealing with the life issues in an unreal way. In such a case migration becomes just another way of running away from one's fundamental issues and concerns. On the other hand, migration can present the creative solution to the inner and outer difficult situation provided that inner psychic work can be done within oneself and one is capable of making realistic decisions about one's life.

In the process of migration there are usually some realistic factors that motivate one to migrate and there are often unconscious, less rational, phantasy-related factors dominated by defensive reasons that impel migration. The migration often fits with the underlying psychological issues and conflicts and can be another method of acting out and concreting the desire to escape inner reality. However, not everybody with the particular type of underlying psychic states of affairs (i.e., like migrants in this book) will necessarily migrate. The inner underlying psychological picture may impel them in other directions; like going in and out of relationships, professions, or engaging in other forms of escapes from life. Some migrants may not be able to engage in the migration process due to lack of skills or other life circumstances may not permit that.

The following excerpts from the composite case of Ela will illustrate how migration concept/process fits into her underlying psychological picture and related defensive set up. While the content of the excerpts from the two sessions is about her inner conflicts and life struggles, the presented clinical process reflects how she is dealing and processing life events including migration. This patient has great difficulties working through any deeper psychological issues. This migrant could not mourn anything in her life including migrating from one place to another. The migration itself was unprocessed and unmourned event like everything in her life.

In order to illustrate the patient/analyst interactions and patient's inner psychic process I will present the clinical vignettes in the following pages. For the reasons of space I will limit the therapeutic process to the composite case Ela. As already stated, I will give excerpts from two sessions in order to illustrate the clinical process, trends, and types of issues that arose in the treatment of composite case Ela. The two sessions came from the same patient that is part of the composite case Ela.

Excerpts from Psychoanalytic session #1

ELA: I disconnected the phone (turned off her cell phone) before you came out to call me in. I had to go to the bank to make a check deposit. I don't know how I stand with the money. I did send another application for a research position.

I had this dream: "The infant is drowning in the toilet. I think the infant was laying on some kind of wooden board. The toilet was big . . . going down through several floors of some kind of building. I could see the inner wall construction. I think that the infant was lying on the two sticks that moved apart. There was also a small Ela there that jumped head down into the toilet. I was just standing there. I did not know what to do. . ." (end)

ANALYST: What are your associations to this dream? How old was small Ela in the dream?

ELA: I saw her face from the old home movie, her face was sad. I think she was 5 years old. I was trying to tell you what they did to me in the past and you talked about the third option. When I was a teenager mother told me "when you have your children, they will have a revenge on you for the way you were to me." I became very compliant and decided that I would not have children myself so that I would not repeat the same issues with other human beings. I started feeling guilty then, I don't know why.

ANALYST: I wonder what are your thoughts and feelings about the children in the dream. The infant and the five-year-old Ela are drowning in the toilet but the adult part of you is not doing anything?

ELA: I started feeling guilty in the first grade of the high school, till then I believed that I was not guilty. I was trying to please everybody, but after the age of sixteen I felt guilty and needed other's forgiveness.

ANALYST: I wonder, if the guilt is about something that happened in the dream.

ELA: Something got killed in me when I was sixteen years old

Analyst: But, what about the killings that are happening right now? In your other dream (from your prior session) you saw me as a prostitute only interested in your money. In this dream the infant part of you is falling down the toilet and you don't do anything. There is a five-year-old Ela that is jumping down the toilet . . . but you don't know what to do.

Ela: I don't like infants or children. I told myself a long time ago that I would never have children. I was sixteen years old and I was bad. This woman (the mother) made me feel that I was the guilty one. But I also remember when I used to go to her bed (as a child) and wanted to sleep with her. It felt very good and safe with her. At other times I felt rejected by her, she was resentful and I don't know why. . . .

(In the latter part of the session Ela stated the following):

Ela: She was dangerous for me. I did not trust her. If she was a good mother I would not hate her. I did not ask to be born into this world. I wanted to go to sleep and never wake up anymore.

In the second session that was presented several weeks later Ela presented the following material.

Excerpts from Psychoanalytic session #2

ELA: Thursday I had a mouse at home. Saturday I came home from an Italian restaurant where I had dinner with C. There was a terrible noise at home. I thought I had an army of mice. But then I saw water coming down from the bathroom ceiling. I ran upstairs and I heard the voice of the super and I knew that things were okay. Next day all was dry. I have no cat. I read my lease contract and I am not allowed to have animals in my apartment. Yesterday, I was crying for two hours. (Sunday)

Long Pause (Crying)

ANALYST: I wonder why were you crying for two hours on Sunday?

ELA: I was reading a book. The book was about the Irish community. It was a romance story. I knew that the ending would be okay and that the woman would end up with a man that she likes . . . it was a good ending. I was crying because of how much I have lost . . . it was about a young woman who was in love with this boy. So there is sadness and regret that I did not have that. I live in hell created by my mother. I don't know what it is like to be in love . . . the book was about how children grow up, get married . . . movement from generation to generation. I only watch. I only have little bit of life. (Crying). . .

ANALYST: In the book there is a struggle between love and hate. Perhaps there is a part of you that feels that you are in a hell-like existence, without love, and with the army of mice inside your inner apartment. Your inner hell was created by your mother. In your last dream (from the prior session) there was a raging fire everywhere and who has created that fire and hell-like existence? Did I create the hell-like experience of raging fire inside of you by my harsh words about the issue of wasting time here? Am I trapping you with my bad words, stopping your development, throwing you into a fire, wasting your time as you have said before?

ELA: I live in hell and I know that I live there. When I was going home (Saturday) I was trying to catch what the little girl was feeling inside and she took me home by my hand (the inner little girl). I know that if I cut myself off from the little girl than I have nothing. My mother interrupted everything. What gives me hope is when I sit with the sadness and despair and I know there is something else there (inside) besides sadness and despair. That I will find joy in life. As a child I played by myself. I had a great imagination and my mother did not allow that. Because of her envy of me she did not allow me to play. Wednesday I was watching the TV show. It is a one hour show about women that killed people. There was this one woman that suffocated her daughter.

ANALYST: The story is about the mother that suffocated her daughter. Is it that I suffocate you with my words . . . Or, is it that there is some part of you that is killing the inner female child part of you? Is this a part that cuts off your capacity to hate here in this room and therefore your capacity to love as well? Is it too scary to activate that part of you that needs to hate because then he whole hell breaks loose? The raging fire from your other dream will destroy you, me and everything else.

ELA: It's a forbidden country; I cannot go into those parts of myself. R (friend from her native country) said that her past created her and she would not like to change anything about herself, she accepted herself. I did not get used to myself at all. I want to kill those bad parts of myself but then I kill the little girl inside of myself as well. For Christmas I always felt safe in my country. It's like I want to go back to some kind of paradise.

ANALYST: You have made all these references to hell and paradise . . . is it that the part of you would like to go back to some kind of paradise/womb structure and never be psychologically born; because being born here in the sessions . . . it's like hell with the raging fire burning things, ugly army of mice or at other times you want to jump out of the mother's womb/hell like place and be free. . .

ELA: I just remembered a dream that I had. . .

DREAM: I was watching a birth. The little girl is born. But it was not a newly born infant; it was not dirty, ugly, with a wrinkled face, like infants are. I think the girl was three years or three months old and she had red hair like me. But I am in hell."

ANALYST: What are your thoughts and feelings about this dream?

ELA: I don't like newly born infants. They are dirty, ugly, and full of wrinkles. I fear my own rage; I feel I could do something to a child. It is like with a cat. I rather have a grown up and fully trained cat. The small kitten would scratch my furniture, pee and shit all over my place and create a lot of mess.

ANALYST: Perhaps feeling these ugly, dirty, messy feelings here is too scary. You want a nice clean grown baby with "no wrinkles." It there a fear that if you activate these ugly parts of yourself here and feel the hell here, maybe the killings will start here like with the other mother that suffocated her messy daughter, or a brother that killed the other brother in the Irish community?

ELA: It was an accusation. He did not do it . . . The unknown character (in the book) shows up to save the situation. In the third book the unknown character shows up and purifies the young man from the accusation and tells the true story about the past. Nobody purifies me from the accusation. Thirty years have passed and I still feel guilty.

ANALYST: Is it that you need some unknown person to come and magically purify you? Perhaps to trust me to help you with your psychological birth is too scary. Do I also want to see only the beautiful parts of you? The ugly mice like parts of you are too scary to feel them here, so you want to get a cat and kill them so you can have a self-created, purified baby that is grown up and very unreal.

Even though there is another part of you that knows that if you kill the bad parts of yourself you may kill the little girl as well.

ELA: I will think about it. Now I have to go to work and pretend that I am an adult and I know what I m doing.

The above clinical material illustrates how by disowning the child part of herself she disconnects herself from her needs and vulnerabilities including her psychic center of existence. The process of disowning the child part and other parts of herself in the first dream (in the session #1 excerpts) leads to intensification of manic defensive processes and "running away" in her phantasy from herself in order to not face her inner psychic reality. The second dream (in the second session) is a visual representation of her manic defensive process, where she is trying to create and produce very quickly a baby that is already grown up and not a newly born infant.

This type of manic inner psychic process could be applied to any life event including physical and psychic migration in this patient's life. Such a manic defensive process is not about embracing true psychic process of change, and going through the different steps and stages of dealing with difficult anxieties, phantasies, and feelings. The underlying motivation is to escape the true psychic process and inner anxiety. The messy process of being psychologically born is too threatening to this patient. In her phantasy she is engaging in the process of jumping over the difficult steps and stages of the psychic process related to psychological birth and psychic change. She is hoping to instantly leap into some ideal and purified situation of psychic birth, which is another magical solution to her inner dilemma of psychic "stuckness."

Inevitably she has dealt with the migration phenomena in the similar way. The migration itself became another undigested situation. This migrant's inner psychic process reflects how she deals with all experiences and events in her life. Possibly in Ela's phantasy life her parents multiple cross-cultural migrations were setting up the model in her mind that one way to cope with difficult life circumstances is by leaving one country for another. Ela's parents' decision to migrate permanently to the United States played into her defensive inner picture and exacerbated her inner issues of splitting, fragmentation and manic escapes.

CULTURE MATTERS

The success or failure of the physical migration to a large degree will be determined by the quality of the environment that receives the migrant. Roland (1988), "In Search of Self in India and Japan" states in his footnote:

> Self psychology is beginning to have something to say about this issue in terms of cultural self objects; that is, that aspects of culture with which one resonates help to sustain a cohesive sense of self. (p. 1)

Perhaps one may say that Freud had primarily focused upon the internal psychic reality and, to a great degree, had excluded the effects of environment upon the developing psyche of the child.

Originator of self-psychology, Viennese-born American analyst Heinz Kohut emphasized that the parent provides missing psychic functions for the child. Kohut developed this idea into the concept of the "selfobject." According to Kohut (1978) the "selfobject" is originally the caretaker that fulfills the specific psychological functions and needs, such as the need to idealize, the need to be valued, validated, etc. This also means that self will always—in varying forms and throughout life—need some form of external support in terms of maintenance of self-esteem and self-cohesiveness.

Winnicott (1971) states that the psychoanalytic literature does not examine "the place where we live in our ordinary life." Furthermore, in "Place Where We Live" (1971) Winnicott states,

> playing and cultural experience are things that we do value in a special way; these link the past, the present and the future, they take up time and space. They demand and get our concentrated and deliberate attention; deliberate but without too much of the deliberateness of trying. (p. 109)

Winnicott felt that the carrier of the primary culture is the early relationship of the mother and infant. The mother is the carrier and "transmitter" of the primary culture.

We may say that the individual culture into which one is born will determine one's enjoyment and pursuit of particular cultural activities. People from different cultures prefer different cultural activities such as a particular type of music, dancing, food, art, sports, literature, poetry, etc. All of these different cultural activities enhance self-development and the quality of one's life.

In the paper "Location of Cultural Experience" (1967), Winnicott points out:

> when one speaks of a man she speaks of him along with the summation of his cultural experiences. The whole forms a unit. I have used the term cultural experience as an extension of the idea of transitional phenomena and of play without being certain that I can define the word "culture." (pp. 98–99)

In Winnicott's theory of the primary culture, the stress is placed on the infant's subjective experience of his primary caretaker. He felt that out of this early mother/child relationship, primary culture emerges with the specific cultural customs, language, emotional, symbolic cultural, and personal meanings. The heart of this primary cultural experience is the child's capacity to unconsciously remember and experience psychologically the mother's holding, containing, and protecting capacity.

Kohut speaks about a child frightened by the hum of a bee and he suggests: "At such times a child needs the parent nearby to calm him and to feel reassured that the drive control is secure" (Kohut & Seitz, 1960, p. 43). Kohut felt that the basis of the child's frightened feelings was linked to the threat of the unmastered drives breaking through onto the world.

Possibly a migrant entering into a new culture feels like a frightened child who needs a caring person who can provide "selfobject" (Kohut, 1978) psychological functions; someone who can contain the migrant's fears about the new and unknown world.

Such a migrant in the new and unknown world, dealing with separation anxiety, could be compared to a child (and adult simultaneously) who is alone and desperately searching for the familiar face of a parent to provide external support for a weakened sense of identity, maintenance of self-esteem, and self-cohesiveness. Such a migrant needs to find in the external environment an "other" who could represent a substitute mother/father and can provide such a cultural "selfobject" function.

However, the migrant's already internalized object relations (internal mother, father, others) will condition his/her capacity to receive help from others and his/her capacity to work through his/her difficult feelings and conflicts.

The new migrant must learn and incorporate a new value system, and often new, unknown communication codes. The regression which is inevitable in each migration (due to multiple losses) makes a new migrant often feel inhibited, vulnerable, and defenseless. In regression to an earlier level of mental functioning, a new migrant's feelings, fears and conflicts might be expressed in relation to primal cultural things such as food, music, or language. The cultural environment represents a part of the migrant's identity. The cultural objects are symbols of belonging and they are often invested with intense emotions, thoughts, and conflicts.

The cultural "transitional space" is a place of experimentation, play, tension release, etc. The loss of such a cultural environment and its valuable cultural objects could be experienced as the loss of the known and caring mother/father. The migrant may feel in his phantasy "eaten up" or invaded by the unknown culture's different world views and value system, and often ambiguous communication.

This may explain why many migrants would decorate their homes with objects that belong to the old culture and carry great emotional weight, which has significance for maintenance of one's self-cohesiveness, self-esteem, and self-continuity.

Food takes on great symbolic meaning because it symbolizes at the deep unconscious early phantasy level the link to the mother's breast. The compulsive eating or drinking may become on the phantasy level, a compulsive search for the lost cultural objects. The newcomer may try in phantasy to escape back to the old culture by eating only "native food" as a way of recreating an idealized breast, as a compensation for the loss of cultural identity, and other multiple losses.

Furthermore, migrants may reject "local food" (of the new culture) and seek out only the traditional native food hoping on the unconscious phantasy level that by rejecting the local food one is rejecting the bad breast that belongs to the unknown and bad culture, while desiring only an idealized breast that belongs to the known and good culture.

Similar mental conflicts and feelings tend to be expressed toward other primal cultural things like music, language, and art, by a regressed new migrant. Not only does the new migrant feel the impact of his/her migration, but also the new world community feels the impact of the new migrant's presence.

The new migrant may be seen as a stranger, invader, or intruder to be feared, persecuted, and treated as the "dehumanized immigrant." The newcomer may be seen as a threat that may endanger the new community's cultural identity, value system, purity of language, world view, and beliefs.

On the other hand, the new migrant may be cast into some idealized and omnipotent role of someone who may resolve the local community's problems. This attitude can easily shift to feelings of anger, fear, and disappointment.

A migrant's past history and experiences will to a great extent determine the quality of his realistic interaction with the new community, without extreme idealization or devaluation. The new community's realistic capacity to accept the newcomer (without extreme idealization or persecution) may allow both parties to authentically participate in the process of gradual assimilation and integration, and thereby getting to know one another genuinely.

CAUGHT IN BETWEEN TWO WORLDS

Migration implies movement into the unknown ground and into an unpredictable future in the new world. Every new migrant to some degree is confronted with basic fears of losing the primary culture, its cultural objects, world view, value system, social behaviors, etc.

It is often inevitable in such a situation that one may experience deep feelings of loneliness, anguish, depression, isolation, insecurity, and a fundamental sense of not belonging. As in Ela's case, the migrant may come with his/her whole family. On the one hand the family may function as a protective shield, providing support and containment. But on the other hand, the family may also function as a coercive and limiting force in a young adolescent's (such as Ela) life. One of the central problems experienced during adolescence is the search for and consolidation of one's sense of identity. Migration in and of itself is difficult, as is any major life event, and therefore may further interfere with the process of identity consolidation.

The migration has greatly contributed to making Ela's adolescence a highly conflicted period marked with all kinds of self-destructive tendencies. Ela experienced her father—the decision maker in the family and the one who decided to move the family to the United States—as the one who deprived her of everything she loved, and as the cause of her despair and depression. She denigrated the new environment and magnified its shortcomings, while exaggerating the charms of the old country.

For Ela, the psychic pain of leaving the old culture behind on the phantasy level felt like an expulsion from home. Her way of counteracting the pain and detaching herself from it was to live in a manic way, denying the unbearable psychic pain via dangerous sports, travel, and identity reinventions.

She had no capacity to experience this partly mental and partly physical kind of pain triggered by the migration experiences and therefore she had little capacity to assimilate the experience of migration.

In fact, Ela's whole immediate family who migrated to America and were to some degree rooted in their Eastern European culture found the trauma of culture change particularly difficult to cope with, and the family had to rely on each other.

Some migrants find it intolerable to accept the regression and live through the humiliating and infantilizing stage before they can enter the new culture and feel accepted.

Ela's father and his family had a prestigious social and professional position in his old culture. In the new culture however, due to linguistic issues and other problems Ela's father had to accept less professional work position(s) and much lower social status. He fell into a deep depression and developed a severe drinking problem.

As already stated, the family as a whole bought a home in an affluent Eastern European part of the city and decorated the new home in a very Eastern European way. The families of migrants often set up their own groups and communities due to their anxiety about the world outside that is often strange and different. The migrant family unit often became more inward looking.

After this permanent kind of migration, Ela's family has closed in and become even more inwardly dependent on each other. Even though Ela's mother was an anxious woman, she was able to make some form of adjustment and created a professional life for herself. However, Ela's father had reinforced the idea that the world outside of the family unit is dangerous, materialistic, and cold.

On the one hand, Ela was discouraged from exploring more ethnic Eastern European neighborhoods, because they were messy, not clean, less affluent, and not up to the standards. But, on the other hand, she was also discouraged from entering a mainstream, materialistic, and cold America that may (they feared would) exploit her and attack her cultural identity.

Ela felt more stuck in between the new world and the old world; in "no man's land." The Eastern European side of her felt oppressive and rigid and the American side of her felt sterile, cold, and materialistic; she did not belong anywhere.

When she came to the United States as an Eastern European migrant she felt marginalized and disrespected, which reinforced her fears and pushed her back onto her family unit, which complicated her already problematic separation-individuation issues. She became an academic over-achiever like her father but, emotionally, the migration reinforced her tendency to fuse with her mother and the rest of the family. But clinging to the family is terrifying as well because the family is overpowering and takes her over, and prevents her from developing into an adult in her own right.

She then attempted to manically get away from the family via sky diving, travel, and identity reinvention, which led to further fragmentation of her sense of self. Possibly migration has reinforced these issues because the fear of the outside world becomes more real. The actual experience of being a migrant and the fact that the new world out there was strange and different than the old Eastern European culture made it more difficult for her to move psychologically away from the grips of her family and into the new world.

This migrant family had no other family members in the United States, who could make the process of migration to a new culture easier. The family became more "closed-in" and isolated from the mainstream American culture.

The family itself became the only stable unit, because everything else was changing so much. This family shared the same experiences of leaving one world and entering another, of losing all their connections and contacts, and depending even more on each other. The anxiety about the external world has undermined the process of separation—individuation of different family member.

SYNTHESIS

The migration in itself is such a deep, complex, long, and ongoing process that working through its impact and effects may never come to a definite end.

Ela's composite case study was able to work through some of her fears and conflicts in her treatment. She was able to move into marriage, sustain an ongoing relationship, and have children of her own.

However, her issues related to separation-individuation are very problematic. Possibly coming to the United States had reinforced all her pre-existing fears of separation, because of her actual anxiety of mixing with the new culture.

Migration has reinforced her claustro-agoraphobic tendency of symbolically wanting to jump out of her mother's body (sky diving) but then being scared of new situations and going back to her mother's body (in her phantasy) in an endless cycle of jumping in and out. The psychological migration into adulthood, and deeper, authentic motherhood, may not be fully possible due to these issues in this composite case.

The quality of physical migration cannot be separated from the emotional development of the migrant. The physical migration may add further complications and undermine the migrant's psychological and emotional development due to the anxiety brought about by physical migration, and to the extent that migrants come with psychic blockages to internal migrations to begin with.

If the newcomer was not able to make emotional and developmental migrations, most likely this will have effect on physical migrations. Possibly we may say that there is dialectic between the emotional and physical migrations. In some situations if there had not been the physical migration maybe the emotional migrations will evolve and lead to psychological development.

The frequent phantasy that the migrants have is the wish that the migration will solve in some measure their economic, psychological, and emotional problems. However, physical migration can become another major physical and psychological trauma if the migrant has not worked through his or her basic emotional and developmental migrations. The quality of physical migration will be very much connected to the quality of the emotional migrations of the given individual.

The migrant carries with him/her the baggage of his past history and his developmental migrations. The success or failure of the physical migration will to a large extent be determined by the quality of the environment that receives him /her and the potential space for one to be able to work through this process.

In Ela's case, the migration was difficult in and of itself, and contributed significantly to making her adolescence a highly conflictual period, and her already-problematic separation-individuation process, and identity confusion became even more problematic.

A COMPOSITE CASE OF BRUNO: A CHARMING COMIC

Introductory Remarks

The impact of migrations on children is much more complex and profound than on an adult population. Depending on the age of the child, prior history, developmental stage and the conditions of the migration process, migrations are assimilated and integrated into one's psyche differently.

Children who migrate when they are very young bear the consequences of migration throughout their life. On the one hand, one may think that the migrations for children are less traumatic because they have family protection and they are capable of absorbing and learning things like language, customs, and culture much faster than adults. However, on the other hand, children do not participate in the decision-making process of migrations. As passive and dependent participants, children may often experience the migration as something that is forced upon them by others and feel exiled because their departure is often involuntary and their return may not ever be possible.

Perhaps such a migration could be called an exile. The exile is often experienced by one as a prison term, or what Bion calls a "catastrophic change" and the outcome of it can be the real catastrophe and not a possible rebirth and creative development. In fact, exile converts the search for new places and a desire to go beyond certain fixed boundaries in search of the new experiences and true knowledge into involuntary migration and punishment. The exiled person often feels like being rejected and expelled from the paradise into a prison-like place. They do not travel toward some promised land, but they feel condemned to remain disconnected from their mother and father land.

In the new country the child goes through his own process of separation from known people and environments. If the child's internal and external objects relations are good enough, and his internal conflicts are not profound, such child may be able to go through the process of grief, mourning, and may be able to better assimilate into the new world.

However, if the early childhood history prior to migration was already problematic, such a child (depending on his stage of development) may display such problems as clinging to others, phobias, difficulties learning, isolation, inclination to accidents, illnesses, sleep and eating disorders, and a propensity to act out and repeat traumas as all kinds of mini-suicidal enactments and gestures.

Often children of migrants suffer the consequences of their parents unworked-through process of grief and mourning and its frequent pathological development. Migrants who suffer economic hardships in the new world often must postpone their mourning process, because the economic survival is the primary issue. Frequently such postponed mourning process is moved over to the second-generation children.

Background and Family History

Bruno was the owner of a very prosperous Manhattan bakery. He sought treatment because he suffered from periodic "black void" depression and a drinking problem. At his work, he had enormous difficulties with managing his financial affairs. In his intimate relationships he was cold, detached, and fearful of deeper emotional involvement and commitment. Outwardly Bruno was very charming, witty, intensely comical and excellent in the game of "Trivial Pursuit." He would know answers to the most trifling and unusual questions that nobody else could figure out.

Beneath this charming comic disguise image was a deadly volcanic-like presence with great capacity for self-destruction and acting-out behavior. Bruno was profoundly disconnected from his internal traumatic childhood experiences. He came from a family of Eastern European migrants.

His most significant past traumas were related to his mother's hospitalization after his birth, her postpartum depression, and her inability to breast-feed him. Bruno's parents both migrated from Eastern Europe to the United States and their four children were born in the new country. However, the family was overwhelmed with economic hardships, marital, and other conflicts and problems, and both parents have decided to send their children back to Eastern Europe for indefinite period of time.

At the time of this extended migration that lasted for several years, Bruno was in his early Oedipus stage of development.

In Eastern Europe Bruno and his older sister and two younger brothers were left in the care of close family relatives. Bruno's feelings of having been abandoned by his parents at such a young age were difficult to bear. He acted out his feelings in many different way*s*. He had many substitute caretakers like aunts, uncles, and grandparents and he lived in different family homes for extended periods of time. With this extended and long exile/migration, new fears, symptoms, and conflicts appeared superimposed on previous fears and nightmares. He remembers some of his childhood fears and nightmares of falling through the hole in an airplane, jumping into a big hole filled with water, being chased by such monsters as Dracula, and so forth. His symptoms expressed his difficulties in mourning repeated early abandonments (before and after the migration process), his fears of being abandon*ed* again, and his confusion between two cultures he could not assimilate.

For a child as young *as* Bruno, migration was a loss equivalent to the fundamental loss of the mother. He experienced the loss on his body level and expressed his feelings through his body. Through the bed wetting he was expressing his depression and his experience of being castrated, empty, and dissolving into pieces, a little boy never contained by his mother.

In fact he had many substitute caretakers and many pieces of himself. Throughout his treatment the themes related to identity confusion and bicultural self differentiation were frequent. He could not assimilate two different cultures and in his psyche one culture was often persecutory and the other was idealized.

Bruno's migration occurred during the early Oedipus stage of development and posed a great danger to his sense of identity. His Oedipal conflicts, feelings of jealousy, fears of castration, and failure got exacerbated by the migratory situation. The resolution of his Oedipal complex got greatly impeded and he developed a belief that he was condemned to a failure, rejection, abandonment, and emotional exile.

In Eastern Europe he had difficulties fitting into the school environment. His awareness of being the different one, the intruder, speaking with an American accent was overwhelming and he was confused about his identity. He was frightened of being deceived, rejected, abandoned, and "brain-washed." Bruno was afraid of new things getting into his head such as the new culture, language, and his adopted set of parents. He often closed himself off by becoming charming, funny, a good boy, or "unlucky" boy full of uncontrolled rage.

Bruno has few memories of his father who died of a heart attack in his fifties. He remembers his father's angry disposition and lack of emotional connection. He would often bitterly complain about his father's not visiting him back in Eastern Europe during his long "exile" migration away from his mother and father. Outwardly Bruno states that he was sent to Eastern Europe away from his migrant parents in America, due to his parents' great economic difficulties and marital problems that eventually lead to his parents' separation and divorce. However, on the deeper unconscious phantasy level he felt abandoned, rejected, and thrown away by his parents.

RELEVANT THEMES RELATED TO MIGRATION, IDENTITY, AND CULTURE (WHICH AROSE IN THE TREATMENT OF BRUNO COMPOSITE CASE STUDY)

Identity and Bicultural Self

Bruno was a man who was profoundly disconnected from his traumatic childhood experiences and his early childhood self. He used powerful mechanisms of dissociation, denial, splitting, projection, obsessive-compulsive, and manic defenses in order to disown his early traumas.

Bruno had frequent dreams about empty homes, broken houses, or castle-like homes located high up on some kind of mountain. In one of his sessions he presented the following dream:

> the house in the country is broken into. The house is dark, cold; there is no food . . . there is nothing there. The windows are broken, the doors are open and stones are thrown into the house. It is like an abandoned house. Other people come to the house and help themselves and wanted to be entertained. . . .

After presenting this dream Bruno said "I have to be a caretaker for everybody and pay everybody. I am the one who is always making it easy for other people; who is always in charge, taking care of other's needs. . ."

This patient felt that his mother, father and siblings always wanted him to be a mediator in the family conflicts. He felt that his family members always wanted things from him, such as money, employment, and other forms of support.

Bruno is a man who denies his own needs, dependency and vulnerabilities. The abandoned, broken, invaded house represents his sense of self. On the deeper phantasy level he experiences his relationships with others as constantly emptying, intruding, and exploiting him.

In this patient's unconscious mind there is a powerful phantasy that he has disowned his internal deprived and needy boy. He has disowned the internal child self by projecting this image out to other people. The needs of this little boy are so powerful that they could destroy everything; therefore, he had to disown that part of himself. However, on the other levels in his life and his business, Bruno surrounds himself with very needy, dependent, vulnerable and greedy people that can carry for him his disowned parts. Thus the needy, greedy people are projected parts of himself, so he does not have to feel his own neediness and dependency. He can instead place himself in a powerful, manic position as the CEO of his business and thereby create an illusionary sense of power and independence.

Whereas, genuine power comes from owning the needy, dependent and vulnerable parts of one's self. Unconsciously Bruno sets up this reality with other people and then colludes with this reality. He feels that the whole world is exploiting and emptying him. He ends up feeling used and exploited as long as he projects and disowns the deprived internal boy.

In yet another session Bruno shares the following dream:

> I am on a beach, but not participating in the beach experience. I see a huge wave coming. I try to get people to higher ground but nobody is listening. The wave hits and washes away the people from the beach. I go to the higher ground—up the mountain. On top of the mountain there is a castle and I go inside. Now I am high up in the air watching the ocean. . . .

In Bruno's associations the ocean represented his overbearing relationships with his mother and father. He had a powerful desire to escape from his overwhelming bakery business full of needy people.

In the patient's deeper, unconscious level the dangerous ocean is the dangerous and dreadful mother, and the high mountain is the mother's breast. On top of this mountain/breast there is some security in the form of the castle. The isolated castle is Bruno's narcissistic escape and retreat, where he can live in isolation on top of the mountain/breast, high up in the air. He has to take this high-up stance in order to monitor the dangerous mother ocean. He has to engage in very precarious maneuvers and desperate escapes into his "high up" castle and narcissistic home. This is not a real, authentic psychological home, but a form of desperate psychological isolation.

For Bruno nothing is secure, nobody can be trusted, and the only secure thing is the isolated castle on top of the mountain/breast. However, the manic castle on top of the mountain/breast is not the grounded authentic psychological home where he can feel secure.

In one of his sessions Bruno stated, "My mother never breast fed me. She lost a lot of weight after she had me . . . she was vomiting a lot . . . she had to be hospitalized."

Bruno fears that from this very early time his mother did not want him and therefore he was the unwanted child. In his infancy she was depressed and did not want to feed him. Today he does not want to experience this "needy baby" part of himself and wants others to experience this disowned, unwanted, and unfed parts of himself. Bruno's relationship to his mother was seriously undermined since early childhood.

The intersection at the beach, near the water where children can play can be compared to D. Winnicott's "transitional area" between the mother and her child, where good feelings *are* experienced, growth can take place and the child can feel able to exist there.

D. Winnicott (1955), in *Group Influences and the Maladjusted Child*, states:

> The baby who loses the transitional objects at the same time loses both mouth and breast, both hand and mother's skin, both creativity and objective perception. The object is one of the bridges that make contact possible between the individual psyche and external reality. . . (1955, p. 149)

Bruno's internal child cannot exist in this transitional area; it has to go on top of the mountain/breast and get into some isolated castle. For him staying on the beach, the transitional space, could end in catastrophe. The pre-existing difficulties in the mother-child relationship were further exacerbated by Bruno's early childhood migration trauma.

Perhaps we can assume that Bruno's early sense of self and his internal psychological home was precarious and problematic. With a problematic self at such an early stage, when such a child is transplanted into a new culture due to migration, such a migration experience becomes very traumatic.

Bruno's fragile developing self got even more fragmented due to the unbearable trauma he experienced as a result of the migration and exile. His enormous anger and rage as a reaction to unbearable trauma of migration/exile got dissociated and he became a very charming, funny young boy. Outwardly, he became the charming boy but underneath that image, there were all kinds of very powerful persecutory anxiety; some of which were directly related to the migration and other traumatic separations.

The trauma of migration in Bruno's case greatly contributed to his preexisting fundamental mistrust of others. He became an appeasing boy in order to cope with a very difficult situation in the Eastern European world and culture which was unknown to him.

Today he lives in a very precarious and unstable world looking for radical solutions to his life problems. He cannot own up to his rage, mistrust, and all kinds of paranoid anxiety, which he projects and dissociates. Outwardly he is charming, polite and seductive, but at the deeper level he unleashes his attacks on others in a silent and hidden way or attacks himself through multiple types of suicidal attempts. He has not been able to recognize all of the unbearable feelings and thoughts inside of himself and make some sense of his internal home.

He lives in this disjoined psychic home where his mind is dissociated from his body, and his early childhood Eastern European self is disconnected from his more American self. Due to early psychic traumas, separations, migration, and problematic relationships with both of his parents, his psychic home is fragmented and disconnected, and his mind is disassociated from his affective self. His fears and difficult feelings are acted out or turn into somatic symptoms and illnesses.

A CLOWN HEAD

Outwardly Bruno presents a neat image of a hilariously funny and very accommodating person. But underneath this facade, in the depth of his unconscious mind, he has powerful phantasies, of breaking or chopping off the analyst's head, or his own head, and other body parts.

He describes his mother as an abandoning but also very tantalizing woman. Bruno states that his mother presents a very clean and warm public image but, underneath that image she is cold, empty, and not able to give anything emotionally. Bruno's mother owns several prosperous businesses which she developed on her own, even though she came to America from Eastern Europe without any financial resources. Bruno has violent, unconscious phantasies toward both of his parents for getting rid of him, and throwing him away into some unknown world of Eastern Europe.

D. Winnicott, in his 1949 paper "Mind and It's Relation to the Psyche-Soma," states:

> Here, in the overgrowth of the mental function reactive to erratic mothering, we see that there can develop an opposition between the mind and the psyche-soma, since in reaction to this abnormal environmental state the thinking of the individual begins to take over and organize the caring for the psyche-soma, whereas in health it is the function of the environment to do this. In health the mind does not usurp the environment's function, but makes possible an understanding. . . . (p. 246)

Bruno used powerful intellectual defenses against internal chaos, fears of annihilation, and rage. He attacks his thinking parts and his feeling parts. He does not want to remember and think any negative thoughts, and he does not want to feel any negative feelings. He just wants to keep everything very positive, very funny and, unfortunately, often very dead. He wants to banish his feelings and thoughts about ugliness, bloody rage, broken body parts, and the savage and uncivilized early Eastern European self that is dangerous and therefore must be disowned.

On a deeper level Bruno fears that nobody will be able to accept his early savage and uncivilized Eastern European self, his ugly, damaged body parts, so he disowns and cuts himself off from his psyche-soma first. But in fact he needs a psychological home for his unbearable thoughts, feelings, bloody parts of himself and, most importantly, the savage uncivilized Eastern European child self.

Just before the long summer break Bruno presented the following dream:

> people without heads, sitting in the bar . . . blood coming from their necks . . . the dismembered arms, legs and other body parts. But I am not afraid. I hear somebody saying about me, "Look at him, he's got a clown hat on again". . .

After presenting this dream Bruno spoke about the upcoming summer break in his treatment. He said that he felt very stuck in the city, feeling emotionally "cut off" and lonely. The upcoming vacation break has reactivated Bruno's memory of the migration to Eastern Europe and the subsequent long hospital experience there. The cut-off heads, legs, and arms are related to the cut-off relationship to his mother and father and cut-off links to other family, friends and culture. Bruno in his phantasy due to his rage wants to cut/chop off the analyst's head or his own head, because he does not want to think and be in touch with who he is and what he feels. He wants to cut the analyst's head off because she has thoughts in her head about going away and leaving him. Therefore, the head, thoughts, and feelings need to be obliterated. But then he feels that he has a "clown hat" head that is filled with trivial matters and funny thoughts.

He feels that this is all located in his head—not his body or his heart—so, if he chops off his head and does not think the pathetic thoughts about breaks, journeys, and going away, then everything will be just fine as long as he is funny and positive.

However, the "savage" and suicidal part of him that wants to destroy everything and has rage-filled thoughts comes back anyhow, and by itself so it seems.

> In another session Bruno presented a short dream: ". . .the showerhead was broken and I have ripped the whole thing out of the wall. The showerhead has old circuits, it needs new circuiting. . ."

During this time Bruno spoke about his somatic issues such as headaches, inner emptiness, and a desire to drink. This patient's clinical material was understood in the following way. Bruno wants to put new circuits in his mind, because the old circuits are damaged and full of rage. He wonders if he can actually change the old circuits in his mind in order to put new links and connections there, or will he be stuck with old circuits and old ways of understanding things. Can he develop new links, new understanding, and move on and have a different frame of mind compared to the old links and circuitry?

The old circuit's wires are filled with rage, and dangerous bloody, fiery, and blazing thoughts. Part of him wants to rip out the old circuits in hopes that the new links and circuits will magically arrive by themselves. The other part of him hopes that through working on his issues he may be able to develop new links, new understandings, and a new frame of mind.

THE PSYCHOTIC AND NONPSYCHOTIC PARTS OF THE PERSONALITY

In *Second Thoughts: Selected Papers on Psycho-Analysis*, Bion (1967) emphasized the simultaneous functioning of psychotic and nonpsychotic parts of the personality. He felt that the psychotic part of the personality is discriminated from the nonpsychotic part essentially by the tendency of the psychotic part to fragment the ego, its projection, evacuation, and expulsion into objects which often lead to confusion between real objects and primitive thoughts. Bion felt that psychosis was the result of attacks on linking. He suggested that the psychotic part of the personality can misuse the capacity to think (alpha-function) by appropriating it from the nonpsychotic part of the personality.

Bion by using the term "psychotic personality" did not refer to a psychiatric category of diagnosis but to a mode of mental functioning based on intolerance of frustration and therefore true thinking, prevailing aggressive impulses, hatred of inner and outer reality, fear of annihilation, and powerful use of pathological dissociation, projection, action and omnipotent thought.

Bion (1967) states the following about the coexistence of a "psychotic personality" and a "non-psychotic" or "neurotic personality":

> I do not think . . . that the ego is ever wholly withdrawn from reality. I would say that its contact with reality is masked by the dominance in the patient's mind and behavior of an omnipotent phantasy that is intended to destroy either reality or the awareness of it. Since contact with reality is never entirely lost, the phenomena which we are accustomed to associate with the neuroses are never absent and serve to complicate the analysis, when sufficient progress has been made by their presence amidst psychotic material. My second modification is that the withdrawal from reality is an illusion, not a fact, and arises from the deployment of projective identification against the mental apparatus . . . the patient acts as if his perceptual apparatus could be split into minute fragments and projected into his objects. . . (p. 46).

Bion felt that the mother's ability to function as a receptive, affective container of the child's sensations and projections, along with her capacity to transform them into bearable anxieties will provide the child with the capacity to cope with frustrations and separations.

We may imagine that a migrant also suffers the loss of containing objects, and may become very vulnerable to psychotic *states,* psychotic acting-out behaviors and psychotic decomposition, based on the individual migrant's inner world and disposition.

In Bruno's treatment the themes and images of falling into a pond, river or falling-off planes and buildings were very frequent. In one of his sessions Bruno said:

> I wanted to jump into the water that is calm and soothing . . . at 4 AM I found myself in the middle of the deep lake—going under. . . . I feared that this was it, I will not make it to the shore this time. . .

Perhaps Bruno was under the grip of the psychotic part of his personality and in a psychotic state of mind where in the dark night he jumped into the deep lake. He wants to keep that part of his internal and external history at the level of not knowing and remembering, even though on another level he knows what took place. He does not want to talk about his suicide attempt and feel, or think or make links between things and events. He wants to keep it at "not knowing level" due to too much terror and rage in this part of himself, even though on another level he knows and remembers his suicide attempt.

The psychotic part of his personality wants to act out his fears and feelings without thinking and understanding what is going on inside of him, because feeling, seeing and thinking is too unbearable.

We could look at the whole process of physical and psychological birth as migrations from the inside of the mother's body and mind to another state of being and functioning. Perhaps Bruno's attempts to jump into a pond or lake could be seen in phantasy as his way of jumping back into the mother's body. He had desired to reverse the process of migration and migrate back into the mother's body, because it's too scary to be an abandoned and rejected little boy, outside his mother's womb.

Bruno's migration at a very young age was also a form of exile from his parents and culture. He felt rejected and abandoned by his parents. Today Bruno's migrations—physical and developmental—often end in some form of emotional and physical exile and eviction, where he ends up without anything; a totally abandoned and rejected little boy. His migrations in life seldom lead to growth, development, and new possibilities in life because he constantly goes back to the position of the abandoned little boy that has nothing. Due to his fears, rage, and lack of trust he undermines himself and often destroys new possibilities in life. It's very difficult for him to develop insight, and knowledge about himself that is part of the psychological awareness of his psychological reality and, therefore, it is difficult for him to grow and develop psychologically, and migrate to a new state of being.

BICULTURAL PSYCHOLOGICAL HOME

As already stated, both of Bruno's parents were Eastern European migrants who came to the United States as young adults to make a new life in the new world. All of their children were born in America. However, due to a lot of conflicts and difficulties with adoption to a new world and economic hardships, Bruno and his siblings were sent back to Eastern Europe to live there with close relatives. Bruno was left in the care of his grandparents and other close family members, and a few years later he was reincorporated into the family here in the United States.

For Bruno his childhood migration was a kind of loss equivalent to the loss and death of the mother and father and, he experienced the loss as a body loss, which increased his castration and paranoid anxiety, which he exhibited as a fear of deceit, fear of anything that is new, that could come from the outside.

He developed a deep distrust of new things, new places, and new people which had roots in his childhood experience of migration and other experiences in which the good country became bad country, and the good mother and father became bad parents who left him in the unknown place. This made him internalize his mother and father as persecutory, harmful objects that were attacking his insides, producing pain and emptiness.

He had dreams about Dracula, and his body parts and limbs being separated from his body just as he was dismembered and separated from the family unit and his place of birth. Dracula represented his own voracious desires and needs resulting from his frustration. He had a lot of resentment and revenge phantasies toward his parents for abandoning him. He was placed in new schools where he felt out of place, different—the intruder—often suffering humiliating initiation rites, and the one who had to fight for a place of his own in a foreign and strange land.

One of the central themes of early life is the search for one's sense of identity. Migration may interfere here and may pose a great danger when one's sense of identity is already very fragile an becomes thrown off course even more by the migratory experience. We may wonder about Bruno's basic and early sense of self and sense of identity. Was his basic self-structure somewhat integrated or split off and fragmented due to early childhood traumas? What happened in his early life from the age of 0 to 3 years is very crucial to his sense of self-development and his capacity to cope with the experience of migration.

The impacts of the migration on the mother and father's minds (when they came to America)—the mother's hospitalizations, family economic and emotional turmoil—were factors that were at play in Bruno's early childhood. And then the long migration/exile was superimposed on his early development. We may assume that with such an early problematic childhood history, Bruno's early sense of self was very problematic and precarious.

Second-generation migrants like Bruno who lived in two different cultures and have an early Eastern European self and, somewhat later develop an American self, may have all kinds of identity confusion issues. On the one hand, they may feel all American and, on the other hand, all Eastern European. We may wonder if Bruno is someone with some degree of the false-American self-identity structure that was placed on top of the deeper one more related to his roots "Eastern European" self-structure.

Today in his life and treatment Bruno suffers such a bicultural sense of self confusion. On the one hand, he feels an American and, on the other hand, he feels an Eastern European when he is with his Eastern European family members.

In his treatment with the Eastern European analyst he is quite American and one may wonder, "Where is his Eastern European self?" Even though in phantasy Bruno wants to get in touch with his early Eastern European self, he is also afraid that if he gets in touch with the deeper emotional Eastern European side, and way of being, he may lose his "American freedom" and become stifled by the old Eastern European world. He has fears of intensifying his therapy with (the) Eastern European female analyst, because in his phantasy this could lead to the analyst/mother (in transference) controlling, tantalizing, exploiting, and abandoning him. He fears that his Eastern European side of the helpless, abandoned little boy may re-assert itself with the powerful, tantalizing, and abandoning mother. He is very afraid of his vulnerabilities and afraid of becoming again the abandoned, confused, and castrated little boy. Therefore in the transference he rather sees the analyst as the "Euro-trash," bad, dangerous mother from the foreign land and he becomes the all American, white, clean, and "made-in-the-USA" man.

Bruno is a second-generation Eastern European man facing many conflicts about his Eastern European self and his American self. There is a fear of being marginalized in the American culture as an Eastern European migrant. He often feels marginal in his American self as an Eastern European migrant and therefore he wants to get in touch with his Eastern European self that is closest to his roots. But he also has powerful fears about Eastern European cultures and, in his phantasy, the traditional, powerful mother figures that will dominate and control him and he may lose his American freedom.

We may wonder if his fears about Eastern European cultures and the traditional, strong mother figures are real or imaginary. Perhaps we may assume that he is seeing the Eastern European culture from a certain distorted perspective based on his family experiences and his perception of what happened to him in Eastern Europe. He fears that the Eastern European culture is stifling but the American culture is not comfortable because he is marginalized as an Eastern European migrant.

He has conflicts within his bicultural selves and different ways of being related to the Eastern European self and the American self which are also in conflict with each other. There are other forms of splitting going on in his internal world which use the bicultural division between the two selves for further splitting and divisions. Bruno's anger and sexuality are split off between the two selves. The early anger, vulnerability, needs and terror of abandonment seems to be split off and dissociated in his Eastern European self. However, he feels more comfortable with his sexual world in his American self.

We may wonder what type of early splitting was going on in Bruno's relationship with his mother and other early caretakers and when did he become aware of his bicultural selves?

We could imagine that due to early childhood traumas and separations from the mother his basic self-structure was already split off and precarious. But even if he had more integrated early sense of self, he still will have to deal with the navigation between the two cultures, but he could navigate this conflict with the more integrated sense of self and more ease, rather than with the more precarious sense of self and more suffering. He has internalized his early Eastern European self and culture from his mother and the American self from friends, school and by living in the American culture.

In such bicultural individuals different conflicted issues could be divided and some things may be allowed and acceptable in the Eastern European self and others in his American self. In his Eastern European self Bruno often wants to please his parents and older generation but in his American self he is more rebellious and defiant toward authority figures or institutions.

He is still very much driven by his internal multiple unresolved conflicts and feelings of anger and he does not have the freedom to choose and make a life of his own away from his internal parents and conflicts.

He has great doubts about his Eastern European part and the place where he spent much of his childhood life. Due to his very difficult experience there, he does not want to know too much about his past, and has made this into an area of no interest.

In one of the therapy sessions he said that, "My father has no ability to communicate in American culture, he is like (an) impoverished, needy, crying, little child . . . and I have to speak for him and take care of him. . ." The child part of Bruno's father represents part of Bruno's internal Eastern European needy boy. Bruno has developed some sense of his American self and that self helps him to survive in the American culture. But underneath of that American self there is a child part of him represented by his father.

Yet in another session Bruno was wondering about the Eastern European character. He said: "The Eastern European character is bold, brash, bravado like, with intense emotions, religious and nationalistic." His explorations felt like a fragile attempt to deal with his Eastern European side that appeared romanticized and sentimental, or extravagantly emotional. Due to his traumatic time in Eastern Europe he is not comfortable with his Eastern European self. He is still very much a man of "Trivial Pursuit" as he likes to call himself and not very much in touch with the more deeper and authentic side of himself that is related to his early roots.

In Bruno's composite case there is some level of semblance of the sense of self and identity. However, even though his sense of self comes together to existence, it is also constantly attacked and undermined by his deadly rage covered up by various defenses.

JOURNEYS TO OTHER PLACES

The images of airplanes, trains and cars, and the themes of journeys to other places were frequent in Bruno's treatment. One could look at a migration as a geographical journey but also as an internal or external change from one situation to another. All kinds of journeys—geographical, psychological, internal or external—are emotionally intense and difficult for Bruno. He has fears of flying, driving, and traveling away from his home.

He was sent away to Eastern Europe in an airplane journey and the fear of this airplane journey lives inside of him. He has fears about airplane catastrophes and planes collapsing and crashing into an ocean. His early childhood was disrupted due to such geographical factors of migrations (besides multiple other factors). He is scared of airplane journeys because they have played into his early trauma of being separated from his mother/father and sent away by plane to the unknown world of darkness.

If from the psychological point of view a journey represents the separation from the mother/father, then his journey was very difficult and traumatic, because there was no contact with the mother/father for a very long time. Now even the small geographical journeys are emotionally intense and difficult for Bruno.

A TAXI JOURNEY

Bruno could not control his journey as a young, helpless child sent away on the airplane to another world of Eastern Europe. He had no control before, but now as an adult man he can control his journeys. Now, even when he is coming by a taxicab, he wants to control the journey and tells the driver to follow his directions precisely.

In one of his therapy sessions Bruno said: ". . . I got stuck in the taxi . . . I told him to go down this avenue, but he did not . . . I wanted to kill him . . . to strangle him because it is more sadistic, lasts longer than shooting. . ."

Perhaps he wanted to strangle the people who took him away from his mother to an unknown world, Eastern Europe. At that time, when he was a young child he could not strangle the airplane pilot or the people that sent him away, but now he wants desperately to control his journeys due to his intense childhood related anxiety.

He wants to be sadistic and strangle people who do not listen to his directions and take him on journeys that he cannot truly control. This extra need to control his journeys and the rage he feels when he is not in control are very much linked to his early migration journeys to Eastern Europe and other smaller journeys.

When not in control of his journey, he either feels great rage or great passivity, where he turns the rage on himself (through psychological or physical suicidal attempts). His passivity is related to the early childhood adaptations that he had to make to his mother and others, and he had to passively accept the migration situation and turn the rage on himself.

The migration trauma and the massive disruption caused by it left the powerful impact on Bruno's psyche. Therefore, one needs to see his psychological issues not only in terms of troubled relationships with his mother and father, but also in the context of this very disruptive early migration and separation from his parents, and the world where he was born.

A JOURNEY TO THE CITY OF LIGHTS

Bruno grew up in his mother's Eastern European home and neighborhood. As a young adult he desperately wanted to move out of there and create a life of his own and have his own business.

In one of his therapy sessions he stated: ". . .the first time when I came to Manhattan I was overwhelmed by so many lights, I was very much drawn to it, away from the monotonous existence of my neighborhood. . ."

Bruno was taken in by the glittering lights of Manhattan and wanted to move away from the mother's Eastern European home to the new and glittering outside world full of possibilities. The glittering city of lights in his unconscious phantasy represented an absent father. The mother's world was dull, boring and monotonous. He wanted to migrate to Manhattan and find a father figure there who could provide him with strength and a way to grow up and become a proper, potent man in his own right.

He wanted to move away from the mother's monotonous Eastern European world to the more exciting world where in his phantasy he could meet a father figure who would open up all kinds of new possibilities for him. Bruno was trying to migrate out of the mother's home to Manhattan which represents his journey to "real America." He was hoping that this "real America" would be some magical new potent world that will somehow transform him. But this migration from his Eastern European world and self to the American world and self seems to be an idealized phantasy, expecting some magical cure through the magical place called Manhattan. He was hoping that the glittering lights of Manhattan would somehow take him away from his depression and monotonous existence.

Bruno managed in his early adulthood to physically move out of his mother's home and neighborhood. He had also opened his own business—a bakery—in a good part of Manhattan. But in Manhattan the same unresolved issues related to his mother would come up again. This magical idealized solution and a migration to a new potent world did not work because his depression came up again. The bright and glittering lights of Manhattan did not provide a cure for his depression and unresolved childhood traumas.

For Bruno his early migration was a form of exile, abandonment, and some kind of punishment. Today in his unconscious mind and phantasy to migrate emotionally or physically is linked to an exile, abandonment, loss of his objects and banishment.

Therefore his migration from his maternal home to Manhattan and to having his own business in this unconscious phantasy had to end in some form of disappointment and failure. He also fears that migration to a new place is about losing everything and is some kind of punishment. He feels a manic pull toward migration and also fears the banishment and abandonment.

Bruno managed to open up his own business in Manhattan. He was able to "physically migrate" to his own bakery/business, but his unresolved conflicts, depression, and traumas got to be played out there again to his great disappointment.

The bakery became on overwhelming responsibility and a prison-like situation for him. As a solution to this problem Bruno has developed a powerful phantasy of going back to Eastern Europe, living there in his mother's home, and maybe opening another business.

The phantasy of going back to Eastern Europe is a way of running away from his business and his internal world and going back to the mother's womb/home to escape from his life difficulties.

In his life he is looking for the radical, idealized, and pathological solutions to his early trauma of exile and abandonment. He hopes to go back to Eastern Europe in a different way this time and get something of value from this journey. The first time when he was sent away by his parents (in his phantasy) he was pushed out from his "mother womb," but now he wants to make this journey on his own and be truly in control. However, this time he is running away from his life difficulties in America and wants to escape from his business and his internal demons.

He is trying to solve his internal problems related to his fears, mistrust, and feelings of rage by trying to escape to some other place. He is constantly fleeing from himself in the illusionary belief that all one needs to do is to change his environment. In such a situation another disastrous outcome can be easily predicted.

OEDIPUS: THE EXILED CHILD

As previously stated, Bruno's long migration/exile to Eastern Europe occurred during his Oedipal stage of development. His Oedipal fears of castration, failure, and feelings of jealousy became more aggravated as a result of the migration situation. The resolution of his Oedipal complex was greatly hindered due to migration and other factors, and in his phantasy he believed that he was condemned to an emotional exile and failure in his life.

In *The Language of Psychoanalysis* (1973), J. LaPlanche and J. B. Pontalis speak about the Oedipus complex as follows:

> organized body of loving and hostile wishes which the child experiences towards its parents. In its so-called positive form, the complex appears as in the story of Oedipus Rex: a desire for the death of the rival—the parent of the same sex—and a sexual desire for the parent of the opposite sex. . . . According to Freud, the peak period for the experience of the Oedipus complex lies between the age of three and five years. . . . The Oedipus complex plays a fundamental part in the structuring of the personality, and in the orientation of human desire. Psychoanalysis makes it the major axis of reference for psychopathology and attempts to identify the particular modes of its presentation and resolution. . . . (p. 283)

The complex was named after the mythical Greek figure of Oedipus (literally "swollen foot" in Greek) who killed his father and married his mother without being aware that they were his real parents. Freud felt that the Oedipus complex is a universal mode of organizing and responding to experience, built in and inborn phylogenetically and is responsible for much of our unconscious guilt.

The resolution of the Oedipus complex typically takes place by identifing with the parent of the same sex and renunciating the parent of the opposite sex and finding in one's life another adult sexual partner. The cause of castration anxiety is the Oedipal rivalry with the father.

There are several migrations in the Greek legend of Oedipus, who is exiled on a migration that separated him from his parents and his native place of birth. Freud placed a great deal of importance on the sexual meaning of the myth and the rivalry, conflicts, and feelings of love, hate and jealousy.

Bion (1963) discovered that the Oedipus sexual crime concealed an intellectual quest for knowledge. He considered that the K-link was an emotional link of the similar kind as love and hate. K-link enables one to differentiate between the internal and external objects, between container and contained, and between feelings of inside and outside.

Bion (1962) felt that there are some basic emotions, such as L—love, H—hate and K—knowledge, that are always present in a link. The concept "link" describes an emotional experience and relationship between two people, or two parts of the same individual. The prototype for a links is the primitive breast or penis.

According to Grinberg and Grinberg (1989):

> The K, or knowledge link, corresponds to the subject that seeks to know an object, and an object that lends itself to being known. It may also represent the individual who seeks through introspection to know the truth about himself. . . . One must distinguish the acquisition of knowledge, which comes about as a result of modification of pain (than the knowledge obtained will be used for new discoveries), from possession of knowledge, which is used to avoid painful experiences, as occurs with persons in whom maniacal defenses and

> omnipotence predominate, and with those for whom true learning from emotional experience is impossible.
>
> Avoidance of pain may be at the service of the activity called "minus K-link"—unknowing, in which denial, envy, and voracity predominate: in such situations no discovery, learning, or development is possible. (p. 66)

This kind of knowledge, that comes from one's capacity to work through and assimilate any difficult experience such as migration or work-through emotional complex (i.e., Oedipus complex), will not be mere intellectual knowledge, K-link, but more experiential *knowing*—what Bion defines as the more experiential "becoming O." Therefore to "know" and also to "be" a migrant, or fully work through the Oedipus complex involves the critical emotional capacity to inhabit painful emotional and mental states, and the capacity for ambivalence, object love, mourning, guilt, and reparation.

When the situation is very painful, as migration often is, then migrants resort to various defensive maneuvers in order to limit themselves to only intellectual knowing, without the emotional knowing, and therefore being true migrants. The extent that a person can assimilate any painful experience such as the experience of migration, work through his/her conflicts, and integrate the dissociated and denied parts of oneself and feelings, such person will be able to grow and develop the capacity to feel his/her pain. Such a migrant will not only intellectually *know* but he will also *be* an authentic migrant. The child's method of resolving his Oedipus complex and his conflicts of subjective desires will have a great impact on the formation (of) his psyche.

According to Ogden (1986):

> The impact of the Oedipus complex on the formation of psychological structure is determined by the child's method of attempting to resolve the conflict of subjective desire. If splitting and reenactment are used as methods of defense against oedipal anxiety limited psychological change occurs. The child endlessly keeps multiple poles of his conflicted wishes alive simultaneously . . . and establishes a series of relationships with part objects embodying each of the aspects of his unrenounced wishes. . . . When one is able to maintain the whole object relatedness, subjectivity, and historicity of the depressive position in the face of Oedipal conflict, one's unwillingness to violate sacred prohibitions in the acts of incest and parricide outweighs one's desire for the enactment of one's Oedipal wishes. (p. 96)

Bruno's long migration which occurred during his Oedipal stage of development hindered his already fragile self and his emotional capacity to resolve his Oedipus complex and his conflicts of subjective desires.

Similarly to the exiled Oedipus, Bruno has concretized and reenacted his own subjective version of the Oedipus complex drama. Bruno's migration was also combined with temporary adoption by his grandparents. Interestingly, Oedipus himself was an adopted child and the adoption saved his physical life but did not prevent him from enacting his tragedy of literally killing his father and marrying his mother.

According to *Psychoanalytic Perspectives on Migration and Exile* (Grinberg & Grinberg, 1989):

> The reenacted Oedipal conflict has a greater possibility of being fulfilled with adopted children. The incestuous desires the child feels are, and yet are not, incest; their struggle to acquire a sense of identity is fierce and more painful. They must mourn the loss of the loved Oedipal object, the loss of their child's body, the loss of their childhood parents, and also the loss of the "other parents" whom they have not known but have both idealized and hated. Finally, they must mourn their own abandonment. (p. 212)

Bruno hated his parents for abandoning him, but his greater conflict and rage came out against the parent of the same sex. Perhaps in order to really appreciate the masterfully told Greek tragedy and myth of Oedipus one ought to look at it from Freud and Bion's points of view.

While Freud placed great emphasis on the sexual aspects of the myth and the conflicts and feelings related to love, hate, jealousy, envy, and rivalry, Bion approached the myth from the point of view that concentrates on the K-link which represents knowledge that is as important in human relationships and experiences as the L-link of love and the H-link of hate (Bion, 1963).

Bion discovered that Oedipal sexual crimes covered up the deeper meaning of the myth which is an intellectual quest for knowledge "K" and liberation. Therefore it is not the mother that is the father's most valued possession and (therefore) the object of Oedipal rivalry, but rather it is the father's true knowledge.

It is of great significance how one acquires the true K-knowledge. Oedipus tried to acquire true knowledge by conquering an image of the Sphinx that is half-human and half-animal and a symbol of his parents' combination. Oedipus felt that by defeating the Sphinx he destroyed the unity of the parental couple. In phantasy he felt that he stole the K-knowledge by destroying the unity of his parents.

Grinberg and Grinberg (1989) state:

> The Oedipus story can thus be seen as an example of the conflict inherent in human nature between the impulse to steal (the) father's most valued and desired possession, exposing oneself to punishment and exile; and the repression of that impulse. (p. 7)

The epic intellectual quest for K-knowledge needs to be seen as a symbolic "K" journey that may have a physical aspect to it. The true and authentic

K-knowledge needs to be seen as a symbol. In Oedipus, and in Bruno's life, his private Oedipal myth became concretized and reenacted.

THE BAKERY: CINEMA PARADISE AND CINEMA PURGATORY

In Bruno's life everything associated with food took on great significance. Every member of his immediate migrant family was into some kind of food business, from owning a delicatessen to a butcher shop. Any special events were often celebrated with a great variety of food, and the dinner table was a special meeting place, and a consolidation of the family of migrants.

Behind these great family "kitchen table" celebrations one could easily discover all kinds of hypochondriacal and persecutory fears caused by the loss of the idealized homeland/mother/breast, nourishing situation. The origin of such a fear of the loss of the idealized object (nourishing situation/homeland) can be traced back to the loss of the mother/breast. The most frequent defense mechanism migrants use in order to counteract their conflicts and fears of loss and abandonment is idealization/devaluation with prominent oral regressive characteristics often expressed in food rituals and celebrations.

Bruno, the owner of a prosperous and centrally located bakery, embodied in his migrant family the idealized aspects of a new wealthy adopted country and the Promised Land. Surely, as an owner of such a bakery he would take care and have proper control of the family's oral needs, hungers, and hypochondriacal anxieties.

He assumed the role of the family's successful son and became their idealized object. However, as he stated, his bakery became his "Cinema and Stage, Paradise/Purgatory," where his Oedipal drama and other unresolved conflicts got concretized and reenacted. The entrepreneurial achievement in Bruno's case became a destructive act against his internal/external objects, accompanied by fears of retaliative persecutory anxiety from his objects.

Being the family entrepreneur appeared to be a pseudo-vocation which had roots in his manic need to repair his emptied and damaged internal objects and his damaged internal image. He assumed the role of the successful son, but did so through the use of manic and psychotic mechanisms, which broke down and submerged him in confusion.

Even with the very prosperous business Bruno's life was very chaotic, and financially he was drowning in an ocean of debts. He was addicted to outrageous spending for which his business did not provide enough money.

On account of his bakery he took all kinds of credits and loans. This made him feel even more manic and euphoric as long as they supported his phantasy of the existence of the ideal object/inexhaustible breast that would unconditionally satisfy all his needs. The ocean of debts that he created represented his internal emptied and damaged representations. He would empty his bakery from all its resources and then he feared the retaliations from creditors and others.

But, on the other hand, he felt in his phantasy that the credit institutions and analyst were the inexhaustible and idealized others to counteract all his frustrations and fears. Perhaps Bruno's case illustrates the possible effects of the migration on the second-generation migrants when the original generation has not worked through and mourned the migration.

The effects of the original migration's pseudo-adjustment, unworked-through process of mourning, and dissociated way of functioning were passed down to Bruno who assumed the role of idealized object and the role of a bearer of the family's unworked through mourning.

As previously stated, one of the places where his own private myth and Oedipal drama became concretized and played out was his bakery that he used to call his "Cinema Paradise." The bakery became his stage where his internal world got projected. Onto the screen of his "Cinema Paradise" he projected his internal mother, father, and his internal needy child, along with other parts of himself.

In the transference Bruno saw the analyst through the images of his parents and his early disowned traumas. In his phantasy Bruno felt that his parents never gave him anything, and rejected him like a "piece of shit."

He had very specific phantasies about killing his father, and seducing and then killing his mother as well. In his phantasy he wanted to kill his father by smashing his head and his mother by stabbing her in her heart because she was cold and had no blood in her veins. The internal child part of himself feels to him like a "shitty, smelly, savage creature" that is extremely needy and full of rage and he constantly tries to disown this part of himself by projecting it onto others or by extreme self-destructiveness (such as suicidal acting out).

In his unconscious mind Bruno would constantly try to kill, destroy, obliterate, and project out the images of his mother and father, and the needy and rage-filled parts of himself. However, the result of it was that he surrounded himself in his life and his business with needy, greedy, dependent, and passive people that could carry his disowned parts and his projected internal world for him.

As previously stated, he would then place himself in a powerful manic position as the CEO of his bakery. In this way (in his mind) he created an illusionary sense of power based on a deeper level on helplessness and omnipotence. The genuine power and liberation that he has been searching for comes from owning his internal world and its needy, hateful, and greedy parts and, from taking full responsibility for them. He fears that if he acknowledges his needs he will be dependent and lose his illusionary sense of freedom. But, on the other hand, when he disowns his needs he cannot fully grow up and become an adult man in his own right. He is trying to attain his liberation by the projections, splitting, dissociation, denial, and disowning of his internal world and his psychological home (-K).

DEFEATING THE SPHINX

As already stated, Bruno's internal world of objects relations and his unresolved issues and Oedipal drama situation gets projected on the screen of his bakery/"Cinema Paradise."

Oedipus, in search of the true knowledge, concretely and literally steals the mother (who is the father's most valued possession) from the father in hope of achieving liberation. But on the deeper level the mother is only a symbol of deeper true knowledge belonging exclusively to the father.

Oedipus felt that by defeating the Sphinx, a half-human and half-animal symbol of the combination of his parents, which arouses very archaic persecutory phantasies, he has destroyed his parents from whom in his unconscious phantasy he steals true knowledge. Bruno symbolically steals the mother from the father, at the expense of the authentic K-knowledge.

For Bruno the authentic psychological, emotional, and physical migrations into an adult life—marriage and successful business partnerships—have been enormously difficult. Due to his unresolved issues with the mother, and his anger at her for abandoning him, and his fears about being rejected again, he is afraid of an authentic relationship with any woman.

On the other hand, due to his anger at his father, and unresolved Oedipus complex (which was additionally more hindered by his migration trauma) in his unconscious phantasy, having a woman of his own is like death because by definition it's like taking the mother away from the father. The only woman he can have is the mother/woman stolen from the father. He does not feel entitled to a woman in his own right because he has not worked through his Oedipal conflicts of subjective desires and his issues of authentically growing up and migrating into adult life.

In his unconscious phantasy he fears that he has stolen the mother from the father and therefore this unresolved Oedipus situation will lead to retaliation from the father (and father's representatives or due to his own persecutory guilt from his internal persecutory object/superego). Therefore, in his phantasy the father (or father representative) or his own persecutory object will bring the collapse of his life for taking what does not belong to him.

Bruno presented the following recurring Oedipal dream:

> I see a big black hole in the ground. I look inside and there is an open coffin. In the coffin I see myself and my fiancé and we are both dressed in our wedding garments. We are both dead.

Shortly after this dream, patient spoke about his girlfriend, and he felt their relationship was stuck in some "dead end" situation, which was reminiscent of his other relationships. Bruno fears in his phantasy that the relationship with a woman will take him into "a grave-like situation," which is clearly depicted in his Oedipal dream. In fact, in a deeper level, being with a woman of his "own" is like being in a grave with his mother. Bruno fears that any close relationship in his life is going to open up his unresolved issues with his mother, father, and so forth, and he will again become the rejected, homeless little boy.

On the other hand, he fears that if he is more in touch with his internal traumas and feelings of rage he may destroy anything of value in his life, including his own life. Bruno has little capacity to trust anybody, any situation, or value things in life. Nothing is safe in his life including his bakery business, close relationships, or any emotionally engaging situation. For Bruno having anything of his own, like having a bakery business or close partnership becomes an all-consuming, demanding, possessive, and dangerous situation. Any life involvement is full of danger and on the phantasy level will control him, possess him, and abandon him.

The bakery on the deeper phantasy level represents Bruno's internal mother and his primary relationship to his maternal figure. On the other level the bakery also represents in his phantasy his punitive father, needy internal child, and other parts of himself that he projects on the bakery cinema screen.

In one of his sessions Bruno stated: "The bakery feels like a prison or hospital. I feel trapped there, like in purgatory. I want to get rid of it. But how can I get rid of it; how can I kill it?"

He believes that the bakery/mother makes him feel stuck, not free to move about and do what he wants to. But he is actually being immobilized by his internal feelings, conflicts, and needs that he projected onto his bakery in the form of his internal objects and parts of himself. He hopes that by killing the bakery through the financial ocean of debts he will get rid of his internal "black void" like depression and other unbearable feelings and conflicts.

By financially killing his "Cinema Paradise" bakery which contains the projections of his internal objects, he is also killing the projected parts of himself in hope that they actually would die. He is trying to kill his projected "feeling self" over and over, but through this method his depressed and needy self will never die. Through his "Cinema Paradise" he is trying to defeat his personal Sphinx represented by his internal mother and father in hope of stealing true knowledge (+K) and getting freedom and liberation.

The bakery situation cannot have a life of its own because he constantly undermines and tries to defeat the success of it. He is constantly at war and tries to destroy the objects the bakery represents which are displaced, projected parts of himself.

In his phantasy he does not feel he deserves to have a successful bakery, financial security, or a life of his own. Instead he feels he deserves to be a rejected and abandoned little boy, exiled, without a home, with nothing of his own, who moves from one place to another.

On the other hand, if his bakery is successful he fears that there is going to be retaliation from the father (or father representatives) because in his phantasy he has stolen the bakery/mother from the father and the bakery is really not a success that he has made. How does this translate into a real-life situation in Bruno's case?

Well, as previously stated, for Bruno the bakery became a controlling, possessive, and demanding situation. The bakery in his phantasy became like the possessive and idealized mother. He would empty his bakery from its financial resources by his outrageous spending which included trips and vacations abroad which left him with insufficient funds to pay his creditors.

He would provoke his creditors (in his phantasy his father's representatives) to make threatening phone calls about cutting off his electricity, supplies, or a possible eviction due to his debts. Part of Bruno wanted to provoke his landlord and different business inspectors to come and take his business so he could be "free and liberated" from being possessed and imprisoned by his "purgatory" bakery.

In his phantasy he felt that he did not deserve to have this business because he acquired it by manipulation and in the depths of his mind he believed that he has stolen the bakery/mother from the father. For one part of Bruno a psychological and physical migration into any situation including intimate relationships, or other businesses or emotionally engaging situations, is full of danger because they could possess, control, consume or trap him. If he obtains things in life such as a bakery or, in the area of human relationships, a life partner by some kind of maneuvers, in the depth of his mind he feels that he has stolen them from the father and they do not belong to him. Therefore, the father figure will retaliate in one form or another and will take the bakery (or other form of "success" in life) away from him. On the other hand, due to his own guilt Bruno will destroy any possibility of psychological migration and growth.

A MAN WITHOUT NEEDS

Before the long summer break Bruno made the following statement: ". . .the bakery feels like a hospital and I am a needy, sick child trapped there. I want to get out and be free . . . the bakery is the black hole that I have to get rid of. . ."

Bruno cannot bear needing anything or anybody. If he needs the bakery or another person he feels a dependency that becomes unbearable to him and he has to get rid of it somehow. Then in his phantasy he can tell himself that he is a man without needs, free, liberated, and with nothing to hold him back or possess him. He cannot bear needing because it's humiliating and unbearable. It reminds him of the time of his exile/migration and dreadful hospitalization period without any proper care (that occurred during that time).

Today Bruno wants to be a man without needs because the needy part feels worse than death; he'd rather kill that needy child part by drinking, denial, and other self-destructive behavior. He projects the internal needy child out and constantly attacks and undermines this part of himself, telling himself that he is without needs.

Bruno has a vague feeling that there is a black psychic void inside of him. He prefers to think that the void and deficit is related to his financial situation in the bakery. He hopes that the "black hole" is simply a huge financial debt/hole in the bakery and he imagines that by killing the bakery he will get rid of his problem. But what he calls his "financial hole" is his self-created emotional hole, which feels very real to him. He feels so much anger that others in his phantasy are rejecting and abandoning him all the time, therefore via projections he evacuated his internal objects and emptied himself out. This psychological process leaves an emotional void inside of him.

He wants to keep his internal drama on the physical and concrete level of a real physical, financial hole represented by his bakery's financial state. He uses manic defenses in order to cover up the big emotional hole/deficit (i.e., image of the Charming Comic). But this process keeps him forever in the position of the empty, abandoned little boy, exiled from his psychological home, and in search of some elusive freedom, liberation and true knowledge.

In his phantasy he truly believes that in order to be free of his psychological hole, feel liberated, and have peace of mind he has to kill his bakery/mother/father (and the symbolic Sphinx) which on another level represent his very self, his own mind, and his life potential. In this process he psychologically kills himself and recreates the theme of the exiled, rejected little boy without a psychological home.

He wants to believe that he is liberating himself from the black hole (depression) and childhood traumas, but on the other level he is psychologically killing himself.

MINUS –K FALSE SYMBOLIC MIGRATION AND PLUS +K AUTHENTIC SYMBOLIC MIGRATION

The childhood exile/migration during the Oedipus stage of development has greatly undermined Bruno's emotional development. Perhaps his private Oedipus trauma and Oedipal quest for true knowledge and liberation would play itself out quite differently if he did not have to endure the exile trauma and the process of adaptation to the substitute family, parents, and new country.

A large part of Bruno's personality is very much invested into reenactments (especially via his bakery "Cinema Paradise" situation) of his Oedipal exile trauma of an empty, rejected little boy with the black hole inside of him, with no mother, father, home, and country of his own; and in search of freedom, home, and liberation.

The other part of Bruno hopes to make an authentic symbolic, psychological, emotional, and physical migration into adulthood and toward some degree of internal and therefore external freedom and liberation.

Part of Bruno is involved in –K (false) symbolic psychological and emotional migrations and the quest for knowledge. Just like Oedipus killed the Sphinx (a symbol of his parents) from whom, in his phantasy, he steals knowledge, Bruno, by killing his bakery (symbol of his parents) was hoping to find a path to liberation and knowledge that would set him free.

For one part of Bruno no emotional link (L-love, H-hate, K-knowledge) can be trusted due to his fears that people will exploit and reject him or, due to his rage, he will attack himself or exploit others. For this part it is too difficult to develop self-awareness, +K authentic insight, and knowledge about what is happening inside of him or others and therefore his emotional growth is very limited. This part of him is constantly engaged in the enactments of his feelings, conflicts, and traumas. He fears all close relationships or psychologically engaging situations.

Therefore all emotionally and psychologically engaging situations need to be closed up and given up because they make too many demands on him. He wants to get rid of his mind, not to think painful thoughts, but be a charming and funny comic or a little boy without anything. On a phantasy level he feels that by closing and killing his bakery he will be able to close his mind. He wants to "close" himself up, and hopes to get peace, freedom and safety in this way. But if the bakery/mind is open then he feels rage, and has fears of rejection, exploitation, abandonment and black hole childhood depression. So he believes that if he closes the bakery/mind because it causes him a financial hole, then the black hole in his psyche will be closed as well. The responsibility for his thoughts, feelings, conflicts, and dealings with partnerships, creditors, working employees is too much for this part of Bruno. But when he closes up the bakery/mind then he remains forever the exiled little boy.

The authentic +K emotional and psychological migration into *the* adulthood is most difficult for Bruno. He fears that such a possibility may not exist and the liberation can be achieved only at the expense of psychologically killing his mother and father and, in the process, destroying his own mind. It's difficult for him to imagine that he can become an adult in his own right and still have parents having their own lives.

Part of him wants to destroy his own possibility of success because the real-life success may expose his internal reality of psychologically killing his parents and stealing from them what does not belong to him, because he did not work through his emotional conflicts. He fears that such an exposure may lead to parental (or parental representatives) retaliation or he will have to psychologically kill himself out of guilt. The only way out of this dilemma is –K, and therefore disowning of his mind, his emotional self, and constant emotional "escapes" (migrations) due to his fear of destructive enactments.

The fear and avoidance of psychological pain, denial, projection, blaming of others, and Bruno's other defensive maneuvers are largely at the service of –K, pseudo-knowledge. In such a situation the emotional growth and new learning discoveries may not be possible. Just like Oedipus steals the mother concretely and literally but at the expense of the authentic +K, Bruno steals the mother symbolically from the father at the expense of the authentic +K (knowledge).

In real life Bruno would constantly try to psychologically steal things by manipulation, seduction, by disowning his feelings, and by pretending to be an intellectually superior adult man at the expense of the true emotional +K.

In his phantasy in treatment he was really the one analyzing the analyst and knowing more than anybody else. But underneath his superior, charming, comic image was a scared little boy with a big black hole inside of him, who was not able to deal with his thoughts and feelings.

Bruno hoped that by killing the bakery (which, in his phantasy, represented his mother/father) he would get rid of his "black hole" and become free from his depression, liberated from his childhood trauma, and finally be a free adult man.

In the depth of Bruno's unconscious mind, due to all of his –K maneuvers, he feels that he does not deserve the bakery or any success in life. He is still filled with the idea of psychologically murdering his mother and father and therefore he always lives at the expense of psychologically killing his parents. To be an adult man in his unconscious mind is based on psychologically killing his mother/father and different symbols of the parental couple (i.e., bakery, marriage, partnership) and taking by force what belongs to others.

Therefore in his phantasy if he does have a life of his own, then he has done it by psychologically killing the parental couple and stealing their K-knowledge, and out of his guilt he has to psychologically and physically punish himself. Hence, true life, authentic emotional K, authentic success, and true psychological migration toward becoming an authentic adult man in his own right for this part of Bruno may not be possible. This part of him feels that he is not deserving of success or a life of his own, but is instead deserving of punishment and emotional exile.

However, the other part of Bruno (via his psychotherapy and psychological migration within) hopes to make a +K authentic symbolic migration into adulthood and toward some degree of internal freedom and liberation.

In Oedipus' drama, the +K-link represents the quest for true knowledge that is symbolized by the mother, and the +K can lead to liberation. The +K (true knowledge) is not to be taken concretely but symbolically as symbolic internal migration/journey toward emotional growth, freedom, liberation, and finding a psychological home within.

For Bruno such a +K, an authentic symbolic emotional migration within, means accepting the mother/father relationship and not stealing the mother from the father, but symbolically "working through" one's relationship with the mother and the father. The +K means working through the internal issues of dependencies and ambivalence, owning up to one's subjective conflicts of desire and difficult feelings, and becoming an authentically responsible adult and, finally, finding one's own partner in life not based on manipulation, stealing or murder, but by working through the difficult emotional and psychological issues.

Synthesis

Bruno's composite case study is on the more advanced level of self-development than the following Zbyszek composite case study, as his sense of self is more cohesive and less chaotic. In Bruno's case some semblance of his self comes together; but that self is constantly undermined and attacked. There is less primitive agonies that appeared in the other composite case study. However, underneath the "Charming Comic" image there is a deadly rage covered up by various defenses of idealization, intellectualization, dissociation, and so forth. Bruno disowns his painful thoughts and feelings, but the more he does that, the more fragmented he feels.

The integrity of his identity is constantly destroyed and undermined for defensive purposes of –K (knowledge). On the other hand, if he internally comes more together, then there is a fear that underlying "volcanic," live rage will erupt and destroy things. In his phantasy he feels that he has to constantly disperse himself, but then he is left feeling fragmented.

For one part of Bruno, the psychological and physical migration to the next level of development, beyond known boundaries and borders is powerfully linked to exile, homelessness, emotional disaster, punishment, and loss of everything. A substantial part of him is paralyzed due to his fears of abandonment, rage, and lack of trust. That part of him hopes to grow up in a manic way by psychologically killing, forcing, seducing, stealing, manipulating, and escaping his internal reality.

The other part of Bruno (via his treatment) is engaged in a more authentic symbolic psychological migration (+K) within himself in search of liberation and freedom. He is trying to get in touch with his childhood exile (migration) more directly and work through his different conflicts, feelings, and fears.

Through a more authentic symbolic emotional migration within, he is hoping to find an emotional home within; he is hoping to find a psychological home where he can live and from which he can (to some degree) appreciate his life and feel some sense of peace and freedom.

Perhaps Bruno's emotional symbolic +K migration into his internal world and into adulthood would be less difficult and less based on psychological killing, possession and stealing, if his real migration/exile was less traumatic and possibly at the different, more advanced stage of his emotional development.

A COMPOSITE CASE OF ZBYSZEK: IRON MAN

Introductory Remarks

Each individual composite case history has a complex picture of factors and forces at play. In this book I try to derive and present an understanding of both constructive and destructive forces that are present in any migration process. In each migrant's story individual premigration histories, psychological traumas, environment, and many other individual factors play into working out the successful migration. In this study I explored what types of people manage to do better with migration trauma and under what circumstances.

To reiterate, the framework that played into my clinical thinking about the composite cases includes the following special areas: a premigration history, identity, and the old and new environment. The premigration developmental and traumatic issues are unique to each composite case. The cluster of premigration issues shaped each composite case's inner reality and therefore the inner identity.

All the composite cases presented here were voluntary migrations. The inner identity of each composite case was shaped by the patients' premigration issues and psychological development. The environment that I am concerned with in this study would include the inner psychological environment but also the outer environment and therefore new circumstances and support systems.

The Zbyszek composite case represents an early adulthood migration that illustrates a more disturbed migrant with a very precarious sense of identity. One of the important reasons for selecting this composite case material was to see what sort of difficulties are presented with more serious levels of psychological disturbance. For such migrant patients the migration process may be the trauma of a particular type. If migration presents the trauma for almost everyone, then for the migrant patients functioning at the more precarious level, the process of migration might be particularly difficult.

Such a migrant's capacity to deal with new situations and new people is very limited and is affected by the types of issues and problems they bring into the new situation of migration.

Zbyszek composite case represents such a migrant who came to the United States in adulthood, and who had underlying psychotic anxieties that were unresolved. In the situation of migration and separation from the old world, the psychotic anxiety can be easily triggered. Even if such a migrant had remained in the old world the psychotic anxiety would have been present in their lives, but perhaps in a more contained form due to the presence of such factors as the holding quality of native culture.

In fact, such migrants may have sought migration as an escape from these underlying psychotic issues, which was the case with the Zbyszek composite being. Even though outwardly he justified the migration on the economic grounds, but the underlying motivation may very well have been a desire to get away from something that was very troubling in his internal world of feelings and thoughts.

Once such a migrant arrives in the new world, there may be a recognition that these unbearable themes and feelings re-emerge in a new way and in a new and different cultural context. In such circumstances the migration represents a form of an escape from an internal and external reality.

Zbyszek represents such a composite case of adult migration with a significant level of disturbance (a very problematic premigration history). Many migrants of this type may seek migration as a form of escape and retreat from these underlying unconscious issues and quite apart from other outwardly conscious motives.

In the new world such migrants find that the very issues that they were trying to escape are still alive and well in the new world. Additionally, the trauma of migration interacts with other unresolved traumas. Such migrants—those with a very precarious sense of identity—have great difficulties in dealing with external changes in real and authentic ways under any circumstance.

Clearly, migration also presents powerful types of challenges to ones identity as can be seen from the clinical material and related discussion. The reader will see the details of it in the following clinical discussions of psychoanalytic work with this particular type of composite case beings.

Zbyszek made his migration as a young adult, therefore (for him) the migration held a very different meaning compared to an older adult or child migrant. To Zbyszek the premigration identity issues were more unsettled and with psychotic dimension of anxiety. The other cases were also significantly disturbed but perhaps less than Zbyszek. He migrated on his own as an adult and perhaps was a little less in need of the family support system that very young migrants would need in order to survive.

Perhaps out of all the cases presented here, he had the least support system (the environmental factor). One may argue that if he had had more support systems he may have made some of his psychological crisis situations less extreme.

He had major psychological issues prior to migration to deal with in any event, which would have come up whether he migrated or not. It's just that migration is a trauma that perhaps created more of the disturbances in these areas that he was already vulnerable in.

However, the migration trauma may have also given him an opportunity to address his psychological issues, and seek treatment which may not have been available in his own culture. Through his treatment some new growth and development came and gave him an opportunity to work through these themes, which may not be readily available in his own culture.

Background and Family History

Zbyszek was in his early 50s when he entered into a twice-weekly psychoanalytic therapy treatment sessions. Zbyszek came from the southern part of Eastern Europe. He had a large mustache, dark hair, brown eyes, and the physique of a man of iron. Back in his native country, he had been a talented boxer, a body builder, and a prize fighter. He competed in many international sporting events. He was married to a woman of Eastern European origins who was a few years older than himself. He was seeking treatment because he had intense fears about leaving his house and fears of being physically attacked by others.

He migrated from Eastern Europe to the United States of America when he was in his early 20s. In the United States he worked in the area of construction and building.

He created an initial impression of a stoical, unflinching, and hard-as-iron body-builder-like stature. Beneath this iron statue image, Zbyszek suffered from powerful fears and anxieties. He lived in a world of perpetual tension and a deep distrust of every person in his family and his life.

Zbyszek's mother was a dressmaker who was constantly overwhelmed by too many responsibilities. She appeared to be a tantalizing, controlling, and abandoning parent. Zbyszek had two older sisters and two older brothers. One of the older siblings died of brain damage at a very young age. The father had a violent temper and was an alcoholic who had great difficulty managing his small business. Zbyszek was much closer to his mother and during the frequent fights between his parents he would take on the role of his mother's protector from the father's violent temper. In fact, during one of the fights with his father when Zbyszek already was a young boxer, Zbyszek almost killed his father. Fortunately, the mother was present and able to stop him at the last moment.

Zbyszek was referred for treatment by Dr. C. He went to see Dr. C after being attacked by three men in broad daylight. Zbyszek has stated that due to this attack he suffered head injury as well as being robbed. After this incident, he was afraid to leave his home and feared that he was losing his mind. He was concerned about his difficulties in trusting people at work. He had intense fears about being exploited, persecuted, dominated, and underpaid. In his intimate relationships he had fears about being seduced, rejected, abandoned, and unwanted.

He dealt with situations in his life in a catastrophic manner. Around holiday times and weekend breaks he had intense fears and phantasies about falling into an abyss, humiliation, attacking others or himself, and so forth. During the summer break vacations, due to his fear of separation, he would drink excessively, engage in brief sexual affairs, or he would get into all sorts of dangerous accidents such as drowning in the ocean, falling off his motorcycle, and so forth.

He reacted to various separations from work, treatment, and in his intimate relationships via manic acting out maneuvers. The nature of his fears, conflicts and phantasies indicated the early nature of his psychological issues, possibly going back to infancy.

In treatment of this composite case study a lot of attention was given to early disowned infantile primitive fears and overwhelming anxieties. Psychologically Zbyszek lived in this early primitive psychological home.

As the treatment deepened some of Zbyszek's initially disowned fears and phantasies became more explicit. At different stages of treatment various disowned and hidden themes become more specific, defined, and vivid. As the work of psychotherapy evolved Zbyszek felt safer and able to bring these deeper anxieties and different aspects of his self (previously unthinkable and unbearable) into treatment. The unfolding themes, phantasies, and images of concrete walls, iron muscles, plugged holes, shifted to holes in the walls, leaking boats, and burning fires.

The images of his body and head are themes that have appeared frequently in his treatment. The head and body were interchangeable in his psyche. The image of an iron-like body had great significance in his treatment, because it was a physical expression of his fears, phantasies, conflicts, feelings, and emotions.

Throughout his childhood, Zbyszek had various oral-anal digestive problems such as psychic anorexia-bulimia, and chronic constipation. He manifested food anxiety and lack of trust in anything that his objects (people) fed him psychologically and emotionally. This mode of functioning was manifested in his reactions to the interpretations. He had difficulty listening to the therapist's words, would not remember them or would experience them as a pain in his body or other physical symptoms.

He had extreme concerns about his anal muscle control and constriction. In his phantasies, he had fears about his body contents leaking out or being forcibly removed, mostly through his anus. He really believed that his real problem was located in his anus and not his head.

The value Zbyszek placed on his body contrasted with the contempt he felt for his psyche and his emotional self. He had a manic need to concretely and physically do things in order to deny the emptiness or terror inside him. He was an action man. He could not tolerate separation without reverting to acting out behaviors and manic reactions.

In his phantasies he saw separation as killing, castration, and catastrophic birth-like situations involving the danger of death. Each separation or holiday break represented a threat of disintegration of his very precarious sense of self, and he entertained death phantasies in which he was killed or the other was murdered, or he was dropped and smashed to pieces. He engaged in a full-fledged flight into manic defenses and flight from reality during the summer and holiday breaks.

He used other objects and human beings as repositories of everything he could not tolerate within himself. Due to his massive projections and disowning of his feelings, he fragmented his internal representations into many parts in order to reduce the danger of taking them back and internalizing them.

This had the effect of fragmenting and emptying his sense of self. Zbyszek would use sexuality in a perverted way. He saw women as body parts and not whole human beings because he could not deal with the emotional side of human relations. He sexualized his feelings, emotions, fears, terror, and despair.

Zbyszek also had intense fears and phantasies of homelessness and poverty. In order to deal with his terrifying anxieties Zbyszek attended different religious services on a regular basis, and prayed to such religious icons like the Black Madonna or Saint Peter. Those religious icons were supposed to be protective figures used in order to ward off psychotic underlying anxiety. He was holding onto the images of the Black Madonna and Saint Peter in a defensive way in order to protect himself from bad internal parental figures and terrifying anxieties.

RELEVANT THEMES RELATED TO MIGRATION, IDENTITY, AND CULTURE (WHICH AROSE IN THE TREATMENT OF ZBYSZEK COMPOSITE CASE STUDY)

A Burning Home and a Catastrophic Migration Experience

Zbyszek had very few early childhood memories. But he did remember well when his family home and small business had burned down due to a fire. He stated that he was less than five years old when the entire family had to migrate to a big city. After the loss of the home, the family was separated for some time. Zbyszek and his older sister were placed in an orphanage.

Within a few months the whole family moved into a one-room apartment. They all slept in one large bed. Zbyszek states that during that time of chaos he saw his sisters' and mother's "naked breasts" and other body parts because they partly undressed themselves in front of him. He further reports that his mother sometimes wanted him to wash her back.

Possibly he felt physically tantalized by this mother who wanted him to wash her naked back. Was she using Zbyszek to deal with her own anxiety and to give her some comfort during this time of chaos and despair? Was this mother being seductive in front of a child who was totally deprived, turning his deprivation into excitement? It seemed as if everyone in this family were exciting everybody else in order to deal with otherwise unbearable and unthinkable catastrophe. They all slept in one bed, and undressed in front of one another. The whole family was playing into some erotic simulation in order to deal with otherwise unbearable pain.

Perhaps due to his internalizing this trauma Zbyszek began to see the whole world as one big "erotic show," and simultaneously a "murder scene" that he would try to escape in any way he could, including physically migrating to America. Zbyszek, already at this young age, in order to deal with the loss of home and with complete chaos, despair, and catastrophe, was trying to turn all this into some exciting scenario. He was trying to deal with absolute chaos and despair by sexualizing and eroticizing his feelings and thoughts.

From this period of his childhood history, including the early years of his primary schooling, he remembered his recurring dreams/nightmares of "falling into an abyss" and waking up in terror. Zbyszek remembered one dream in particular from this time: "I am sucking my own penis. I feel the warmth of semen on my face. I even tasted it, but I do not get any satisfaction. I feel bad."

Shortly after this dream Zbyszek had the following memory. He stated that at the age of 6 or 7 years old he would masturbate frequently. He was able to shape his body in a form of a cradle and imaged his semen all over his chest and face which provided great relief. He imagined that he was able to produce and even taste his semen. Perhaps Zbyszek experienced such early deprivation that he had to feed himself with his own breast/penis in order to turn deprivation into some kind of excitement and feed the deprived infant inside of himself with his own semen. Zbyszek found a way of feeding himself and thus created a narcissistic wall of self-sufficiency around himself, where he had his own breast and penis for feeding and masturbatory excitement. But in actuality, Zbyszek was unable to care for the infant inside of him that needs the mother's care, love, and the proper milk and food in order to grow.

To Zbyszek, to give up his method of self-care today, his narcissistic wall of self-sufficiency is very frightening. He cannot allow anyone to engage in his psychological feeding, because opening to another means also opening to his own unbearable feelings of despair and anger. Therefore, he needs to be self-feeding, self-attacking, and self-exciting, and need no one else.

Zbyszek believes that his intense curiosity about his mother's body developed around this traumatic time when he was dealing, however ineffectively, with the trauma of loss of house and catastrophic migration, by sitting at his mother's bedside while she was asleep, and watching her legs for hours, and "wanting to see her womb and where father's penis goes. . . . I was disappointed that I could not see it." He further states that during this period of time he started masturbating. "I would make different positions, put my legs behind, into a 'cradle' like position and would masturbate to have an ejaculation on my chest."

THE DEVELOPMENT OF A PSEUDO-EROTIC PSYCHOLOGICAL HOME (ANALYTIC THEMES WHICH AROSE IN THE TREATMENT OF THE ZBYSZEK COMPOSITE CASE STUDY)

According to Klein, "A good object established in a secure form gives the ego a feeling of richness and abundance. It is a precondition for developing an integrated and stable ego" (Klein, 1955). Klein claims that a good internal object is a precondition and a foundation of a stable ego/self and our authentic inner psychic home. The foundation of the psychological home is very much dependent on the first agent in the infant's life, the mother/caretaker and the quality of care that she provides.

The first psychological home must be provided by the mother's mind first. The mother's mind and her own psychic home and her capacity for holding and containing her child's feelings and fears enable the child to find his or her own psychological home. We may say that the original psychic home is first in the mother's mind.

If the mother is unable to contain and hold the child in her mind, and therefore let the child "in emotionally," then the child who is unable to enter the mother's psychic home becomes psychologically homeless.

Winnicott writes: "A good enough mother meets the omnipotence of the infant and, to some extent, makes sense of it. A True Self begins to have life, through the strength given to the infant's weak ego by the mother's implementation of the infant's omnipotent expressions" (Winnicott, 1960, p. 145).

The mother has to "lend" her mind, as it were, to the child, her own psychological home, in order for the child to evolve, to internalize and develop his or her own psychological home.

Bion speaks about *Alpha-Function*:

> an alpha-function converts sense data into alpha-elements and thus provides the psyche with the material for dream thoughts and hence the capacity to wake up or go to sleep, to be conscious or unconscious. (Bion, 1962a, p. 115)

If the alpha-function fails to convert raw sense data or *beta-elements* into meaningful integrated experiences, then we have an accumulation of *undigested* beta-elements.

One cannot develop a mind of one's own, one's own psychological home, unless the mother's alpha-function and her capacity for maternal reverie enables the child to develop an alpha capacity to hold on to the beta presymbolic and preconceptual elements and feelings, and digest and convert them into meaningful integrated experiences.

We might speak of the physical birth of the infant from the fused physical state with the mother in the mother's body into the world of physical reality. The child, through the birth process, migrates from the mother's body to find a new physical home in physical reality.

But what about the psychological birth of the infant who is able to find his or her own mind and therefore his or her own psychological home? In this sense, the mother has to facilitate that process of migration from the mother's mind by providing, holding and containing through her own mind to enable the child to develop his or her own mind.

We may see human development as a succession of migrations away from the first objects. One could say that the child goes through a physical migration from the mother's body, but also a psychological migration from the mother's mind, into developing the child's own mind and psychological home. Thus the *psychological home* of the mother is now internalized by the child and becomes part of that child's own separate psychological home. The child develops his/her own new psychological home, one that has been given roots in the mother's psychological home.

When this process fails, as it did in Zbyszek's story, then we are left with the problem of psychosis. Zbyszek does not have a mind and internalized psychological home that can encompass his feelings, thoughts, fears, and conflicts. His mind cannot deal with internal stress and turmoil, and he is trying to obliterate his mind through powerful projections, splitting, evacuation, eroticization, dissociation, and the creation of a very concrete subjective reality.

Through primitive eroticization, body sensations, and stimulation he provided containment for his mind. He created for himself his own primitive erotic psychological home. Otherwise, he was terrified of madness, confusion, and total despair. Underneath this *primitive erotic psychic home* that provided a form of containment for his mind was total bleakness. His *erotic home* was a desperate attempt to keep out the unbearable feelings and unthinkable thoughts.

In treatment Zbyszek felt that if only he could see his analyst's body parts, this somehow would address his problems and take away his physical hunger, and would give him deeper satisfaction and provide some answers to his perpetual questions. But looking at the body parts and sexual gratification did not provide answers to his deeper questions such as who is he, what is inside the mother/analyst's mind. On a phantasy level, Zbyszek was trying to enter the analyst's mind and to find there a psychological home for himself. He felt that the only way to do so was through her body, in a concrete physical and sexual way. In order to find out what she is like inside, what she thinks of him, and in order to find himself as a human being, and find his psychological home. Zbyszek's mother was not the kind of mother who was available emotionally to her child. Therefore Zbyszek had a very powerful phantasy and a desperate desire to physically enter her body, given that her mind was emotionally unavailable, in order that he might find out about her mind and possess her mind.

Perhaps we might say that Zbyszek had been excluded from his mother's mind, had not been taken into her heart, and therefore had a desperate need to figure out what is inside others' bodies (mother/analyst/others) in order to find a psychological home that one day might become his own internalized home, "a room of his own."

Zbyszek concretized his fears, needs, feelings, and emotions because he could not feel them. He believed that he wanted to see his mother's womb, and that doing so would provide some magical cure. He looked at the analyst in a very concrete, physical and sexual way as a defense from what he really did not know, but wanted to know, namely, was he really wanted by the mother.

One could speculate here early childhood pathology. A healthy child who wants to know his origins, who wants to know where he comes from in his mother's body is more in touch with the feelings, emotions, needs, and its symbolic expression. Zbyszek's thinking, has been very concrete, non-symbolic, and covered by pseudo-sexuality. He would turn human beings into concrete mechanical machines made of body parts and part objects. This function is a powerful defense against emotional and human contact and against getting in touch with much more terrifying questions, such as who he is, does he exist in the mother's mind, and whether he matters.

THE ZONAL BODY CONFUSIONS AND THE CREATION OF AN ANAL PSYCHOLOGICAL HOME

According to Steiner,

> withdrawal to a narcissistic world where differences between the sexes and between the generations do not exist is . . . offered as a refuge. Meltzer (1966) . . . had described these states in terms of the idealization of the anus and the creation of an anal world in which all differences are abolished. The distinction between good and bad and hence between love and hate is also abolished. The individual thus develops perverse relationship in which good objects are rejected and bad are idealized. (Steiner, 1993, p. 98)

For Zbyszek, the real psychological, emotional, and physical world is too terrifying therefore he created a world of an idealized anus-body, erotic subjective psychological home. He is a man suffering from zonal body confusion, where the mind, body, penis, breast, womb, and anus are confused and interchangeable. Zbyszek presented a dream:

"I am wearing doctor's gloves and I want to check my anus. I feel the damage is there. I put my fingers there."

During this part of treatment the patient spoke about his memory from Eastern Europe where he visited a military doctor for a medical examination. He feared that the doctor may discover that his anus was damaged. In his conscious thoughts he felt that his problems were related to his anus not his mind. He felt that he had damaged his anus in childhood by inserting a toothbrush there, while bathing in order to stimulate himself. He felt that this masturbatory practice left a permanent damage to his anus. He also feared that he damaged himself mentally in the process. The anus is really representing his mind with all terrible thoughts, feelings, hate, contempt, that feel like "shit" to him and he wants to get rid of them. In his phantasy he wanted the analyst to examine his anus, to concretely find out if his problem is there. In another dream, Zbyszek saw a vagina:

"I saw a very strange vagina. It was in the form of a vase, with a long neck, round rim made of a plasma-like substance."

On a deeper, unconscious level, Zbyszek does not know what a vagina or anus looks like. He is confused about male or female anatomy. Even though he watches pornography, in his mind he cannot hold onto the images of different parts of human anatomy. These images on a deeper unconscious level look scary to him, like plasma, or fecal waste. He is afraid of real sexuality and of what goes on inside the human body. He has confusional primitive fears about his mind and body. In his phantasy he fears that his mind is made of plasma; he fears that there is nothing of value there, and nothing can be taken in and internalized. For him to feel that his mind is made of plasma was an expression of his fundamental lack of identity. He uses others as repositories of everything that is unbearable to him, disowning huge parts of his self, after which he feels emptied of his internal images, feelings, and possessions. The internal or external physical movement represents to him the risk of moving his feces experienced as concrete aspects of his self, which could leak out exposing him to emptiness.

In the sessions he experienced the analyst as a screen/mirror/breast that returns his image of "nobody" made of transparent plasma or that devours and takes him over completely. We may say that this man lives in the psychological home of unbearable, unthinkable fears, chaos, confusions, and paranoia. He was exposed in his childhood history to traumatic events and had extremely unstable parental figures he could not trust.

BIRTH CHANNEL

Grinberg and Grinberg (1989) write:

> Using migration as a metaphor, human development itself can be seen as a succession of migrations whereby one gradually moves farther and farther away from his first object. . . . Birth is the first migration in the life of every individual. To leave the womb and lose the continuous, unconditional supply of food via the umbilical cord is a traumatic and persecutory experience for the infant. . . . (Grinberg & Grinberg, 1989, p. 191)

Zbyszek's phantasies contain scenarios that suggested his desire to remain inside the analyst's body and remain psychologically unborn, and not have to go outside. On the one hand, on the phantasy level he wants to be constantly in the analyst/womb because everything outside is very dangerous and persecutory. Thus he needs to be fused and merged together all the time. But this fusion is very precarious, because as soon as there is difference, he could be expelled and pushed out.

Possibly in his "psychological birth," he was pushed away from the mother too quickly and he felt unwanted by her. But the womb is also not a safe place for him, due to either too much fear, hate, conflicts or a combination of the three. It appears that his "psychological birth" was a catastrophic type of migration from the mother's mind and her body.

All human beings possibly have universal phantasies and desires to psychologically and physically migrate from the mother's body, mind, and heart, and migrate beyond known limits in search of freedom, knowledge, and liberation. At the same time, there is a fear of movement forward, and fear of bearing the pain of new knowledge, and being a true and authentic migrant. There seems to be a conflict between parts of the personality that seek true knowledge and those which oppose the desire to "migrate" beyond fixed psychological, emotional, and physical borders in search of liberation.

Ideally the birth is the first physical and psychological migration of the human being's life and emergence from the mother's body. It is the loss of the "ideal paradise" and the personal birth of the most primitive fears. After the first migration experience, there is a series of other migrations and adaptations, such as finding the mother's breast and being weaned from it, finding the first object of love and desire and letting go of the forbidden object of desire (parents), finding one's own mind, self, and so forth.

Human development may be seen as the process of multiple migrations in search of a true and authentic psychological home that is in the depth of one's heart and soul. We tend to imagine that there is some kind of external "Promised Land" for which we are searching. But this "Promised Land" is totally an internal space in the center of our heart and soul.

Grinberg and Grinberg (1989) write:

> The migration from one object to the next, from the breast to the penis, transfers to the penis the quality of object relations that had been sustained with the first object . . . what matters is not only how the child has said a final "goodbye" to the breast but also how he had been able to separate after each suckling. If the mother has good supportive qualities, the child will be able to carry out the various developmental migrations on a firm basis and any actual migrations in his future . . . if in early infancy the mother has functioned as a good container, the baby will feel greater inner freedom to choose between staying or emigrating . . . if the mother has failed . . . the child may feel compelled to stick it out in submission to a maternal object . . . or else will try compulsively . . . to travel from one place to another . . . in search for idealized maternal objects. (Grinberg & Grinberg, 1989, p. 193)

Perhaps we can say that if the mother was not a "good enough" supportive figure and container, and the real father was not there to modify the situation, that this may result in the future illusionary search for the new idealized containers and a manic psychological and physical migration as a way of escaping from the persecutory mother. On the other hand, a deprived child and future deprived migrant may be compelled to cling to the old world and its objects. The migrant leaving his native country (symbolically the womb) needs to come into contact in the "new world" with the caring others that will hold him and contain him. If this is inadequate or missing, one may suffer an emotional breakdown.

Zbyszek reports that before his migration to the America, back in his native country, he got a good paying job and the possibility of advancing in sports as a professional trainer. But he suddenly made a desperate move to migrate, not really knowing why, nor what really motivated him on the deeper level.

Shortly after his migration, he married a woman of the same cultural background who was older than him. His wife had already lived in the "new world" for some time, which represented some safety for Zbyszek. He looked up to her as a mother figure who had done the journey of migration. He hoped that she could guide him and provide him with help in his migration process.

We could imagine that in addition to conscious and external reasons for migration, Zbyszek also had all kinds of unconscious reasons and phantasies. One such unconscious phantasy for Zbyszek was a desire to find the safety of the mother's womb and a new rebirth. On the other hand, he had a strong desire and phantasy to find a potent father in a form of a rich new promised land.

Zbyszek presented the following dream: "I was looking for a subway entrance. I opened the door there are two men sitting up there. Before going to a subway, I see a gate, there is a prostitute there. I play with her breasts."

He produced this dream just before a holiday break, which was difficult for him to tolerate. Around this time he experienced me as a cold, detached, wall-like structure, going away on vacation with two other men. . .

For Zbyszek, finding the subway entrance in his phantasy is finding the passage back to the mother's body. But there is no space for him; two other men are there. The mother is closed off, seductive with no feelings, like a prostitute with empty breasts.

On another occasion, he stated: "I cannot stop watching TV birth channel. I want to go into the vagina. I want to be in the womb. I want to see it again and again, the opening of the womb, cutting the cord, and so forth."

Zbyszek had a powerful wish to be in the womb, get inside the analyst's body to be protected from dangerous feelings, in this desperate refuge/womb. Inside the womb there is no safety, because a dangerous other men (father) is there, and all his difficult feelings come back in the womb. On the other level, he is very scared of the woman having a womb/holes/vagina. He does not know what is there: he could fall through the hole forever; he is trying to escape from the human being connection to the physical body connection. If one becomes a whole human being for him, not reduced to different body parts, then unbearable thoughts and feelings come up (rage, terror, etc.). Therefore everybody has to be a partial person that he can control. But then he has fear about body parts (wombs, vaginas) that they will devour and imprison him or he'll devour them.

For Zbyszek, the migration on the most regressive phantasy level is a desire to go back to the mother's womb. He wished to physically relocate himself to the mother's body because being outside of her in the real world was too painful. The wish to migrate to a better place, represented by the United States, is a wish to start over and go through the process of being reborn. On the other hand, his migration was also a wish to escape from his unbearable internal world, cold and seductive mother, and violent father. He is a kind of "manic migrant" who is in constant search of exciting objects and experiences, and he uses migration as an escape from the internal demons and tormenting dreams and feelings.

Possibly his birth was a catastrophic birth of coming from the womb-like paradise into a physical realm experienced as hell. He has a psychological fixation on his anus because that is connected in his phantasy with the fundamental rejection by the mother who did not receive him emotionally but turned her back on him. On the phantasy level, Zbyszek feels that he was pushed out of his mother's body as a messy "shitty baby blob" and he came through the anus and not a proper birth channel.

Possibly, the migration was a wish for a proper rebirth and also an external physical and psychological escape from this cold, dangerous, and prosecutory mother. At the same time, he is also fused internally with his mother and his internal representations cannot escape his internal reality. He is fused with his internal images and identifies with them, but is also simultaneously cut off and dissociated from them due to his fears of being controlled, overtaken, devoured, etc. He tries to escape through physical migration, but is unable to do the internal separation by working through his issues and terror. He tries to deal with his internal reality through the "physical moves"/migrations because he fears that the internal problems may not be solvable.

CREATION OF AN "IRON MAN" DEFENSIVE IDENTITY STRUCTURE

Due to the very traumatic early childhood history and very unstable and disturbed parental objects, Zbyszek could not trust anyone. He felt that his head had been "damaged" very early in his life, and that he had to rely on his body. He sees the psychological damage to his head on the physical level, but he is unaware of the emotional damage that he has experienced in terms of not having emotionally available parents. He disowned his mind because his emotional self was unbearable and become focused on his body. He does not want to authentically feel or think, because when he does then he has to own up to his feelings side. We may say that he does not have an emotional home but lives in the "home of the unreal" because he has disowned his feelings and his mind. He fears that his head has been concretely and physically damaged, but what got broken is the underlying emotional state that is fragmented. He radically cut himself off from emotional functioning and lives in the world of "concrete reality" and a pseudo-erotic anal psychological home.

As a young adolescent, Zbyszek decided to become a boxer and a body builder. He said that he was talented in sports and had all necessary ingredients for becoming a great success. He developed a huge iron-like body that he idealized and eroticized. He developed muscles like iron in order to deal with his fragile emotional world. His body became his armor, both weaponry and a wall of protection. He psychologically moved into his body in order to find a safe place there. On a phantasy level, he felt that if he has a body like iron, then there is no "hole" that can be penetrated, and the only way one can find out about his feeling side is by going through the anal entrance hole.

He created "iron muscles" like a second narcissistic skin so no one can get inside him. He felt that thus he has closed off any possible openings to his body. In his phantasy, he feels he has to control all openings to his body due to his fear of leaking out his emotional and body contents. He has to put similar controls over his mind, so nobody enters through his mind either. But then he is unable to receive any help and nourishment from others because he has closed his mind and body and nobody will receive him in any way. But if he opens his mind, he is afraid of being controlled, used, exploited, and taken over, or feeling his unbearable emotional states.

LEAKING BOAT

Zbyszek's body and its iron-like wall of muscles are frequent themes in his therapy sessions. The images of doors, gates, holes, or some other entrance were appearing on a regular basis in his therapy.

In one of his sessions, Zbyszek revealed that he used a female tampon in order to plug a hole in his anus. He also described the following dream:

> "There is a hole in a boat and a man does not know what to do. But the woman takes out the tampons and plugs the hole."

This dream evoked the patient's memories of using a female tampon, before leaving his house and going to work. He had fears of uncontrollable diarrhea and fears of leaking out his body contents. He feared that others will find out about his secret of using a tampon and humiliate him for using a female tampon. The image of a leaking boat plugged by a tampon has a great meaning for Zbyszek's therapy because it is a physical expression of his primitive fears and phantasies, and his state of mind and body. His sense of self and his basic identity felt to him like a "leaking boat" with holes in it, and that needed to be plugged by the tampon. Underneath the Iron Man body there was a powerful phantasy of a leaking boat plugged by the tampon, which was his fragile emotional self. He felt that he needed to plug the hole in his body with a tampon in order to prevent himself from falling apart, but on a deeper level, it was a hole in his mind that he needed to plug with something. He needs something concrete, like a tampon in his psychic phantasy in order to prevent himself from falling apart psychically and concretely from falling through his anal hole. He fears that his very self will fall through his anus so he needs a tampon to plug the hole inside his body. The boat is his sinking personality with the big holes in it and his fears of collapse.

Winnicott (1963) speaks about unthinkable and primitive agonies, such as going to pieces, falling forever, a return to an unintegrated state, loss of sense of real and loss of capacity to relate to others. According to Winnicott, psychotic illness is a defense against primitive agonies, and the fear of break down is the fear of a break down that has already happened.

Winnicott writes (1963):

> It is wrong to think of psychotic illness as a breakdown; it is a defensive organization relative to a primitive agony, and it is usually successful except when the facilitating environment has been not deficient but tantalizing, perhaps the worst thing that can happen to a human being. (D. Winnicott, 1963, p. 90)

Furthermore, Grinberg and Grinberg write:

> Among the major sources of psychotic organization, one finds the traumatic experience of separation, the child's loss of important objects at a precocious stage of development, or the mother's failure or inability to alleviate the child's anxieties. The child experiences great distress and in his desperation feels that he is falling into a void. (Grinberg & Grinberg, 1989, p. 135)

The fear of falling through the hole and falling forever is one of the primitive agonies with which Zbyszek was confronted.

Hence, he imagined in his psychic phantasy that his anus hole had to be plugged because there might be inner dragons, demons, or even worse than that, namely some "nothingness" or some internal black hole. Even demons and dragons are defensive figures and images that are filling up the unbearable emptiness and the underlying fear of falling forever. The psychotic person, such as Zbyszek, fills up the unbearable inner emptiness with demons and dragons, and so forth, in order to defend from the underlying fear of breakdown. His psychosis serves as a defense against his primitive agonies of falling forever through a hole, his fear of a boat sinking, and the water coming through, and his mind coming apart. He tried to fill up this emptiness, nothingness, and lack of holding by a tampon in his anus.

One may wonder what went wrong in Zbyszek's basic identity formation. Was his primary caretaker/mother herself a "leaking container" without any or with very limited capacity to contain her infant's fears and anxieties. Or, perhaps his basic identity problem is related to his incapacity to relate to the mother rather than the mother being defective herself. One can only hypothesize what went wrong in his mother-child relationship from this patient's treatment. Was this mother unable to cope with her own anxiety and therefore was using her son as a container or as something to project her own unbearable feelings and fears into? One could imagine that it is very possible that this mother was unable to contain the child's fears and anxieties. However, on the other hand, some children are very difficult to contain due to their inner makeup, irrespective of how good the mother may be.

Zbyszek had early childhood memories of being left home by himself, because his mother had to go to work. He remembers one incident:

> "somebody was trying to break into the house, and kill me. I was ready to jump out of the window, but my brother stopped me at the last moment."

We can imagine that Zbyszek's mother was overwhelmed herself and therefore not quite able to provide a containing, safe, and caring environment.

AN IRON MAN: DELUSIONAL OBJECT

According to Rosenfeld:

> The psychotic structure is like a delusional world or object, into which parts of the self tend to withdraw. It appears to be dominated by an omnipotent extremely ruthless part of the self, which creates the notion that within the delusional object there is complete painlessness but also freedom to indulge in any sadistic activity. The destructive impulses within this delusional world sometime appear openly as cruel, threatening the rest of the self with death to assert their power, but more frequently they appear disguised as omnipotently benevolent as life-serving, promising to provide the patient with quick ideal solutions to all his problems. These false promises are designed to make the normal self of the patient dependent on or addicted to his omnipotent self and to lure the normal sane parts into this delusional structure in order to imprison them. (Rosenfeld, 1971, p. 250)

In order to protect himself from the tantalizing and abandoning mother, violent father, and the deprived, needy, and rage-filled child within himself, Zbyszek developed an iron man muscle-like body, a psychological wall around himself, and a ruthless, omnipotent "Iron Man" part of the self-delusional object. Zbyszek presented the following dream:

"I was near a pool of water, where people needed food. I went to get water in a Nazi metal cap for my head, but water was running through the holes in it. I did not have any food."

Around this period the patient spoke about his childhood deprivations. He stated that at home there was not enough food for the family members and when there was a chicken for dinner he was only allowed one chicken wing. His mother used to make his clothing herself, in order to save money.

Today Zbyszek cannot properly feed deeper parts of himself. His head (represented by a Nazi cap) is damaged and things are leaking out of his head. He tries to get rid of his thoughts, feelings, and the desperate child inside of himself, and obliterate himself completely. His head is like a "leaking Nazi cap" and nothing stays in his mind; mental content gets wiped out.

He had to become a very strong, frozen "Iron Man" (delusional object) in order to deal with the powerful underlying fears of being a small, weak, and paranoid child. He fears that if he "melts"—becomes softer and more emotional—he may leak out everything that is inside of him, he may stop existing, he may become nobody. Therefore, he has to be an Iron Man with a muscular, iron-like body, and remember at all times that he is that strong in order to deal with the unbearable internal situation. But how long can an Iron Man last? Zbyszek is getting older (he is in his 50s) and is scared that the Iron Man defense is crumbling, disintegrating, and his rage, fears, and needs may be coming out.

The reaction formation of an Iron Man is his way of dealing with the underlying powerful anger at "idealized" women and people who exploit, use, and humiliate him. He has to consciously believe in the reaction formation of an Iron Man but unconsciously he knows that his rage is explosive. Underneath an Iron Man are hungry people (parts of the self); there is a hungry child whom he cannot feed and look after because he needs to be an Iron Man without any needs, feelings, or hunger. The representations in his internal world are devastated and attacked. He cannot make any reparation to his internal representations. He is getting older and the Iron Man defense is coming apart: at times he forgets that he was an Iron Man. The Iron Man may not protect him much longer and all his feelings may leak out and all his thoughts may come up.

Through the Iron Man's omnipotent structure and narcissistic organization he "kills" his needs, feelings, emotions, and the vulnerable child part of himself. He feels that if he engages in the treatment, something bad will happen; if he produces more insights, feelings and thoughts may come up and he may get (in his phantasy) killed, imprisoned, and so forth. He constantly fears that the Iron Man defense against his deep depression and despair, his tormenting dreams and feelings of inadequacy, may not last much longer. He has been using sex, drinking, and an Iron Man structure to protect himself from his fears of castration and being nobody.

A succession of the following dreams presented by Zbyszek in treatment revealed the devastated internal world underlying the reaction formation of an Iron Man.

"I had a gun, and kept on shooting into the empty doorway. An old, fat man opens the door and offers me alcohol. I shoot him. The house is empty . . . I wake up."

His internal emotional home is empty here. There is no food in his psychic home; only an old man who wants to give him alcohol. The fat man is the needy side of him and he wants to kill that part. In another dream:

"I am lying on top of a dead woman . . . the body is decaying, swollen. I am feeling all alone and scared."

Consciously, Zbyszek idealizes women but underneath he fears exploitation, humiliation, and mind control, and therefore he feels rage toward women and others.

In still another dream he states:

"I am flying in a helicopter over a "Ground Zero"—like scene. There is police . . . ambulances . . . some emergency going on. . . ."

Zbyszek is trying to fly above his feels and stay above the internal catastrophe because if he allows himself to go into that area he may lose his life, so he needs to be above it at all costs.

In Zbyszek's devastated internal psychological home the Iron Man psychic organization kills his internal father, mother, and a child inside himself (which represents his deepest emotions and life force inside the self) with alcohol and primitive sexualization. When he kills the parental images for leaving him hungry, and the needy child, he is then faced with the "empty" psychological and emotional home. He feels that he is a son who has been abandoned, and did not receive proper care and love. He was left feeling hungry, desperate, and abandoned. So he wants to "break the door"—possess the mother/woman in a concrete way—and meet his emotional needs in a perverted way through sex, incest, violence, and dehumanization.

He has no basic integrated "self" to hold and contain his feelings, emotions, and fears. His basic self has holes in it and he tries to eliminate this basic structure by constant evacuations (of feelings), enactments, drinking, and sex in order to be above his feelings. He fears that through the psychotherapy the child part that has needs and feelings may be born inside an "Iron Man." Then he cannot be an Iron Man who has no fears and feelings. Even though on the one level he "idealizes" his body, on the other level he is constantly attacking his body and his mind. He has to constantly attack his emotional perception and experience in order not to allow any emotional registration to take place. When feelings of rage, hate, and so forth come up, he has to continuously dispense them.

Zbyszek's body is developed into an iron body, and then idealized as a defense against feelings, emotions, and conflicts. However, the physical body of an Iron Man cannot solve his emotional problems and the fact remains that he is at war with himself and cannot find a safe place for himself where he can find his psychological and emotional home. He has been able to find a physical and external home in the United States. Through the process of psychotherapy, his psychological migration within, he is trying to find an authentic psychological home, the mind of his own, and a place where he can exist without fear at least for very short periods of time.

Bion speaks about the "containing object" (1970). He saw the mother/infant relationship in terms of the links between the container and the contained (the child), where the mother functions as an affective container of the child's sensations and unbearable anguish, and transforms them into bearable anxieties. The mother's alpha capacity transforms the fear of dying into aliveness, hunger into nourishment. If the mother has good alpha capacity and good reverie, then the child most likely will be able to cope with frustrations and separation. If that process fails (as in Zbyszek's situation) the child will inhabit psychotic states. It the mother fails in her containing functions of the child's fears and projections, this often produces a deficit in alpha-function which transforms the content of sensory and emotional experience into alpha-elements that help in the creation of thoughts, memories, and dreams. The loss of such an early "containing object" in extreme situations may lead to ego disintegration and the blurring of ego boundaries.

The risk is felt most strongly in situations like Zbyszek's, who suffered major deprivations and separations early in his life, resulting in feelings of helplessness, terror, and inarticulate suffering. The real physical migration here, that creates a dramatic change in the human being's life, with its multiple losses, may reactivate very primitive anxieties and phantasies such as fears of being swallowed by the new cultures (mother/container), or fears of being torn apart by it, leading to states of panic, terror, and, on occasion, an outbreak of madness. The childhood and adolescent history of the migrant, his internal object relations, personality, age, and many external factors related to migration will influence the quality and possible outcome and consequence of real physical migration.

Grinberg and Grinberg write:

> Youth is without doubt the best and worst age for everything, migration included. Statistical studies on the mental health of refugees and emigrants show that the greatest illness rate occurs in persons who emigrate between the ages of twenty and thirty. This is understandable if one takes into account the fact that at that stage of life the central problem is the search for and consolidation of one's sense of identity; and if an event such as migration intervenes, one's sense of identity is thrown off course. (Grinberg & Grinberg, 1989, p. 126)

We may wonder if migrants like Zbyszek, with a very fragile sense of self and a latent psychotic mechanisms, may have been able to continue living a rather "normal" life back in their old world, maintaining a rather pseudo-psychological balance, and existence. We can only speculate if Zbyszek's separation migration had touched off the psychotic aspects of his personality and caused a breakdown of the fragile mental equilibrium. A deprived child such as Zbyszek, who suffered the prolonged absence of the maternal figure, perhaps becomes a "deprived migrant," with an increased predisposition to psychosis. A "deprived migrant" such as Zbyszek, due to losses of the reliable persons and known environment, may experience fears of collapse, fears of death and falling forever in the "new world" and culture when "selfobject" (Kohut, 1978) support is lacking. A migrant such as Zbyszek, who suffers the loss and absence of the containing other, and who cannot tolerate separations, may become exposed to psychotic states. The new country, like a new mother/container, may not provide the needed help and containment which may lead to fears of disintegration and real psychotic breakdowns.

THE HOME OF BIZARRE AND CONCRETE OBJECTS

According to Bion, who writes on psychotic thought disorder:

> attacks are directed against the apparatus of perception from the beginning of life. This part of his personality is cut up, split into minute fragments, and then, using projective identification, expelled from the personality. Having thus rid himself of the apparatus of conscious awareness of internal and external reality, the patient achieves a state which is felt to be neither alive nor dead (Bion, 1963, p. 39).

Such a psychotic personality becomes depleted by the projected out fragments of the perceptual apparatus which lead to an alienated existence and creation as called by Bion, "bizarre objects." Such bizarre objects are experienced by the psychotic person as possessing an independent existence of their own. The psychotic feels imprisoned in the world of bizarre objects, which lead an uncontrollable, independent life; he lacks an integrated state of consciousness that could provide a key and open the door to freedom.

Zbyszek, due to his paranoid anxiety, creates such bizarre objects via massive projective identification into concrete things and space. Here the mind is trying via projection to get rid of unbearable fears and terrors because there is a very limited alpha capacity structure with which to process these unbearable and unthinkable fears.

So they are constantly evacuated, but then they begin to exist in real objects, which now become bizarre objects and they carry the beta-elements.

If they can be thought out, talked about, and become more thinkable, such bizarre objects can become more real and living objects.

The analyst in Zbyszek's mind was turned into such a bizarre object as "the wall" and a "red car" on the emotional level. In this patient's mind the analyst becomes a "concrete wall" that separates him from the real analyst. He believes that the analyst set up the wall around herself and, therefore, she did not give anything to him emotionally. But in fact, Zbyszek is so desperately cut off from his feelings that he feels like a wall inside, with unbearable thoughts and fears underlying the wall.

In yet another dream he speaks about "a well-made red car, made with the metallic back pipes being repaired and fixed. . . ." For Zbyszek, his psychotherapy was like the "red car," a mechanical thing that was being repaired and fixed. He does not see psychotherapy as an alive process, but a mechanical repair shop. In fact, seeing and treating psychotherapy as a mechanical car device is a defense against becoming engaged in the process on the feeling level. He can only engage on the mechanical level of a "car repair" process and not on an alive and emotional process. The car focus is the "mechanical substitute" for himself.

Underneath these concrete, bizarre objects, the psychic home of such a psychotic patient as Zbyszek is filled with physical pain, terror, fears of psychic holes, and body intrusions. The concrete objects and concrete physical actions represent his unbearable thoughts and anxieties, and they need to be converted into a psychic realm of more thinkable thoughts and bearable feelings.

In treatment he is trying to connect to different things in the analyst's room (red carpet, brown table) but he is unable to make an emotional connection to the analyst as a person. He is not making an emotional connection but, rather, a "concrete connection" through things, which on another level is scary as well. He cannot allow anybody the entry to the emotional side of himself, represented by the child, due to the unbearable fear of being taken over, controlled, or humiliated.

His concrete connection is based on a desperate grasping onto things in the room or tearing them apart (in his phantasy) because the emotional connection with the living person is too frightening.

In his treatment, one hopes that things will become less concrete and move more to the psychological and feeling realm. What he mostly experiences in the session is psychosomatic pain in his head, stomach, heart burning, and a "strange arousal" at the same time. He does not have any real feelings, just physical pain, and sexual arousal. His rage and hate are expressed in the primitive way, through wanting to "pee," "shit," and humiliate the self or the other. He cannot process his sensations (beta-elements) in his mind; therefore he expels them through bodily substances. He has turned his primitive sexuality into an addiction. He eroticized his self-destructiveness and turned the whole thing into "despairing pleasure." For Zbyszek, sex is a way of expressing hate and to humiliate others by "anal penetration."

In his psychic home his internal objects intrude into him and annihilate him. He turns unbearable thoughts and feelings into concrete physical things, physical migrations, accidents, and other physical traumas. The movement toward his fears and thoughts being made more thinkable is very slow and scary. One could imagine that a real physical migration for Zbyszek, with such a precarious level of existence, was a path to get away from his unbearable internal and therefore external reality. Possibly his physical migration to the United States was a physical, concrete, and manic escape from his mind and the unbearable internal and, therefore, external existence.

A HOLE IN THE WALL

After the summer vacation break, Zbyszek came back with intense fears and phantasies about things "breaking down," "falling apart," "pain in his body," and so forth. He thought that his body was "breaking down" due to his sports injuries, but underneath that thought was the fear that his mind was going to "fall apart." For Zbyszek, body and mind are closely interlinked and he did not separate the two. He felt terror that his Iron Man muscle defenses were falling apart in the treatment. The pseudo-muscles that he created as a cover up for his fragile emotional self were falling apart.

At the same time he did not yet trust that some authentic muscles and the authentic sense of self could be developed instead. The Iron Man muscles did not protect him in his life and did not help him to deal with his psychological and emotional issues.

Zbyszek states that in the last day of his vacation, he almost lost his life. He said: "I almost lost my life. I went to the ocean and the waves were pulling me back. I was ashamed to scream for help, but I forced myself to do that. The life guard saved my life."

When Zbyszek is more in touch with his internal life, he feels that he is drowning in the internal ocean of conflicts, fears, and unbearable emotions. His vacation break was another manic escape/migration from all difficult fears and feelings in treatment. It is humiliating for him to ask for help. He is a boxer and a body builder; he does not want to need anybody and he wants to psychologically feed himself. His body building was designed to give him a second skin and his own self-protection, his own muscles, but this second skin may be coming off.

During this time, he presents the following dream: "The skin under my eye is coming off. I try to put it back but it came off again . . . the siding is also coming off of my house."

Around this period in treatment patient spoke about his preoccupation with his extensive home renovations going on. He had concerns about his kitchen, toilet, and the siding of his home coming off. In the context of his dream and clinical material I have arrived at the following understanding.

The iron muscles that he has developed to protect his fragile self are falling apart and his fears and feelings of rage are leaking through the muscles of his body/house/self. He fears that the muscles are giving in, and there is no internal structure to hold him from within, and he fears the collapse of his own self. It was around this time that Zbyszek started wearing a t-shirt with his national flag on it. It is possible that he was looking for some kind of external identity picture/structure to hold himself together. On the phantasy level he hoped that the "flag" was going to give him some holding structure, identity, and prevent the feared state of fragmentation.

In one of the meetings with Zbyszek during this period of time, he said in a voice full of terror: "I found a hole in my wall, behind my closet. I fear my tenant is plugging into my electricity box."

On the phantasy level, Zbyszek feared that I have made a "hole" in his psychological wall of iron muscles and I will take away his power now. On the other level, he is the one who plunges himself into others psychologically via his projections and wants to live out of other people's nourishment. He fears that he has no mind of his own and would like to steal others' capacity to be in the world. He fears that his parents did not give him power to be a functional adult in life. He believes that in order to get anything of value, one has to magically steal the power that will make him potent in the world.

The treatment became a dangerous "ocean of feelings." Perhaps the iron muscles were giving in? Zbyszek felt that if he changed his sitting position in the sessions that might contain his fears of drowning. In a psychotic and a concrete way he was using his physical moves (little physical migrations) in order to cope with his anxiety. He was looking for physical and concrete solutions to his emotional underlying issues.

He was also greatly preoccupied with the analyst's physical moves including her sitting positions. He would say: "I cannot concentrate when you cross your legs. I want to see deeper." Zbyszek was preoccupied with body entry, because he feared there was no entry into the other's mind. In his phantasy he wants to physically enter into the other's body through any physical entry (anus, vagina) because he believes there is no emotional entry. Physically entering into the other body still does not solve his problem because he still feels emotionally rejected and unwanted. He thinks in a concrete way that if he sees deeper into the analyst's legs, just the way he wanted to see deeper into his mother's legs after the loss of family home due to a fire, he may get better ideas as to what is inside a woman's body and mind, and if he is emotionally wanted. The physical "deeper seeing" into the analyst's legs will give him a magical cure and provide answers to the deeper questions that he has. His intense concern on the psychological level is related to wanting to know if he is wanted and desirable by anybody. He thinks that he needs some physical and sexual entry, but it's really the emotional acceptance that he is seeking.

On the other hand, during this time he was also very preoccupied and angry about not having a room of his own in his brother's house, which he himself had partially financed. In fact, on the deeper unconscious phantasy level Zbyszek was very preoccupied with a deeper desire to have a "psychological room" in the analyst's mind and body.

However, in order to find his own "psychological room" he needs to have an "external room" first represented by access to the analyst's office, and her capacity for holding and containing before he can develop an internal holding potential space (internal room) of his own. He is looking for concrete external space which, at a deeper level, is an internal psychological potential space, an internal emotional room where he can live and be safe. He fears that if there is no room in the analyst's mind, then he cannot develop a room inside of himself. But if the analyst can hold him in her mind, then he can internalize this holding space that in time becomes his own and can hold him. In his phantasy he feels that nobody kept him inside their mind. His birth parents rejected him and therefore he feels homeless with no internal safe holding room of his own.

In fact, for most of the time, Zbyszek lives in a "blank room." The internal blankness is a consequence of having to evacuate (via projections) most of the contents of his mind, and therefore he is left with the "blank room." Underneath this blankness created by massive evacuation there is still a deeper fear of "falling forever" where there is nothing to hold the center.

According to Winnicott (1974), psychosis is a defense against this most basic "fear of breakdown that has already been experienced." A migrant, in order to become authentically assimilated into a "new world," needs to have an internal potential space in order to promote an imagination and creative attitude toward the migratory experience. A deprived migrant with traumatic past experiences may have very little capacity to work through the trauma of migration and may suffer mental or physical illnesses.

Due to unresolved childhood trauma, personal problems, and conflicting relationships with both parents, integration into a new culture has been morbidly traumatic for Zbyszek and he became profoundly depressed, paranoid, and detached. In order to deal with massive changes due to migration, Zbyszek, like a deprived child and deprived migrant with no capacity to create potential space and therefore no capacity to symbolize, he used the primitive defense mechanisms of dissociation, splitting, projection, and so forth. He used powerful dissociative mechanisms of idealizing all aspects of the "new world" and devaluing the "old world"—regarding it as persecutory—as a way of escaping the underlying persecutory fears and phantasies, intolerable thoughts and feelings.

By belittling the losses, denigrating the old world and admiring the "new world," he was trying to negate the unbearable anxieties that are perhaps to some degree inevitable in every experience of migration. The content of his dissociation was easily reversed where the "old world" was idealized, the new was persecutory, and he was easily disenchanted with the "promised land." The breakdown of dissociation between the idealized and persecutory aspects lead to confusional anxieties not knowing what was good or bad and what was love or hate.

He has managed to find a "physical room"/home for himself. But the road to finding an internal "psychological room" and therefore a degree of freedom and independence is extremely difficult, long but, hopefully, to some degree possible. The true integration into the "new world" may be possible but to a very limited degree. He will need a good internal object as a part of his psychic reality in order to create a foundation for the capacity to hold and contain his feelings, emotions, fears and dissociated parts of himself, and the capacity to tolerate separations in an authentic (not manic) way.

Synthesis

How does someone like Zbyszek deal with a situation of real physical migration? What role has migration to America served in his situation? Perhaps the real physical migration thrust upon him a "new catastrophic birth," one that he has unconsciously equated with death and ceasing to exist, feeling like some "plasma" like creature on the mother's breast. On the other hand, perhaps the migration was an ultimate escape, a desperate move to run away from the unbearable internal situation.

In his case, we might talk about a category of a composite case where underlying problems are more of the "psychotic nature" and such migrants use the migration to escape these issues. Migration to them is much more problematic than in the case of somebody who makes a more realistic migration. Zbyszek's migration, apart from external economic reasons, was an unrealistic manic escape from his unbearable internal emotional home. He runs away from who he is, he wants to lose his emotional self, and does not want to get in touch with who he is. To Zbyszek, his emotional psychological self/home is unbearable and, yet, not to know who he is and to be psychologically homeless are also unbearable.

In treatment, when he is faced with situations of breaks or vacations, he uses similar manic escape solutions. He uses vacations as attempts to run away from multiple anxieties that are present in his treatment. But going away is not safe either, because he is fearful that he may kill himself or somebody may attack him. He cannot deal with his feelings of loss, separation, and often when away, he gets into semi-suicidal situations.

On the other hand, he cannot live in his psychological home because there is rage, pain, fear of death, and killing. He tries to get out of this home, and to escape through masturbatory excitement, yet to not have his psychological home and be homeless was equally unbearable.

We may safely assume that an individual cannot be in the world and part of the real world if not at home within oneself. On one level, migration in its various forms had been for Zbyszek a manic escape from his internal world, a way of jumping out from a "sinking boat" which represents his mind and body. His internal objects represented by such powerful dream images like anaconda, dragons, and demons suffocate, annihilate, and devour him from within. These are not safe internal representations that have love and concern, but they suffocate his internal life. He is often afraid to leave his physical home but he is really imprisoned in his rigid psychological home that he cannot leave.

The internal persecutory mother and father images represented by anacondas and dragons are outwardly covered up by the idealized religious icon images (to which he prays too) and unreal figures of black and white Madonnas and the Holy Father, St. Peter, St. Paul, and so forth, that he can love in some ideal and unreal way. He uses idealized religious icons in order to defend from the underlying psychotic anxiety and in hope that they will give him magical cure and magical potency in the world. He uses these idealized religious images to create some sense of structure for himself and to give himself some way of holding and containing. Underneath of these idealized structures are very dangerous creatures like dragons and anacondas. The imago of holy icons can very easily shift in his mind into dangerous dragons that suffocate and devour him.

He does not have a proper internal father identification that would allow him to become a man in his own right. He is more of the pseudo-man who identifies with the fused mother-father internal representation. His psychological home is concretely represented for him by his real physical home, and he experiences great fears when he has to leave his physical home. When he does come out, he has fear of being attacked, humiliated, robbed, and so forth. There is no safety inside his psychic home, nor is there any safety outside the real world as well.

He does not feel a real sense of care and concern for self or others. He is engaged in desperate attempts to run away from this internal reality.

We may safely assume that his migration to the United States was a wish to run away from this internal reality. But when he came here he was confronted with the same internal world and same problems in his relationships that are cold and rejecting. However, on the other hand, due to his treatment and the psychological migration within, he is a bit more in touch with the intensity of his anxiety and a bit less prone to act these fears and feelings out in a such a massive way. The internal chaos and unbearable, unthinkable anxiety are a bit more thinkable rather than constantly enacted.

One hopes that he may one day develop an internal "room," a "psychic space," where he can become aware of what is going on inside of him and make sense out of his psychotic anxiety. He needs to gradually develop a psychic home and a sense of self where he can live and be in touch with his feelings, fears, and conflicts. The Iron Man defense physically protected him in his life but did not enable him to move, grow, and develop his emotional psychic home.

Being more in touch with his emotional self gives him a chance to get in touch with something more authentic and real. Due to his treatment he is more in touch with his dream material. Through his dreams, which were absent in the first part of his treatment, things are more thinkable, symbolized, where before they were all enacted in such a massive way or eliminated by very primitive defense mechanisms. He was seriously uncontained in his chaotic early childhood situation, and was never able to process any of his unbearable thoughts and feelings. There was a massive acting out in the family situation, and he did not develop the capacity to think, process, and work through his issues. He has developed very primitive defenses to deal with the unbearable thoughts and feelings. Zbyszek has been able to find and develop a physical home for himself in this country. Now he is in the process of an emotional migration within, in hope of finding a room of his own, and his internal psychological and emotional home.

Chapter 4

Concluding Analysis of Composite Cases

In each presented composite case study, migration created a crisis in the patient/subject's life and identity. Each composite case illustrates different developmental issues and different generations (1st, 2nd and 1½) of migrants. By analyzing each case study's problems and difficulties one can better infer what are the healthier solutions to the process of migration and who makes a successful migration to a new world.

One may deduce that a more successful migrant does not carry the type of emotional and psychological baggage that is presented in these composite migration stories. So a healthier migrant is not necessarily making a major escape from his internal issues via migration and, if to some degree he does, then he would have to work through them in a new culture, because these issues will not go away in the new environment.

In any case, the migration process represents a form of crisis and the identity will get destabilized. They are some migrants that may have the capacity to recover from such a crisis and identity destabilization rather quickly. But when someone is making a "major escape" from their internal issues via migrations, the impact of the migration will create more internal and external problems.

What literature and the above case studies suggest is that if one is moving a physical and psychological home from one culture to another, one inevitably will have to readjust both internally and externally to a new place and physical home. One will have to work through different types of anxieties, losses, and changes. In a successful migration the identity of the migrant is preserved and enhanced by the migration process.

In situations where a migrant's identity is already problematic the migration will become an additional trauma, intertwined with pre-existing problems.

ELA'S COMPOSITE CASE

Ela's composite migration story represents a so-called one-and-a-half generation migrant. She migrated to America with her parents when she was in her adolescence. She had real knowledge of what it is like to be born and live in Eastern Europe. Ela had deep roots to her home country and her Eastern European identity was already evident. She was comfortable in her home country and her migration was involuntary and felt like an exile from her native home.

Ela's early separation-individuation process from her mother was already severely problematic in her home country. The process of migration made Ela's separation-individuation process even more problematic, and she got caught up into all sorts of manic escapes from her internal mother via identity reinventions, etc. Because this fundamental separation issue was not worked through in her home country before migration, her manic defenses after the migration became even more extreme.

In fact, after the migration to America, the whole family became more closed off and suspicious about the external world. The parents had their own unworked-through traumas before the migration, and after migration her father's drinking problem increased, the mother became more anxious, and the whole family became more enmeshed.

The premigration family issues worsened and the parents and children were forced to fall back upon each other. One could observe this phenomena in families that move around (i.e., diplomats) from one place to another. The only consistency in their life is each other, because everything else in their life is transient, so they hold on to each other. If there are separation issues in such a family to begin with, they get compounded and made worse. Such families share each other's experiences of loss and at the same time they feel stuck with each other.

In more settled situations, there may have been greater opportunities for more separation and individuation situations. The parents would feel more held and contained by the surrounding culture and the children would feel more contained by being in one familiar place, and therefore, the parent/child separation issues could be dealt with better. In the migration process the context of a containing culture, support networks, etc.—all of that gets disrupted and undermined—makes the separation-individuation more difficult to address.

In Ela's family the parents became more anxious; the father turned to alcohol, the mother clung to her daughter; there was not enough of cultural holding and containing of the mother-child relationship. So the separation-individuation process got even more compromised. Ela resorted to extreme measures of the separation-individuation process by manic escapes to other countries, jumping from planes, changing identities, and becoming a different person every two years but never succeeding in her desire to authentically separate and become a mature adult.

Ela felt she was an exiled migrant child, and when she became an adult she had phantasies about going back to Eastern Europe. She had feelings and phantasies that her life would have been less complicated and better off in Eastern Europe than here. She believed that her first cousins and other relatives in her home country grew up with less conflict because they were part of one culture. She felt that some of her relatives did economically and professionally much better in her native country than her family here.

Exiled migrant children, when they become adults, may not want to feel like exiles any longer. They often want to undo the trauma of migration/exile and be more in control of which part of the world they live in. Such one-and-a-half generation children migrants, when they become adults, may have phantasies of reversing the process of migration by going to one's native home. However, going back is not an easy process, because now such migrants have the American part of their identity that does not feel at home in Eastern Europe anymore.

It is possible that in Eastern Europe Ela's process of separation-individuation and her identity issues would be easier to address. Being part of one culture, she would not have to deal with the complexity of the bicultural Eastern European and American identity conflicts.

Had this family been able to work through their issues of separation-individuation, and the multiple anxieties about the immigration process, there may have been a greater possibility for a healthier outcome of the migration in this case study.

BRUNO'S COMPOSITE CASE

Bruno represents a second generation migrant who had to endure the conflicting relationship between a home country of his parents and the home country of his birth.

Bruno was born in the United States and as a child migrated back to Eastern Europe—the home of his parents—where he felt like an intruder and an outsider who did not belong there. He suffered major identity crisis and identity confusion between his American self and his Eastern European self; he did not know who he was or where he belonged.

He was born into the American culture but both of his parents, who were migrants, were born into and represented the Eastern European culture. In the first few years of his life Bruno did not have any first-hand experience with his parents' native culture, but had only experienced it via the internal world of his Eastern European parents. Not long after Bruno's physical birth his mother became severely ill and had to be hospitalized. He developed a phantasy that his very birth was dangerous and led to his mother's disastrous illness. Even though intellectually he knew that his mother has fallen ill, on the other more emotional level he believed that his birth caused it and, therefore, his psychological birth is dangerous and may mean disaster to somebody else.

He has a phantasy that he was a savage baby that caused so much damage to his mother and put her to a hospital. He is afraid to get in touch with that very early part of himself that he calls his "savage Eastern European" self. He is scared of this savage part of his early self that became very active during his migration/exile in Eastern Europe where he got into many dangerous accidents, like when he jumped into a deep pool of water, etc.

In his mind he connects his "savage self" to his Eastern European self and the American self is another part of him that is placed on top of the earlier savage self. When he was sent away to Eastern Europe he developed some sense of an Eastern European identity while there. He has been able to use this internal split between the Eastern European self and his American self for splitting all kinds of other internal conflicts about himself.

He has not been able to integrate his Eastern European and American experiences because both experiences were very painful. He was sent away from the United States and had to cut himself off from who he was here as a young boy in order to deal with the feelings of being in Eastern Europe, where he felt neglected and suicidal. He has learned how to use cultural differences and different aspects of being Eastern European and American as the basis for lots of other forms of splitting and organizing inside of himself.

In his phantasy Bruno tends to put unbearable feelings and emotions into his earlier savage Eastern European self that he does not want to be in touch with. The cross-cultural Eastern European migration has reinforced the preexisting splits in his personality; he has used the cultural differences as receptacles for further splitting of different aspects of himself.

It may be quite common for second-generation migrants to use cultural differences for various forms of internal splitting. The second-generation migrants learn from their migrant parents (both consciously and unconsciously) different cultural aspects of their parents' home country which can create a cultural split situation. Such a second-generation migrant may have phantasies where part of them comes from another world and another part is more American; and they may use these cultural differences for all kinds of internal divisions.

In Bruno's case such a splitting was encouraged and reinforced by the fact that he was sent away to Eastern Europe and had to live there for a few years; so he places different painful experiences into different cultural compartments based upon Eastern European and American self, major internal splits. There are other forms of splitting in Bruno's internal world, but the bicultural split is the most pronounced inside of him.

We may wonder how much this cultural migration/exile experience has complicated Bruno's ability to achieve a more cohesive sense of self. His migration was involuntary so he felt exiled from his mother's home and sent away to Eastern Europe from where he could not come back for a long time. He was at the mercy of his mother to take him back home. This must have generated in him great feelings of impotence and helplessness. Any migrant in exile may feel psychologically impotent with no power to make decisions about their lives and decision to get home.

We may assume that the more trauma that is experienced in a migrant's life, the more difficult it will be for him or her to deal with different cultural aspects and bicultural identities. If we consider the hypothetical situation of the second-generation child born in the United States and brought up in a more loving family with overall healthier development and less trauma; such a child most likely will take from their parents a sense of a different culture from which the parents come from (i.e., language, food), they still will have to deal with the issue of bicultural identity, and the question of who they are. They would carry the primary family culture passed to them unconsciously and consciously by their parents and, then, the American culture to which they feel connected from birth onwards.

While such a second-generation migrant children still have to deal with the whole issue of bicultural identity, they do not carry the extra baggage of severe trauma as someone like Bruno does. It is not easy to navigate through two different cultural identities, so the related difficulties should not be underestimated in any case, especially if the cultural differences are significant. The implicit assumption in all of this is the idea that we all have a need to be more rooted in some sort of continuity that goes beyond our parents and their generation.

We may wonder if the negative implications or results of migration can be reversed or healed in one generation. In any event, migration is a long and complex process that inevitably may not be satisfactorily worked through in one generation. It seems inevitable that the first generation migrants will unconsciously pass on the trauma of migration that they have never worked through themselves to the next generation.

This further supports the view that migration is a complex process and human beings have to work through that over long periods of time and often, over generations. For children of migrants who are part of their parents' migration the consequences of migration may not be visible for some time.

Bruno's mother made a decision to send her children to Eastern Europe in hopes that they would be better looked after by the close family relatives there. The mother herself grew up in the more extended family setup where different family members were close to each other. In America she had to adjust to a more nuclear family set up for which she was not quite prepared for, as an American mother may have been. In this respect the Eastern European culture allowed for more extended family setup situations and other support networks.

Bruno's migration back and forth between Eastern Europe and America was very traumatic because it represented a separation from his mother and father for a long period of time. He had earlier traumas and then the migration experience became an additional factor placed on top of other conflicts. He used the migration experience to split off all kinds of unbearable aspects of himself into different cultural categories.

First-generation migrants, who do not have relatives and other supportive networks in this country, may often be faced with very difficult decisions related to their children's care and future. In Bruno's case he was moved back and forth between Eastern Europe and America. Additionally, he still had to deal with being a second-generation migrant, with his parents' migration trauma, and what they could not work through was passed down to him.

ZBYSZEK'S COMPOSITE CASE

Zbyszek's migration story represents the first-generation migrant going through the migration process. Zbyszek had identity issues and a fragile sense of self before his migration. In this composite case, to some degree, migration was a manic attempt to run away from his internal and external problems. However, migration to another environment did not solve his problems but, instead, the same problems were reproduced in the migration state.

The external migration did not bring about the internal shifts that he might have unconsciously hoped for. His problems did not disappear but, now, with the trauma of migration they became more complex. We do not know how his life would have unfolded in Eastern Europe and if he would be able to maintain his pseudo-psychological balance. He decided to undergo migration to the United States, but he could not escape from his emotional issues that became more intensified here.

We may wonder how the themes of migration impacted Zbyszek's psychological home? Zbyszek is the first-generation migrant who has been living in the United States for over twenty years. However, he has not put forth enough effort to learn the English language. We may wonder how much of it is related to not wanting to deal with the genuine migration issues. He is still so caught up with his native/mother tongue, and his homeland; in essence, he has not been able to leave Eastern Europe behind. Yet, on another level, he is not able to connect with his Eastern European roots in any real emotional way. It is too unbearable for him to deal with his feelings about Eastern Europe. He is stuck in between two worlds and living neither here nor there.

In order to make a successful migration one has to deal with both realities, the reality of the place that one left, and the reality of the new place and, one's feelings and thoughts about both. In this case, part of leaving Eastern Europe would be connected to taking on another mother tongue/language.

Zbyszek is unconsciously very much bound to his internal mother image (represented in his dreams by the anaconda, etc.) that pulls him back into her world. He cannot quite make the psychological migration from this internal mother/anaconda image into more authentic relationships with other people (including his wife and the analyst) because the same fears (in terms of suffocating anacondas) come up there as well.

On the other hand, by holding on to the mother tongue he wants to be in a more familiar and therefore safer world, with which he has ambivalent feelings to begin with. We may wonder to what degree he is psychologically staying in the old world because he is terrified of the outside new world and, to what degree he is staying there (not quite escaping from the outside world), because he needs a place where he can feel more comfortable without blocking out the world outside.

How much is he willing to deal with the new world and how much does he want to close his eyes to that reality and imagine that he is in the old world?

Even though the Eastern European culture is part of the Western culture that America represents, if we look closely there are also lots of differences. In broad categories we put these cultures together, but on a deeper level there really are distinguishing aspects of each culture (i.e., different sense of space, ego boundaries, etc.). Such cultural differences represent threats to one's sense of cultural identity and especially in the case of the first-generation migrants.

Particularly, the first-generation migrants who are dealing with identity crisis related to migration, and identity problems related to their pre-existing psychological issues, are often very unsure in many ways as to who they are. They frequently cut themselves off from their earlier Eastern European self due to painful emotions and depression that they are experiencing. This in itself puts their identity at risk.

So much of their self gets disowned and acted out that they no longer know who they are. They have identity issues within the earlier Eastern European self and then the crisis of migration gets super-imposed and interwoven with all of their internal conflicts and issues.

In Zbyszek's case, as well as in the other composite migration cases, each composite being experienced basic concerns about who they were, and other concerns about their sexuality, identity, etc. On top of these early basic identity issues migrants have to deal with an Eastern European and American identity factor that is superimposed and often in conflict with each other.

Zbyszek maintains his Eastern European side and clings to it almost like to his mother tongue, unwilling to move out and learn a different language.

The American mother tongue represents to him some unknown, threatening world. He fears that if he learns English he will be thrown into an alien, unwelcoming world that he cannot yet trust.

The process of connecting to his roots by making real links and connections with his past memories and feelings is frightening to him. The process of making such real connections to his roots would include getting in touch with his feelings about people and places that he left behind in Eastern Europe.

We might say that it would be a normal part of the migration process for the migrant to undergo on an ongoing basis a process of working through their thoughts, feelings, and memories about places and people left behind; the life they had in a different world in contrast to the new life they have in the new one.

As already stated, Zbyszek (to some degree) is stuck in between two worlds. There is a genuine fear in him that prevents him from authentically dealing with his feelings about leaving Eastern Europe. One aspect of his having to psychologically leave Eastern Europe relates to his concerns about taking on another mother's tongue as there is a big part of Zbyszek that is still wrapped up with his internal anaconda mother and her language. He cannot quite make the emotional migration from the internal mother into the relationships with other people in the outside world due to his fear of being taken over, etc.

There is a deep split-off depression connected to his Eastern European side that is still too painful for him to revisit. He is not quite able to make this internal/external transition by working through his depression and his feelings about Eastern Europe.

A more successful migrant would have to work through (internally as well as externally) the "migration melancholy," and the process of giving up an external physical home in one world, and forming a new home in another world. One would have to work through all of the internal feelings connected with this type of move in order not to become overwhelmed by the implications of the migration process.

One function of Zbyszek's physical migration was a desperate attempt to escape from his early internal depression and other unbearable feelings. He became an "Iron Man" without feelings and vulnerabilities.

One of the elements in finding an authentic psychological home for Zbyszek has been the process of working through his psychotic anxiety, and developing some capacity to understand his psychotic fears, so he can be more in touch with his real feelings. The other element of finding a psychological home would be related to addressing his feelings about his Eastern European self and his feelings about the migration process more directly.

This man came from another world and has a whole Eastern European side of him that is part of his internal psychological home and needs to be reclaimed and worked through. One important aspect of his future treatment would be related to more directly working through the real trauma of migration and his Eastern European part of the self.

In the treatment of any patient coming from another culture it would be enormously important for mental health practitioners to be aware of the challenges the migratory process presents. If a therapist is not sensitive to these issues, they may actually collude with patients, and not deal with anything connected with the painful feelings about migration, and instead engage in some kind of pseudo-assessment of the patients' issues.

While such treatment may help a migrant patient in many other areas, the patient will always be disconnected in a fundamental way from the deeper identity related to one's original roots.

For migrants (particularly first and second generations) the areas related to one's roots may be too painful to revisit and they might be willing to become Americans too quickly. The indigenous therapist who may not have a personal awareness, in terms of the importance of this area, may engage in some pseudo-analysis of a migrant patient. This could possibly reinforce and enlarge the split in the patient's psyche.

A more successful migrant would be more in touch with his native roots and, at the same time, would be able to make necessary internal and external adjustments in order to assimilate into the new world. Indeed, it is possible for a migrant to successfully adjust to the new world without losing the essential and important parts of their native identity.

The migrant who converts too quickly into an American and denies his native roots (due to painful feelings/memories) may suffer a sudden psychological breakdown and collapse of the self. A migrant who has a phantasy that he needs to discard all that is related to the old world may become a pseudo-American, with an American accent that never rings fully authentic.

As previously stated, in Zbyszek's treatment this is another area of his psychological home that needs to be explored to a greater degree. The themes related to his migration and his native identity have been presented in his treatment in more latent form. Through his treatment Zbyszek has been able to get in touch with his more immediate disowned phantasies and psychotic fears. Being able to work through some of his unthinkable fears has enabled him to find a bit of an anchor within his psychological home.

Underneath all of these more immediate fears and conflicts there is this other area of his psychological home related to migration and his Eastern European identity that needs to be more fully reclaimed. The cultural issues have not yet come up in his treatment in a more direct way because he felt he had to hold on to pieces of himself in order to survive psychologically.

Even though Zbyszek has ambivalent feelings about his home culture, he has not run away completely from his connection to a home country. Instead, he has created more of his own artificial Eastern European world around himself. He speaks mostly in his native language and surrounds himself with Eastern European family members and friends. Perhaps he has chosen an Eastern European analyst in hopes that such an analyst will be able to show him how to live in the new culture.

In spite of this, he still does not go more directly to the real, emotional Eastern European part of his psychological home, as it is yet very much connected with his depression. He is afraid to have a more direct contact with this real emotional internal Eastern Europe. In order to find a proper psychological home, he needs to psychologically migrate back into this part of himself and work through his feelings related to the real, emotional Eastern European part of his self.

Part of Zbyszek is blocking out this part of himself. In his therapy he makes only isolated references to his Eastern European family members who still live in the old country and their problems. He has not been able to reflect more authentically on his move/migration from Eastern Europe to the United States and what that has meant to him.

We may safely assume that if the migrant totally disconnects from the old world and his feelings related to the migration process then there is no possibility of a successful migration and integration into a new world. An authentic migrant would need to periodically revisit the idea of migration and reconnect/reprocess his or her feelings about the world he or she has left behind. In order to make a proper migration one would have to work through, on an ongoing basis, the painful feelings of loss and having to move from one's cultural homeland.

The essence of a successful migration is the migrant's capacity to feel the losses and mourn the places and people left behind, and continually (and periodically) work through one's mixed feelings.

In Zbyszek's treatment he needs to incorporate into his psychological home all of his feelings related to his real Eastern European self. He has not arrived at that stage yet, but a big part of him wishes to explore this side of himself and reconnect with his past, which would enable him to make a more authentic move into the real American culture.

His pseudo "iron muscles" (identity) are becoming less useful in his life, and they are being slowly replaced by the more authentic emotional muscles.

Chapter 5

What Leads to Successful Migration to a New Culture and What May End in Failure

We may wonder what the characteristics are of migrants who successfully integrate into a new culture versus those of migrants that have limited success in the process. Generally speaking, migrants with unworked-through childhood traumas, conflicting relationships with their mother, father and others may often suffer great dependency (clinging or manic escape) on the family and the old world (see Ela's case study), which makes a transition and integration to the new world morbidly traumatic.

As my case studies show, those who have identity problems, mental disturbances, personal problems, and who lack professional skills prior to migration, when faced with the additional impact of migration, may fail to assimilate the trauma of migration and integrate into a new culture. They often become profoundly depressed, paranoid or detached.

As seen with the composite cases that I described, migrants who have a tendency to cling to what is stable and known will have greater difficulties in the process of transitioning and integrating into the new world. On the other hand, the migrants who are in a continuous search for new, exciting experiences may be the manic type who use migration as a way to escape from internal tormenting feelings, and therefore the authentic transition and integration into the new world may not be quite possible (see cases of Ela and Zbyszek).

We may conclude that the sign of better mental health would be an integration of both modes of functioning with a healthy dependency and a desire for new experiences. So one can have flexibility to be one way or the other according to the given cultural context and circumstances.

The extreme attitudes in any of these basic modes of behavior will lead to such pathologies as agoraphobia and claustrophobia (i.e., Ela's composite case) and an authentic integration into the new world may not be quite possible.

As this study shows, the traits of a premigration personality could influence the outcome of the process of migration. There can be a greater or lesser predisposition to migration based on one's history, early multiple migrations, individual constitution, personality type, environment, and various internal/external motivations (as seen in the composite cases of Bruno and others).

The individuals with a well-integrated self/ego, a strong desire for new experiences, and the capacity to face risks, losses, and changes in the new world may tend to migrate.

On the other hand, individuals with identity disturbances such as schizoid personalities, who often have a limited sense of rootedness, may have a greater tendency to migrate. The paranoid personality type may be prone out of fear of persecution (i.e., Zbyszek's composite case) to migrate.

One may deduce from this study that migrants who have the capacity to form healthy relationships and attachments to new places will have a greater chance of successfully integrating into a new world and psychologically growing and benefiting from the experience of migration.

Based on this study I arrived at the conclusion that almost every migrant must face and endure such difficult feelings as loneliness, guilt, sorrow, and isolation, and simultaneously continue to function in the new world. Migrants who have the "capacity to be alone" (D. Winnicott, 1958) and the ability to cope with such difficult feelings as hatred, guilt, shame, etc. will have a greater chance at proper integration to a new world.

According to Winnicott's paper "The Capacity to be Alone" (1958), capacity to be alone is an important characteristic of maturity in psychological development; tolerance or ambivalence of one's feelings and the capacity to identify with each parent are important qualities related to a greater sense of maturity. For these capacities to remain intact in the face of the migration process, the migrant will need to have good internal object representations as a part of his psychic world, which will create the foundation to better tolerate separations and the impact of changes due to migration.

The migrant with the above capacities will be able to better deal with multiple losses of family members, culture, feelings of frustration, and inevitable exclusion in the new world to which he is a stranger.

The losses of valued cultural symbols (i.e., language), which are essential parts of the old world, might be experienced as loss of potency equal to psychic castration. As my case studies show, in all object losses in the migration process there is a loss of parts of oneself, which may threaten one's sense of identity. The lost parts of oneself related to the old world may never be recovered. This contributes to feelings of migration nostalgia (Grinberg & Grinberg, 1989) and a notion of not fully belonging to the new world and to oneself. After the migration the integration into a new world is such a long, complex, and often painful process, that one may never fully integrate and belong to the new world. The feelings of nostalgia, loneliness and mourning may be an ongoing, lifelong process that is part of each migrant's reality. Just like a migrant's native accent never fully fades away, so his bittersweet longing for the old world may become his constant companion that never vanishes.

In the mourning process, migrants come face-to-face with their feelings of guilt, sadness, and anger. The desire to become more complete by recovering some of the lost aspects of oneself is at the center of the "work of mourning" (Freud, 1917).

The concept of the "work of mourning" was first introduced by Freud in "Mourning and Melancholia" (1917). The migrant must give up some parts of his individuality that are related to the old world in order to become integrated into the new world.

As seen in the cases described in this study, the complications in the evolution of the migration process may be related to intense feelings of guilt, loneliness, hopelessness, and other conflicts of subjective desires. When a migrant manages to adapt too quickly, when he is not emotionally and developmentally ready for integration, paradoxically at the point when he can finally enjoy an apparently balanced life (as in the case of Bruno who had a prosperous bakery), he falls into a state of profound grief and depression. In such situations the manic defenses become exhausted and the underlying depression frequently sets in. A common phenomenon related to migration is expressed by a migrant's frequent fears and phantasies of homelessness and poverty as seen in Zbyszek's case. Migration can be at times a concretization of "orphan phantasy" (Grinberg & Grinberg, 1989) or some heroic act of independence from the home country for some migrants.

In any event, migration constitutes an enormous change and in the process of change, there are periods of pain, disorganization, and frustration.

A migrant having a family network or a spouse in a new world may be better able to confront and endure changes, and work through the melancholy of migration. A migrant with professional skills and the ability to speak English (or the language of the new country) may cope more successfully with the migration process. Occupation and stable work can be a stabilizing and organizing factor that may restore a migrant's self-esteem and make him feel that he has a place in the new world.

As previously stated, the migration process unfolds through different phases. The initial stage is often full of intense feelings, fears, and phantasies about the unknown world, leaving one vulnerable to periods of confusion and disorganization. After some time, which varies for different migrants, the difficult feelings previously disowned become more bearable and accepted. Migrants may suffer feelings of sorrow for the lost old world along with the "growing pains" of incorporating the elements of the new world (Grinberg & Grinberg, 1989).

Finally the realistic migrant is able to recover the desire for working, creating, thinking, and being with others in the new world. The past becomes part of one's living history and does not interfere with living in the present. The native culture becomes to some degree integrated into a new culture, and thus the migrant is able to assimilate to the new culture without having to disown one or the other.

Generally speaking one may deduce from this study that if the migrant's personality is healthy, the motivation for migration realistic, and the new world reasonably hospitable, one can gradually assimilate to a new world. If the migrant's emotional state is realistic (without extreme dissociations such as shown in the case studies) and, if he/she can accept his limitations, then he/she will be able to learn from new experiences and make room for psychological enrichment and real assimilation.

We may infer from analyzing the problems presented in the case studies that if a migrant works through the period of mourning for oneself/others, for his lost native home, and works through the grief of migration, he will reorganize and re-establish his sense of identity; he will feel that he belongs to a new world.

One may deduce that being able to follow a normal path of working through the migration process will lead to increased psychological development and greater maturity. Such a migrant comes to live in a new culture with his own individuality and his own cultural peculiarity, while maintaining a realistic and stable relationship to his old world and culture.

While the mourning process for the old world may never be altogether completed, the authentic process of working through the migration trauma promotes ego enrichment, identity expansion, and transformation (as it would in working through any trauma). To the extent that the migrant can assimilate the experience of migration as the time moves on by re-owning feelings and aspects of himself, and by reorganizing his identity, he will grow and be an authentic migrant living in an expanded and enriched bicultural (or multicultural) psychological home.

MIGRATION TRAUMA

Migration is a difficult process for almost everyone, irrespective of one's internal psychic world or external environment. It presents a significant challenge on psychological, emotional, conscious, unconscious, physical, economic, and many other levels. Perhaps the notion of trauma can be applied to prolonged events such as migration.

According to Rycroft (1968), in psychoanalysis, trauma is any unexpected and painful experience which a given person is unable to assimilate and which produces anxiety and could lead to the development of a psychoneurosis.

In his paper "Studies in Hysteria" (1895) Freud stated that trauma could be connected to one traumatic event or can be caused by the accumulation of few partially traumatic events.

Migration is not an isolated traumatic event observable at the time of departure from one's country or the time of arrival in the new country, but the accumulation of several often traumatic events. Migration can be seen as a "cumulative trauma" (Khan, 1963) in which a migrant's reactions are not always expressed and visible, but the consequences and the effects of such trauma run deep in any migrant's life.

The concept of cumulative trauma was introduced by Khan (1963) in his book "The Privacy of Self." According to Khan (1963), an individual may experience several small traumatic events that are not experienced as trauma. However, such partial traumatic events can suddenly accumulate into a traumatic impact (i.e., mother's constant inability to contain and hold her child can build up to the trauma of abandonment).

In any migration a constellation of factors and events combine to produce anxiety, fears, and sorrow, and these conditions may not be clinically apparent from the beginning of the migration process. There could be a latency period of varying lengths of time between the traumatic event of migration and the visible after-effects of this process (i.e., delayed mourning period).

In my view the migration process itself can be seen as "migration trauma" in its own right. Just the fact of leaving one's home and moving to a foreign place presents a difficult task and psychological challenge. However, if one is forcibly exiled to a different location or had to leave due to persecution in their own country that would present a greater type of trauma with a large "T." Many migrants had extreme traumatic experiences in their own country. For instance, Jewish people who experienced systematic persecution during World War II era; or the United States collaborators during the Vietnam War had to escape with the United States forces because if they had stayed they would likely have been killed.

Migrants psychologically carry within them such past trauma experienced in their own countries as they engage in the process of migration. When migrants leave the old world under such a traumatic circumstance, that type of trauma is a localized trauma related to the country of origin. Due to persecution and a threat of being killed such a migrant has to make a traumatic escape because his/her life is threatened. This represents localized trauma of war and persecution related to a country of origin. The migration trauma with the big "T" is related to such a situation where the migrant is forced to move due to exile or persecution. For instance, Freud during World War II era never wanted to leave Vienna even though his situation was dire. According to DeSalvo (2009) who in her book "*On Moving: A Writer's Meditation on New Houses, Old Haunts, and Finding Home Again*" states the following:

> Still, he thought emigrating "would be like a soldier deserting his post." In rebuttal, Ernest Jones told Freud that though the second officer of the Titanic did not want to leave his ship, nonetheless, the ship had left him. Jones's words, along with Anna Freud's capture (she was released, though for a time she thought that she would remain a prisoner and no doubt be executed), helped persuade Freud to leave, and he began to wish he could "die in freedom." (p. 119)

Even after Freud's home was captured by Nazis and his son got arrested he still wanted to remain in Vienna. Ernest Jones's comments helped Freud to reluctantly leave Vienna. On the other hand, if one has a choice of leaving one country for another for professional or personal reasons, such a migrant would be less traumatized. However, when people make choices to leave one world for another, there is always some element of more subtle migration trauma with a small "t," which the migrant may not have realized at the time of leaving. Even when a migrant moves to a new world which offers greater economic and professional opportunities, nevertheless the whole idea of giving up the native place where one lives for a new place has a traumatic dimension itself, which a migrant may not have initially appreciated. However, on the more subtle level, in such a situation (as above) the idea of the migration trauma with the small "t" is operative.

If we compare migrants who actually wanted to leave their culture to migrants who did not want to leave their native world, but were forced to do so, we may conclude that in the later situation migration trauma was with a big "T" trauma. The forced type of migration represents a risk to the migrant's live, and therefore converts the whole process of migration into a big "T" migration trauma.

The migration process itself can be seen as migration with a small "m" and big "M." Generally the migration journey within the same culture and country may be seen as migration with the small "m." In migration with the small "m," where there is relocation from one place to another within the same country, there also will be internalized native culture within such a migrant. This type of migrant will have the internalized culture of different caretakers who are carriers of their native culture. For instance, an individual would have internalized his mother and father's different psychological capacity that will also represent inner culture with a small "c." Therefore, each individual within the same country has different internalized culture from another individual. However, the internalized culture in the migration process from one location to another within the same culture is not going to present significantly problematic issues. Such a migrant will still be part of a similar cultural framework. In contrast to cross-cultural migration from one country/culture to another county/culture will present additional traumatic dimensions (with the big "C" cultural factor) and create cross-cultural conflicts in migrants, lives (as already elaborated earlier in this study).

In conclusion, this study is about migration process with the big "M" which in my thinking, to various degrees, is a traumatic process in its own right, independent of any earlier trauma experienced in the country of origin. The migration process itself can be seen as trauma with a small "t" or, in other cases, when there is a threat to ones existence as trauma with a big "T."

Final Remarks

As my clinical case studies show, migration exposes any individual who experiences it to a state of disorganization and reorganization that may not always be resolved or achievable. The migrant's ability to reorganize after a temporary disorganization due to a stressful situation will determine to a great degree the success or failure of the migration process.

Based on my clinical case studies we can infer that in the assessment of the migrant situation in psychotherapy it would be important to consider three broad categories for mental health practitioners. The three basic categories are:

I. Premigration—history, traumas
II. Migrants' Identity—within this broad category there are two basic sections to be considered:
    a. A precarious sense of identity (different levels of precariousness)
    b. A well-integrated sense of identity (different levels of integration)
III. New Environment—would include such factors as new culture, economics, support networks, job status, and type of migration (exile/voluntary).

It is important to consider the three categories together, since they seem to be linked together and in a dynamic interaction with each other. A given migrant may have a difficult premigration history and significant traumas but, his/her identity may be well-integrated due to one's ability to work through difficult situations.

In the "Identity" category, the migrant with a well-integrated sense of self (one needs to consider different levels of integration) will already be living in the true psychic home and his migration process will take a healthier path. Nonetheless, such a migrant will still have to work through the process of assimilation of migration, re-owning of his feelings, mourning the losses, accepting both worlds, and navigating through different cultural identities.

Whereas, a migrant with a precarious sense of self (one needs to consider different levels of precariousness) will have much greater difficulties with the process of migration, and the migration itself will be the manic type and much more problematic. Such a migrant will have to re-own significant parts of their personalities and work through the major internal splitting of the self (as seen with all cases that I described in this study) in order to become more integrated.

Based on my psychoanalytic study I believe that migration is a profound challenge and, in many ways, perhaps a trauma for almost any migrant, therefore even in a relatively healthy migrant, the migration process may open up early primitive anxiety. In a well-integrated migrant there may be temporary periods of regression into more anxious states, but then he or she will have the capacity to work through difficult situations. Such a healthy migrant will therefore be able to work his or her way back toward a healthier sense of self, which has already been developmentally achieved.

In such a situation, the migrant's personality was already stable before the migration process, therefore after temporary regression such a migrant has the capacity to re-establish his better integrated sense of self. This capacity is especially significant during unstable transition periods.

Compare those healthier migrants to those that were previously described in the precarious identity section, those who have never successfully dealt with basic identity issues in the first place. When they experience a migration, they are presented with yet another trauma that further complicates the premigration identity problem.

Consider, for example, Zbyszek's case. He had never developed a true psychological home prior to his migration to the United States, and as a result his migration led to further internal splitting and other issues.

In any event, for mental health practitioners it would be important to recognize that migration is a difficult process which can be quite disturbing for almost anyone, and it requires a deep process of working through difficult mental states and conflicts.

This may not be recognized by some mental health practitioners who have not thought about this issue or have not experienced the migration process themselves. The migration process is just like other challenges in life; it requires constant re-working through of difficult feelings and conflicts. The capacity to be able to work things through helps us to deal with challenges of life and migration.

The idea that if one is psychologically healthy then one will not feel psychic disturbances inside is a simplistic and empty notion of psychic health. It's natural to feel anxious and disturbed when traumatic events take place, but a healthy migrant or other will have psychological capacities to work through difficult feelings and situations.

To recapitulate and elaborate further, the three broad distinctions which may be helpful in the thinking process and the assessment of the migrant's situation are as follows:

I. Premigration Situation

This category will include the migrant's history, traumas, and also one's capacity to work through difficult life situations which could lead to a better integrated sense of identity. Therefore those who had various traumas in the premigration period but also had the capacity to work through difficult emotions and conflicts will develop a more cohesive sense of self. Compare such migrants to those who lack such a capacity and therefore develop a more precarious sense of identity. This first broad category seems to be linked to the second identity category.

II. Identity Category

A) <u>Migrants with precarious sense of identity:</u> all of the composite cases presented in this study represent migrants with different levels of precariousness of identity. Migrants with a precarious sense of identity lack many basic emotional and psychological capacities to work through difficult and traumatic life situations.

Such migrants often lack the "capacity to be alone" (Winnicott, 1958), the capacity to mourn, form healthy attachments, or endure difficult emotional states. This type of migrant may have the tendency to engage in "manic escapes" or cling to others, and they often may become depressed, paranoid, or both.

B) <u>Migrants with a more integrated sense of identity</u> (with different level of integration):

The migrants in this category will already have the emotional capacity to mourn, to form healthy attachments, to endure difficult feelings of loneliness, and to be alone. Migrants in this category will have a basis of the true psychological home with different levels of integration. Nonetheless, even a well-integrated migrant may still have to work through the difficult process of migration and its different stages (as previously mentioned).

However, such a migrant may have a much greater chance of going through the healthy process of migration and assimilation of migration. Compare this to the migrant with a precarious sense of identity migrant who will have a much more difficult task to work through the migration process; his/her migration will have more manic qualities.

III. New Environment

This category is comprised of such factors like the new culture, the nature and functions of migration (exile/voluntary), economies, support networks, and job skills. The migration to a new environment with good opportunities for migrants and, people, who receive them well, will make a difference in the migration process.

However, this category seems to resonate with the identity of the migrant and the kind of person he or she is to begin with. So, if a migrant with a highly distorted paranoid ideation and functioning comes to an affluent and welcoming society (i.e., Zbyszek's case), he may not be able to take advantage of a good situation because of the level of his identity precariousness. For all of us, the external culture provides us with a holding environment (psychologically speaking) and when we leave our native culture we are faced with a great loss, even though we may have the "capacity to be alone."

As seen in the cases of Ela, Bruno, and Zbyszek, the external culture in which we live with its value system and worldview provides a very important framework for human functioning and existence. When one moves from that cultural framework to another type of framework one becomes much more aware of how important that cultural framework is. The cultural holding environment gets lost to some extent and all migrants need to deal with that loss.

The situation of Bruno involves not only cross-cultural migrations between the USA and Eastern Europe but also parental abandonment and neglect trauma. The more standard migration situation is where the parents accompany the child on cross-cultural migration from one country to another like in Ela's case. In Bruno's case the migration trauma was layered over by the fact that he had to give up his parents and was sent to an unknown (to him) Eastern European world. The parental neglect and abandonment created additional trauma in its own right, and independent of migration trauma situation. I suspect that if Bruno had moved to Eastern Europe with his mother or entire family, his whole migration process would take on a much less traumatic dynamic.

In Ela's case there was a trauma in the migration process itself, even though she migrated with her entire intact family and without parental abandonment trauma. Bruno's situation is much more complicated, because he was traumatized on different levels related to cross-cultural migration trauma and parental neglect resulting in the lack of containment, continuity, and parental stability.

Even though in the new culture one might be with well-intentioned people, on another level their thinking, value system, their recognition of a migrant's functioning may not be there and therefore the cultural holding environment always gets lost to some extent. Generally, people feel more comfortable with people who recognize their value system, worldview, and inner psychic structure.

Therefore, the holding environment that the culture provides is important; even though we are all individuals, we also live in culture and groups. The cultural environments are far more important than we often recognize and we feel the loss and significance of them when we migrate to another culture.

Even though the new culture may be affluent and receptive, with many opportunities, there will always be a disjunction between the migrant's native culture (internal/ external) and the new culture. Any migrant will have to readjust and reconnect to things that are profoundly different in the new culture. Migrants will have to deal with the loss of cultural environment, mourn, and work through the losses.

The categories (I, II and III) seem to be interlinked in dynamic reflective mutual interaction, and they seem to have a direct effect on each other. Therefore if there is a problem or some kind of deficiency in one category, this may have an effect on the other two categories of the migration experience.

We may wonder again what the true psychological home is and how the construction of such a home happens in the context of migration.

To recapitulate, the authentic psychic home is the capacity to think about your own psychological processes and to be in contact with them. To have a psychic home is to have a mind which can be in contact with his or her own psychic states as well as to be aware of those of others.

One aspect of psychic home would be the capacity to own up to different psychic states and have an authentic sense of self. The healthy mind with the capacity to think freely about everything, which is in contact with his own psychic states—and the psychic states of others—is our authentic home.

The subjects of the composite cases presented in this study did not have an authentic sense of self before their migration leading to their motivation to seek treatment. Through their treatment they begin to gradually own up to previously disowned parts of their selves and therefore parts of their respective psychological homes. They developed more capacity to think about some of their psychic states which were previously acted out because they were unbearable and unthinkable.

As my clinical study shows, migrant patients with a precarious sense of identity who disown parts of themselves and therefore their mind (not just repressed difficult feelings) are not able to process events, experiences, and therefore mourn their losses. Over a period of time they were able to own up to the unbearable psychic states and to have some measure of a healthy psychic home.

Migrants with a very precarious sense of identity engage in a powerful splitting of their whole mind (not just repressing difficult feelings) and keeping things internally apart. It is only when various anxieties are gradually addressed in treatment that there is the capacity to bring things together which otherwise have been sharply kept apart by composite beings like Zbyszek and others.

One has to have a sense of self and a well-integrated identity in order to be able to mourn one's losses. The migrants who were the subjects of the composite cases in this study, who had a precarious sense of identity, did not have this advanced psychological capacity to mourn because the parts of their self (psychological home) were missing. For instance, in Zbyszek's composite case there was a radical disowning of aspects of himself (psychologically speaking). In his phantasy, he felt that there were holes in him that had to be plugged with different things. He feared that his whole self may leak out, so he was trying desperately to plug his psychological holes so he would not disintegrate. This is a very different order of things, as compared to being able to own up to one's difficult repressed feelings and mourn one's losses.

The first task for Zbyszek was to plug the psychological holes by owning his projections. However, he found that once his psychological holes had been plugged, he had to deal with difficult psychic states that are frightening, so he unplugs the psychological holes again (via projections) by disowning parts of himself. A big part of him (in his phantasies) feels stuck in this process of plugging and unplugging holes which needs to be worked through before he can develop more advanced psychological capacities.

Migrants with a well-integrated sense of identity will already have good foundations of an authentic psychological home and, therefore, the basic emotional capacity to work through the migration process. In order to work through the migration trauma and reconstruction and expansion of a psychic home, such migrants will have to re-own difficult repressed feelings, mourn their losses, accept (over a period of time) the new and the old world, and navigate through different cultural identities. The sufficient capacity of the migrant to be able to work through the crisis of migration will lead to quality of rebirth, recovery, and future further development of the authentic psychological home.

Mental health professionals working with migrants need to be aware of the psychodynamics of migration and different levels of self-integration. There may be reluctance in some migrant patients to explore the issue of migration due to painful feelings related to the process of migration. Some therapists may unknowingly collude with migrant patients' desire to become Americans too quickly in order to feel accepted.

Broadly speaking the greater the therapist's awareness of the trauma the migration may represent, the greater the possibility of authentically helping such migrant patients. Sometimes, migrant patients may not explicitly articulate this trauma and just focus on simple day-to-day concerns related to adapting to a new mode of living in which case the therapist may not recognize its significance and collude with the patient's need to minimize the trauma.

Mental health professionals' capacities to be aware of the significance of the migration process, its dynamic, and trauma elements (as knowledge of other traumas) would greatly facilitate the migrant treatment, construction of an authentic psychological home and true integration in to a new culture.

In this study I have arrived at the conclusion that migration was traumatic for all the cases that I have studied. The migration had an element of psychological trauma to a greater or lesser degree. This leads me to believe that migration seems to be a psychological trauma for almost everybody, regardless of whether or not they are healthy or unhealthy before the migration experience. However, the way people deal with such a psychological trauma of migration will vary with each individual.

There are many factors to be considered such as the premigration history, the migrants' identity issues, the nature of the new environment, and many others that will actually shape the nature of what I call the trauma of migration.

Nonetheless, based on my psychoanalytic study it appears that the migration process is a trauma to varying degrees for almost everybody.

This general statement is based on conclusions that I have drawn from having worked intensively with migrant patients in psychoanalytic psychotherapy and psychoanalysis. My book tries to show how different people with different premigration histories and different psychological profiles have actually coped with the migration trauma.

I discovered that migration was a trauma to a greater or lesser degree in all circumstances in all patients that I have treated. The migration process is a highly disruptive event (although it has some positive aspects to it) that opens people up and challenges them in a way they may not have been challenged before.

Even though in this book I have focused on migrants that represented people with different levels of psychological disturbance, based on my overall experience with a wide variety of patients, it is my suggestion that migration be regarded as a trauma of greater or lesser degree for almost everybody who undertakes it.

Due to psychological challenges that migration presents, which are clinically observable with the patients that I have worked with, I feel that it is plausible that my general conclusions about migration trauma may be extended to the general population.

Welcome All

Epilogue

"The Guest House"

As human beings we are always internally growing and psychologically migrating from one developmental stage to another (in health). Dealing with life changes through the process of internal growth represents the inner psychological migration. However, taking the real physical journey of migration can make more tangible some of the creative and traumatic aspects of the migration process (inner and outer). The reality of the physical journey that takes place introduces the real physical and psychological losses and often presents a degree of crisis. Migrants and nonmigrants are all faced with the developmental migrations and dealing with life changes throughout life. However, migrants may have to do a greater amount of psychic work due to the additional factor of physical migration. The physical migratory journey is inevitably intertwined with the psychological migration and the desire to find a home of one's own.

The idea of finding a psychic home and the notion of having a mind of one's own that can tolerate and welcome the inner emotional experience is well captured by the following poem of Rumy's called "The Guest House." We can all as human beings aspire to live in such a well-integrated state of consciousness with the capacity to welcome and not only just endure difficult and pleasurable states of mind.

The migrants presented in this book were living in relatively precarious inner worlds with poorly developed sense of self. Their psychic homes were fragmented and impoverished with only a dim awareness of their psychic realities. They were all enduring the process of migration and working through their fears and conflicts in order to find a semblance of a psychic home within. To have a psychic home and a mind of one's own in order to be able to think real creative thoughts, digest inner experiences, have insight, and understand the emotional truth requires a lot of inner psychic work.

In migrants (or other human beings) precariously cut off from one's sense of self, there was not enough of an integrated mind present and therefore they were mostly enacting and not experiencing their fears, feelings, and mental states. In such a psyche only bits of consciousness can be maintained and most of the psychic content gets enacted and evacuated. That kind of mind is often used for evacuation and discharge of tension rather than capable of real creative thoughts and emotional experience.

Migrants (or other human beings) living in such a precarious state of consciousness tend to live to various degrees in the concrete world experiencing mostly sensations but not emotional experience. In a relatively well-integrated migrant (or other human being) there will be a sense of self and personal operational life center, than such an individual can experience the emotional life within. Such a migrant will have the inner capacity to tolerate and even welcome their inner world chaos, difficult emotional psychic states, and find some meaning in inner and outer life.

All migrants in this book were deeply involved in their search to find some inner sense of psychic home that could possibly become "the guest house" for the exiled parts of the self from the old and the new world to be admitted back into one's conscious awareness. It is possible that a better integrated psychic home becomes "the guest house" that can welcome and not only endure difficult states of mind, emotional truth, and true alive knowledge.

The Guest House

This being human is a guest house,
Every morning a new arrival
A joy, a depression, a meanness, some momentary awareness comes
as an unexpected visitor.
Welcome and entertain them all!
Even if they are a crowd of sorrows, who violently sweep your house
empty of its furniture, still, treat each guest honorably.
He may be clearing you out for some new delight.
The dark thought, the shame, the malice, meet them
at the door laughing and invite them in.
Be grateful for whatever comes because each
has been sent as a guide from beyond.

—Jelaluddin Rumi
Translation by Coleman Banks[*]

---

* Reprinted with permission.

Glossary[1]

Alpha-function: term originally used by Bion (1897–1979) in order to describe the process by which raw sense data is converted into mental contents which have meaning and can be used for thinking. The alpha-function is facilitated by maternal reverie and its failure leads to the accumulation of unassimilated, "undigested" beta-elements.

Beta-elements: a concept used by Bion to describe raw, "undigested" sense data. The experience is generated from raw sense data by meeting with pre-existing expectation which results in meaningful conception.

Containing: Bion developed a model of the relationship between contained and container in the 1970's. The origins of a contained-container notion goes back to the mother and infant relationship where the mother's mind functions as a container for the uncontained infant. He spoke about interpenetrating form of contact between the infant and mother's consciousness, the individual and the social group, or the process of getting thoughts into words. The mother as a container needs to be in a calm receptiveness (reverie) in order to take in infants' own feelings and give the meaning to them. When the mother is not capable of containing infants' feelings and providing meaning, than infant experiences that a sense of meaning has been stripped away resulting in what Bion called "nameless dread." In Bion's theory he suggested three forms of the container-contained relationship such as parasitic, symbiotic, and commensal. By "symbiotic" he understood relationships in which one depends on another object to a mutual benefit. By "parasitic" he meant to depict a relationship in which one depends on another object to produce a destructive third.

1. The terms and definitions developed and constructed for this glossary are based on descriptions provided by the following resources: *The Language of Psychoanalysis* (1967) by J. LaPlanche and J.B. Pontalis, and *A Critical Dictionary of Psychoanalysis* (1968) by Charles Rycroft.

By "commensal" he understood a relationship in which two objects share a third, with the advantage of all three. Originally he applied this model to show the different possibilities related to the development of a new idea or a person who cherishes the idea, in relation to the establishment that responds to the idea.

Countertransference: the therapist's transference on his clients' and the therapist's emotional attitude toward his clients. An analyst can use his emotional responses toward his clients as the key to the clients' unconscious communication and as a clinical tool, which makes it useful in interpreting clinical material.

Development (nonlinear): human behavior can be seen developmentally, and adult human behavior can be viewed as an elaboration of infantile behavior. The developmental process can be seen as the evolution of innate developmental processes and the impact of environmental experience on these processes. For instance, the concept of a developmental line (A. Freud, 1965) does not adequately capture the nature of the nonlinear shift that occurs in movement from the paranoid-schizoid position to the depressive position of M. Klein. These positions are not static entities but are processes; the operation in one mode presupposes simultaneous operation in the other mode. The depressive position mode is undergoing continual development over the course of a person's life. The operation in the depressive mode implies the dynamic, simultaneous operation (at times back and forth) in the paranoid-schizoid position.

Holding Environment: term originally introduced in the 1950s by D. Winnicott. The concept of mother infant relationship became the foundation of his theory of holding environment. He was concerned with the psychological "holding of the baby in the mind of the mother," in conjunction with other mother's functions such as feeding, dressing, and bathing. Winnicott felt that due to the good-enough holding, the baby may grow greater capacity to develop a sense of "I am" and better capacity to integrate psychic experience. He felt that good-enough holding by environment is the foundation for future important developmental processes. The theory of the good-enough holding environment which originated with the mother/infant relationship extends outwards to external society, groups, and culture.

Idealization: is a defensive process against recognizing ambivalence and feelings of guilt and depression; the failure of this process leads to disillusionment and depression. In idealization, an ambivalently regarded object is split into an ideally good and wholly bad one. The concept includes the idea of the construction of an ideal, perfect object which is not a real object.

Identification: the process by which an individual extends his identity into someone else or borrows his identity from another or confuses his identity with someone else's. The primary identification is the process wherein the individual (in infancy) has to distinguish his identity from his objects. The secondary identification is the process of identifying with an object whose separate identity has been discovered. Secondary identification with parental figures is seen as a part of the normal developmental process.

Linking: term used by Bion in order to describe the function of linking between mental contents and of linking one object with another. The prototype of all the links is the primitive breast or penis.

Links: L-love, H-hate, K-Knowledge—Bion (1962) felt that some emotions (i.e., love, hate and knowledge) are basic and are always present in a link. The concept "link" describes an emotional experience and relationship between two people, or two parts of the same individual. The prototype for all links is the primitive breast or penis.

Manic defense: it is a type of defensive behavior where an individual defends himself against anxiety, guilt and depression by such operations as denial, the operation of an omnipotent control phantasy by which they imagine themselves to be in control of anxiety-provoking situations, projection of "bad" aspects of the self on to others and identification with a powerful other from whom a sense of power can be borrowed.

Regression: (i.e., oral) a process of reversion to an earlier mode of functioning. It is a defensive process by which a person seeks to avoid anxiety by returning to an earlier stage of ego development, and therefore earlier patterns of behavior and modes of functioning. For instance, the regression from the Oedipal level to the oral level is a defensive process against castration anxiety.

Reparation: is a process of recreating an internal ambivalently invested object which has been harmed in phantasy. In Kleinian theory reparation is one of the natural processes by which the individual resolves his ambivalence toward others and reduces his feelings of guilt.

Representations (internal): a mental representation is a relatively stable internal image of anything that has been previously perceived. An object-representation is the "mental image"; a representation of any person who is a human object for the human subject.

Transference: the process by which a client in psychotherapy displaces on his therapist feelings, fears and ideas which were derived from historical, previous figures in his life. A client endows the therapist with the significance of another, usually paternal, maternal and other prior objects.

Working through: the process by which a client in psychotherapy over an extended period of time discovers the deeper and fuller implications of some therapeutic interpretations and new insights. For instance, mourning is the process of working through the loss of another and recognition that the lost person is no longer available.

References

Ablon, J.S. (2005). Review of An Open Door Review of Outcome Studies in Psychoanalysis. *International Psychoanalytical Association*. pp. 79–80.

Abram, Jan. (1996). *The Language of Winnicott. A Dictionary and Guide to Understanding His Work*. U.S.: Jason Aronson Inc.

Akhtar, S. (1999). *Immigration and Identity. Turmoil, treatment, and transformation.* Northvale, NJ, London: Jason Aronson.

Akhtar, S. (1999). *Immigration and Acculturation. Mourning, Adaptation and the Next Generation.* Rowman & Littlefield, Lanham, Maryland, London: Jason Aronson.

Anderson, R. (1992). *Clinical Lectures on Klein and Bion*, New York, NY: Routledge

Bacal, H.A., & Newman, K.M. (1990). *Theories of object relations: Bridges to Self Psychology*. New York: Columbia University Press.

Balint, M. (1959). *Thrills and regressions*. London: Hogarth, and The Institute of Psycho-Analysis.

Berry, J.W., Dasen, P., Poortinga, Y., & Segall, M. (2002). *Cross-Cultural Psychology: Research and Applications.* (2nd ed.)

Bick, I. (1968). The experience of skin in early object relations. *International Journal of Psycho-Analysis*, 49: 2–3.

Bion, W.R. (1962a). A theory of thinking. In *Second thoughts. Selected papers on psychoanalysis.* Reprint. London: Kamac (1984. (Folder).

———. (1962b). *Learning from experience.* London: W. Heinemann.

———. (1963). *Elements of psycho-analysis.* London: Heinemann.

———. (1967). *Second thoughts: Selected papers on psycho-analysis.* London: Heinemann.

_______. (1970). *Attention and Interpretation.* London: Tavistock.

_______. (1977). *Two Papers: The Grid and the Caesura, ed.* J. Salomâo. Rio de Janeiro: Imago Editora.

Davis. M., Shepherd R., & Winnicott, C. (ed.) (1984). *Deprivation and Delinquency.* London: Tavistock, 1984. New York: Methuen.

_______. (1989). *Psycho-Analytic Exploration.* London: Karnac Books. Cambridge, MA: Harvard University Press.

DeSalvo, L. (2009). *On Moving: A Writer's Meditation on New Houses, Old Haunts, and Finding Home Again,* New York, NY: Bloomsbury.
Deutsch, H. (1965). "Some Forms of Emotional Disturbance and Their Relationship to Schizophrenia," in *Neuroses and Character Types,* International Universities Press, New York.
Erikson, E.H. (1950a). Growth and crises of the healthy personality. In *Identity and the Life Cycle,* pp. 50–100. New York: International Universities Press, 1959.
———. (1950b). *Childhood and Society.* New York: Norton.
Falk, A. (1974). Border symbolism. *Psychoanalytic Quarterly*, 43: 650–60.
Flanders, S. (1993). *The Dream Discourse Today.* New York: Routledge.
Fonagy, P. (2002). *An Open Door Review of Outcome Studies in Psychoanalysis.* (Rev. ed.). London: International Psychoanalytical Association.
Freud, S. (1917). *Mourning and Melancholy. S.E.*, 14: 237–260. London: Hogarth Press, 1957.
———. (1895). "*Studies in Hysteria.*" S.E. 2.
———. (1900–1902). *The Interpretation of Dreams.* S.E. IV-V.
———. (1911). *The Handling of Dream-Interpretation in Psycho-Analysis.* S.E. XII.
———. (1916 [1915–16]). *Introductory Lectures on Psychoanalysis. Part II. Dreams.* S.E. XV.
———. (1917 [1915]). *A Metapsychological Supplement to the Theory of Dreams.* S.E. XIV.
———. (1923 [1922]). *Remarks on the Theory and Practice of Dream Interpretation.* S.E. XIX.
———. (1925). *Some Additional Notes on Dream-Interpretation as a Whole.* S.E. XIX.
———. (1933 [1932]). *New Introductory, Lectures in Psycho-Analysis*. S.E. XXII.
Freud, S., & Breuer, J. (1895). "Studies on Hysteria." *S.E.* 11 (1893–1895), 1–306.
Grinberg, L., & Grinberg, R. (1989). *Psychoanalytic perspectives on migration and exile*, trans. N. Festinger. New Haven, CT: Yale University Press.
Haynal, A.E. (2002). *Disappearing and Reviving: Sandor Ferenczi in the History of Psychoaalysis*. London. H. Karnac Ltd.
Herbert, R. (1966). *Psychotic States: a psychoanalytical approach*. London: BPCC Wheatons Ltd, Excter.
Hinshelwood, R. D. (1989). *A dictionary of Kleinian thought.* London: Free Association Books.
Khan, M.M.R., "The Concept of Cumulative Trauma" (1963). Repr. in *The Privacy of Self,* Hogarth Press, London, 1974.
King, R.A., Peter, B. Neubauer, Samuel Abrams, & A. Scott Dowling, eds. (2003). *The Psychoanalytic Study of the Child.* Binghamton: Vail-Batlou Press, Inc.
Klein, M. (1946). Notes on some schizoid mechanisms. In M. Klein, P. Heimann, S. Isaacs, & J. Riviere (Eds.), *Developments of psycho-analysis*. London: Hogarth Press, 1952.
———. (1957). Envy and Gratitude. In *Envy and Gratitude and Other Works,* 1946–1963. New York: Delacorte, 1975.
———. (1955). "On Identification." In *New Directions in Psycho-Analysis.* Ed. M. Klein, P. Heimann, R.E. Money-Kyrle. London, Tavistock.
Kohut, H. (1971). *Analysis of the Self.* New York: International Universities Press.

———. (1978). *The Psychology of the Self. A Casebook.* New York: International Universities Press.
Kohut, H., & Wolf, E. (1978). "The Disorders of the Self and their Treatment: an Outline," in P. Ornstein (ed.) *The Search for the Self,* vol. 3, pp. 359–85. New York, International Universities Press, 1990.
Kramer, Peter D. (1993). *Listening to Prozac: A Psychiatrist Explores Antidepressant Drugs and the Remaking of the Self.* New York: Penguin Books.
———. (1997). *Should You Leave? : A Psychiatrist Explores Intimacy and Autonomy—and the Nature of Advice.* New York: Penguin Books.
Kurzweil, Edith. (1997). *The Freudians: A Comparative Perspective (Psychiatry and Social Psychology Series).* Transaction Publishers; Reprint edition (January 1, 1997).
LaPlanche, J., & Pontalis, J.-B. (1973). *The Language of Psycho-Analysis.* New York: W.W. Norton & Company, Inc.
Mahler, M. (1971). "A Study of the Separation-Individuation Process." In *The Psychoanalytic Study of the Child* 26. New Haven, Yale University Press, 1974.
McGoldrick, M., Pearce, J.K., & Giordano, J. (1982). *Ethnicity and Family Therapy.* New York: Guilford Press.
Meltzer, D. (2009). *Dream Life—A Re-examination of the Psychoanalytic Theory and Technique.* The Harris Meltzer Trust. London. Karnac Books Ltd.
Mitchell, J. (2000). *Madmen and Medusas: Reclaiming Hysteria.* Great Britain: Penguin Group.
———. (1974). *Psychoanalysis and Feminism.* London, Great Britain: Penguin Group.
Ogden, T. (1986). *Matrix of the mind: Object relations and the psychoanalytic dialogue.* Northvale, NJ: Aronson.
Oliver, M. (1992). *The Journey.* Beacon Press Books, published under the auspices of the Unitarian Universalist Association of Congregations
O'Shaughnessy, B. (1981). A commemorative essay on W.R. Bion's theory of thinking. Reprinted as W.R. Bion's theory of thinking and new techniques in child analysis. In E.B. Spillius (ed.), *Melanie Klein today, vol. 2. Mainly practice.* London: Kamac (1988).
Rey, J.H. (1979). "Schizoid phenomena in the borderline," in J. LeBolt and A. Capponi (ed.) *Advances in the Psychotherapy of the Borderline Patient.* New York: Jason Aronson. 449–84.
Roland, A. (1988). *In search of self in India and Japan: Toward a cross-cultural psychology.* Princeton: Princeton University Press.
———. (1996). *Cultural pluralism and psychoanalysis: The Asian and North American experience.* New York and London: Routledge Kegan Paul.
———. (2011). *Journeys to Foreign Selves: Asians and Asian Americans in a Global Era.* Oxford: Oxford University Press
Rosenfeld, H.A. (1971). A clinical approach to the psychoanalytic theory of life and death instincts: an investigation into the aggressive aspects of narcissism. *International Journal of Psycho-Analysis* 52: 169–78.
Rubin, J. (1996). *Psychotherapy and Buddhism: Toward an integration.* New York: Plenum Press.

———. (1998). *A psychoanalysis for our time: Exploring the blindness of the seeing I.* New York: University Press.

Rumi, J. *The Guest House.* From *The Illustrated Rumi* by Coleman Banks and Michael Green, copyright 1997 by Coleman Banks and Michael Green. Broadway Books.

Rycroft, C. (1993). *Critical Dictionary of Psychoanalysis.* Second Edition. London: Penguin Books.

Schafer, R. (1997). *The Contemporary Kleinians of London.* New York: International Universities Press, Inc.

Sharpe, E. (1937). *Dream Analysis.* Hogarth Press.

Siegel, A. (1996). *Heinz Kohut and the Psychology of the Self.* London: Routledge.

Small, Meredith. (1999). *Our Babies, Ourselves: How Biology and Culture Shape the Way We Parent.* New York: Anchor Books, Random House.

Spillius, E. (2015). *Journey in Psychoanalysis.* New York: Routledge.

Steiner, J. (1995). Psychic Retreats: Pathological Organizations in Psychotic, Neurotic and Border Line Patients. New York: Routledge.

Suzuki, L.A., Ponterotto, J.G., & Meller, P.J. (2001). *Handbook of Multicultural Assessment: Clinical, Psychological, and Educational Applications* (2nd ed.). San Francisco, CA: Jossey-Bass.

Tausk, V. (1919). "On the Origin of the Influence Machine in Schizophrenia." *Psychoanaly Quarterly.*

Wharton, Barbara. (2005). Ethical issues in the publication of clinical material. *Journal of Analytical Psychology*, 50(1): 83–89.

Winnicott, D. W. (1945). Primitive Emotional Development. Ibid.

———. (1949). Mind and its Relation to the Psyche-Soma. Ibid.

———. (1950). Aggression in Relation to Emotional Development. Ibid.

———. (1951). Transitional Objects and Transitional Phenomena. Ibid.

———. (1955). *Deprivation and delinquency.* London: Tavistock.

———. (1955). *Group Influences and the Maladjusted Child: The School Aspect.* London: Tavistock.

———. (1958). The capacity to be alone. In: *The maturational processes and the facilitating environment: Studies in the theory of emotional development* (pp. 29–36). New York: International Universities Press, 1965.

———. (1958). *Collected Papers: Through Pediatrics to Psycho-Analysis.* London: Tavistock, 1958. New York: Basic Books, 1958.

———. (1960). Ego distortion in terms of true and false self. In *The maturational processes and the facilitation environment.* New York: International Universities Press, 1965.

———. (1963). Fear of Breakdown, IRP 1 (1974): 103–7.

———. (1963a). Communicating and Not Communicating leading to a Study of Certain Opposites.

———. (1965). *The Family and Individual Development.* London: Tavistock.

———. (1967). The Location of Cultural Experience. *Int. J. Psycho-Anal.*, 48.

———. (1971). *Therapeutic Consultations in Child Psychiatry.* London: Hogarth Press and the Institute of Psycho-Analysis.

———. (1971a). *Playing and reality.* London: Tavistock.

———. (1971b). Playing: Creative activity and the search for the self. In *Playing and Reality* (pp. 53–64). London: Tavistock, pp. 53–64.

Index

About the Author

Grace P. Conroy is a psychoanalyst and psychotherapist in private practice in New York City. She has been engaged in working with multicultural population, teaching and supervision for over twenty years.

Immigration, cross-cultural work, and identity development are her particular interests. For more information about the author please visit www.graceconroy.com.

www.ingramcontent.com/pod-product-compliance
Ingram Content Group UK Ltd.
Pitfield, Milton Keynes, MK11 3LW, UK
UKHW012039150926
475560UK00001B/90

9 781442 231511